TOYNBEE'S
INDUSTRIAL REVOLUTION

TOYNBEE'S
INDUSTRIAL REVOLUTION

A Reprint of *Lectures on the
Industrial Revolution in England,
Popular Addresses, Notes and Other Fragments*

by

ARNOLD TOYNBEE

With a new Introduction by
the late Professor T. S. Ashton

REPRINTS OF ECONOMIC CLASSICS

AUGUSTUS M. KELLEY, PUBLISHERS
NEW YORK 1969

Published in the United States of America by
Augustus M. Kelley, Publishers, New York

Library of Congress No 68-59517

This is a reprint of the first edition, published in London by
Rivingtons in 1884, from which only the Memoir by Benjamin
Jowett and the Prefatory Note by Mrs Toynbee, occupying pp
v-xxxi of the original, are omitted. Two lectures on Henry George,
which first appeared as *"Progress and Poverty"*, *a criticism of Mr
H. George* (London : Kegan Paul, 1883), were added to the fourth
edition in 1890. A 'new and cheaper edition' was published in 1908,
when the book had gone through five editions. The edition also
contained a memoir by Lord Milner, who had already written
Arnold Toynbee, a Reminiscence, published by Edward Arnold
in 1895 and again in 1901, and who was also the author of the
Dictionary of National Biography article on Toynbee, which
appeared in 1899. The 1908 edition was reprinted many times,
serving as a textbook of English economic history, until it finally
went out of print in 1927.

This edition published 1969

Printed in Great Britain by
Redwood Press Trowbridge Wiltshire

INTRODUCTION TO THE 1969 EDITION

Arnold Toynbee, the second son of a distinguished naval surgeon, was born in Savile Row on 23 August 1852, and spent most of his childhood at Wimbledon. A fall from a pony at an early age was to set limits to his physical activities in later life : nevertheless, it was by his own choice that, at the age of fourteen, he was sent to a school that trained boys for a military career. After two years, however, he abandoned thoughts of this. Other plans of preparing for the Civil Service or the Bar came to nothing, and until he reached twenty he lived at home, spending most of his time in wide but undisciplined reading in history, philosophy and literature. In January 1873 he entered Pembroke College, Oxford, but after a few months was forced by a breakdown to spend a long period of almost complete idleness in the country. When in January 1875 he returned to the University it was as a commoner of Balliol, where for four years he was to enjoy the guidance of Jowett, T. H. Green, and Nettleship, and to become the central figure in a brilliant group which included Alfred (later Lord) Milner and F. C. Montague. (It is to the recollections of these two, together with those of Jowett, that we owe most of what we know of his undergraduate life.) Continued delicate health – and perhaps lack of previous systematic training – prevented his reading for Honours : according to Jowett, 'an hour or two in the day of serious study was as great a strain as his faculties could bear'. But the lighter requirements for a pass degree left scope for the full enjoyment of what Oxford had to offer. At an early stage he came under the spell of Ruskin, then Professor of Fine Arts at the University, took an active part in Ruskin's bizarre project of road-repairing at Hinksey, visited workhouses, introduced pupil teachers to wider fields of learning, and engaged in other altruistic activities.

An ordinary degree is not normally a passport to an academic career. But Toynbee's incisive mind and intuitions made such an impression on the Master that, in 1878, he was appointed to a Tutorship at Balliol, a post to which he later added that of Senior Bursar. His chief responsibility was to teach Political Economy to men preparing for the Indian Civil Service, and this led him to make a close study of the classical economists. The remaining four years of his life were crowded with a wide range of commitments. He worked for the spread of trade unions and co-operative societies; became a Poor Law Guardian; stood as a Liberal candidate for the Oxford Town Council; paid a visit to Ireland to study the Land Question; acted as a visitor for the Charity Organisation Society; spent months of his vacations living alongside the poor in the east-end; and gave lectures, with a success that surprised him, to large gatherings of working men at Newcastle, Bradford, Sheffield and Bolton, as well as in London. Such stress could not be sustained for long. His health broke down again and he died, at the age of thirty, in March 1883. Apart from Toynbee Hall in Whitechapel, his monument is this slender volume of Lectures, first published in 1884.

With the single exception of the one on the Yeomanry, the Lectures are not from Toynbee's own pen. He expressed himself more effectively in speech than in writing, and the short pieces of prose he left have few of the swift, vivid phrases which, by all account, entranced those who listened to him. No scholar would care for his work to be assessed almost exclusively on evidence drawn from the notebooks of his students. But Toynbee was fortunate to have among his pupils W. J. (later Sir William) Ashley and Bolton King, whose notes, recorded with Boswellian devotion, form the basis of this book. Of his abiding concerns other than history mention can be made only of one. He was deeply religious, and though his cast of mind was so

strongly rational as to prevent his believing in mirac
was firmly attached to the Church of England, seeking
to effect reforms in doctrine and structure and, in Jowe
words to demonstrate that 'rational faith can be as intense .
irrational, and that the narrowest convictions are not always
the strongest'.

His economic creed was derived, though not uncritically, from
Adam Smith, Malthus, Ricardo and J. S. Mill. From Smith
he drew his fundamental belief in the salutary effects of competition. 'The essence of the Industrial Revolution', he said, 'is the
substitution of competition for the mediaeval regulations which
had previously controlled the production and distribution of
of wealth'. But he held that if pushed to extremes competition
might lead to social ills, including sweating, truck and unemploy-
ment, and was hence strongly opposed to laissez-faire. He was
a whole-hearted supporter of Free Trade, and regarded the
Repeal of the Corn Laws as having been the chief instrument
of the economic advance and stability England had enjoyed
since 1850. He followed Malthus in asserting that the Old
Poor Law had been responsible for both the increase of numbers
and the degradation of the English poor. And he declared that
the harsher measure introduced in 1834 was 'the most beneficial
Act that had been passed since the Reform Bill'. In his day
the reaction against abstract reasoning was at its height; a
group of economists were seeking to substitute inductive and
historical ways of treatment for the 'logical artifices' of Ricardo
and his successors. Toynbee is to be thought of as a member
of the historical school, but he owed too much to Ricardo –
as this book discloses – to wish to see deduction swept away.
If its exponents would submit to scrutiny of both premises
and conclusions in the light of ascertained facts there was a
place for *a priori* reasoning in economic history. Indeed, unless
one started with theories, or at least hypotheses, historical
research must be a futile exercise. He reminded radicals and
free traders that 'All the most forcible arguments in favour
of industrial freedom are deductions from certain familiar facts
of human nature', and that 'Cobden on the platform was
as deductive as Ricardo in the study!' He accepted Ricardo's
doctrine of rent and carried on a correspondence with Henry

George, but had too much robust sense to support George's project for a single tax on land values. Finally, his debt to John Stuart Mill was deep : evidence of it is to be found, in particular, in the Lectures on the Wages Fund and the Future of the Wage Earning Classes.

In at least one respect Toynbee differed from Adam Smith and his followers. Smith thought of the workers as oppressed by law, but nevertheless was opposed to combinations of labour. Toynbee was a strong advocate of trade unions. But in stressing the obstacles placed in their way by the State in the eighteenth century he was almost certainly mistaken. For as George Unwin was to point out, a generation late : 'The passing of the Combination Acts, and the early prosecutions of trade unionists should not blind us to the fact that it was the comparative freedom of England in the eighteenth century which alone made the combination of wage-earners possible. At the very moment when the workers of England were laying the foundations of a free organisation, by the establishment of the "tramping ticket" and the "house of call", the Governments of France and Prussia were putting a veto on any such spontaneous popular development, by transferring these same institutions into the hands of the police, and utilising them as part of the machinery of a more or less benevolent despotism'. Even after the Act of 1800, as we now know, the trade unions were left to continue their activities with relatively little interference.

There has been an even stronger change of opinion about agricultural and agrarian development. Toynbee believed that the English yeoman had broken the power of the king and the squires in the Civil Wars, but after 1688 had been driven off the soil by the landowners and aspiring merchants, seeking the prestige and political influence that ownership of large estates conferred. Gradual at first, the movement accelerated after 1760 and reached its height towards the end of the century, bringing with it destruction of the open fields, enclosure of wastes, consolidation of farms, a decline in the demand for labour, and a vast increase in the number of paupers. Toynbee was right in asserting that the motives behind the changes were largely political and social – right, too, in saying that the small-holders declined because they sold their holdings, not because they were, on any significant scale, evicted. But his account of the military and political attainments of the yeomanry is romance rather than history. And recent enquiries have shown that the transformation of agriculture was a secular process, possibly quickened but not markedly concentrated, in the second half of the century; so far from the number of labourers and smallholders on the land having fallen, it increased at this period. The myth of what Toynbee called 'the agrarian revolution', though still to be found in reputable works, is clearly on the way out.

To Toynbee's assertions that the steep rise of prices between 1780 and 1820 (better 1814) was unaccompanied by an equivalent increase of earnings, and that bad harvests depressed the standard of living, little objection can be raised. But when he speaks of the huge taxation imposed on the workers, and goes on to say that, after this period, half the labourers' wages went in taxes, one may wish for the evidence. His statement that the whole of the capital transferred to the exchequer through the national debt was withdrawn from productive industry would hardly be accepted today by anyone acquainted with the theory of public finance. And his explanation of the shortage of cottages and the rise of rents at this time is too simple. It is true that farmers were increasingly disinclined to take labourers to live in their farmhouses; and that some landlords also pulled down cottages lest their occupants should become a burden on the rates. But material stringencies played a larger part. The war had cut off supplies of timber from the Baltic, had led to a shortage of bricks, tiles and glass, and the rise in rates of interest had put the capital on which they relied beyond the reach of builders. At the same time the number of young people seeking homes had greatly increased. In view of these hard economic and demographic conditions it hardly seems necessary to give great weight to 'the selfish and grasping use of a power which exceptional circumstances had placed in the hands of landowners, farmers, and capitalists'. It would be easy to specify other questions to which modern scholars would give answers different from those in these Lectures. Were the low prices of foodstuffs in the early eighteenth century detrimental to industrial growth? Is it true that in the old days the employer maintained his men when out of work? Did the domestic system offer greater continuity of income and closer personal relations between employers and workers, than the factory? But it is a truism that history has to be written anew by each generation. And, like his, the answers we give may be revised by our successors.

Toynbee's main purpose in the Lectures was to survey the early economists against the background of their own times and to indicate how far they moulded and were moulded by the course of events. Less is said than we might wish of the technical innovations, the sources of capital and enterprise, and the rise of financial institutions – the last perhaps because he was not given time to complete his project. A notable feature of the book is the extensive use of international comparisons. Toynbee counselled his pupils to be alert to the problems of the day and to speculate on the future. And just as now historians of this period write with one eye on the slowly developing nations of Asia, Africa and South America, so he spoke with an enduring concern for a working class slowly emerging to independence and influence. His great achievement was to bring seemingly disparate theories, technical changes, and social trends into conjunction and to give them a local habitation and a name. This, it is to be borne in mind, was done by one little more than a youth. Since his day many have written books on the Industrial Revolution, a few with distinction. But who among these, if his life had ended at thirty, would have been so much as heard of? The reprint of this remarkable pioneer work will be welcomed by economic historians of all shades of thought, in England and elsewhere.

T. S. ASHTON

LECTURES

ON THE

INDUSTRIAL REVOLUTION

IN ENGLAND.

a

LECTURES

ON THE

INDUSTRIAL REVOLUTION
IN ENGLAND

*POPULAR ADDRESSES, NOTES AND
OTHER FRAGMENTS*

BY THE LATE

ARNOLD TOYNBEE

TUTOR OF BALLIOL COLLEGE, OXFORD

RIVINGTONS
WATERLOO PLACE, LONDON
MDCCCLXXXIV

CONTENTS.

c

RICARDO AND THE OLD POLITICAL ECONOMY.

THE INDUSTRIAL REVOLUTION.

RICARDO AND THE OLD POLITICAL ECONOMY.

I.

The change that has come over Political Economy—Ricardo responsible for the form of that Science—The causes of his great influence—The economic assumptions of his treatise—Ricardo ignorant of the nature of his own method—Malthus's protest—Limitations of Ricardo's doctrine recognised by Mill and Senior—Observation discouraged by the Deductive Method—The effect of the Labour Movement on Economics—Modifications of the Science by recent writers—The new method of economic investigation.

THE bitter argument between economists and human beings has ended in the conversion of the economists. But it was not by the fierce denunciation of moralists, nor by the mute visible suffering of degraded men, that this conversion was effected. What the passionate protests of *Past and Present* and the grave official revelations of government reports could not do, the chill breath of intellectual criticism has done. Assailed for two generations as an insult to the simple natural piety of human affections, the Political Economy of Ricardo is at last rejected as an intellectual imposture. The obstinate, blind repulsion of the labourer is approved by the professor.

Yet very few people even now understand the nature of that system. I have called it the Political Economy of Ricardo, because it was he, more than any one, who gave to the science that peculiar form which, on the one hand, excited such intense antagonism, and, on the other, procured it the extraordinary influence which it has exercised over English thought and English politics.

No other book on the subject ever provoked the same fierce, intellectual disparagement and moral aversion as the *Principles of Political Economy and Taxation;* no other book, not even the *Wealth of Nations*, obtained the same immediate ascendency over men of intellectual eminence. Evidence of the first statement may be sought in innumerable refutations by economists and moralists; evidence of the second it seems worth while, in view of recent controversies, to recall once more. To Colonel Torrens, an economist of remarkable vigour and independence, Ricardo was still in 1844 " his great master;" to John Mill, writing about 1830, his book was the " immortal *Principles of Political Economy and Taxation";* to Charles Austin, many years later, there was, with one or two exceptions, nothing in that great work which he desired to see altered ; and to De Quincey, writing soon after his first perusal of the book, it seemed the revelation of a new science. " Had this profound work," he writes in the *Confessions of an Opium Eater,* " been really written in England during the nineteenth century ? Was it possible ? I supposed thinking had been extinct in England. Could it be that an Englishman, and he not in academic bowers, but oppressed by mercantile and senatorial cares, had accomplished what all the universities of Europe and a century of thought had failed even to advance by one hair's-breadth ? All other writers had been crushed and overlaid by the enormous weight of facts and documents ; Mr. Ricardo had deduced, *à priori,* from the understanding itself, laws which first gave a ray of light into the unwieldy mass of materials, and had constructed what had been but a collection of tentative discussions into a science of regular proportions, now first standing on an eternal basis." Not merely the members of the school to which Ricardo belonged, and literary philosophers like De Quincey, but even the Tories themselves, the ancient natural enemies of the economists, joined in the applause. Christopher North, in *Blackwood's Magazine,* in a professed eulogy of Adam Smith, placed Ricardo above him.

At first sight nothing appears more strange than this antipathy to, and this adoration of Ricardo. The bitter antagonism, the unqualified admiration seem alike inexplicable. Why should a treatise so remote, so abstract, so neutral, not filled with passion, like the *Wealth of Nations,* not eloquent in denunciation and exhortation, stating conclusions without eagerness, suggesting applications almost without design, why should such a treatise as this excite an uncompromising moral repugnance ? Because it *was* remote, abstract, neutral, because, while excluding from its consideration every aspect of human life but the economic, and dealing with that in isolation, it came, nevertheless, though not with the conscious intention of its author, to be looked upon and quoted as a complete philosophy of social and industrial life. And this isolation, this artificial separation of elements, carried by the same habit of mind into the explanation of economic facts themselves—this separation it is, which explains the persistent criticism of many of the leading theories of the treatise. The moral wickedness of the whole tendency of Political Economy, and the intellectual fallacies of the theory of value, have been denounced almost in the same breath, and for precisely the same cause.

But again, we may ask, why should a treatise so destitute of sympathy, observation, imagination, even literary style—a great part of it is nothing more than bald disjointed criticism of other books—dealing as it did with the most interesting, the most vital of human affairs; why should such a treatise as this dominate the minds of nearly all the distinguished men of a distinguished time? Because, I answer—though no one answer will serve as a complete explanation—of its marvellous logical power, the almost faultless sequence of the arguments. Systems are strong not in proportion to the accuracy of their premises, but to the perfection of their reasoning; and it was this logical invulnerability that gave to the *Principles of Political Economy* its instantaneous influence. Ricardo has been recently compared to Spinoza; and what was said of Spinoza may be said of him: grant his premises and you must grant all. The contrast in the case of Ricardo, between the looseness and unreality of the premises and the closeness and vigour of the argument, is a most curious one.

For a complete explanation, we must push our investigation further. We have seen that admiration of Ricardo was not confined to any one class or school; but, undoubtedly, the influence of his book was increased by the fact that in method and spirit it coincided completely with the mental habits of the most vigorous and active thinkers of that age. Indeed, Ricardo was their disciple. " I am the spiritual father of James Mill, James Mill is the spiritual father of Ricardo, therefore I am the spiritual grandfather of Ricardo," was an utterance of Bentham's; and it is exactly true. James Mill exercised over Ricardo the greatest influence. Ricardo's disciple in Political Economy, he was his master in everything else. It is probable that it was only through the encouragement of

Mill that Ricardo, by nature unambitious and diffident, resolved to undertake the composition of his famous treatise. It is certain that it was by Mill's express exhortation that he bought his seat in Parliament; and Ricardo's speeches in the House of Commons popularised—for he was far more persuasive and lucid as a speaker than as a writer—the principles of his treatise.

Though in Parliament only four years, Ricardo revolutionised opinion there on economic subjects. "It is known," says a writer a few months after his death, "how signal a change has taken place in the tone of the House of Commons, on subjects of Political Economy, during his short parliamentary career." "It was only," said Joseph Hume, the most distinguished disciple of Ricardo in Parliament, "by the advice and in hopes of the assistance of a distinguished individual, whose recent loss the kingdom has to deplore," that he (Hume) called attention to the subject of the combination laws. "The late Mr. Ricardo was so well acquainted with every branch of the science of Political Economy, formerly and until he had thrown light upon it so ill understood, that his aid in such a question would have been of the utmost value." "Surprising as it may appear," says a writer in the *Westminster Review*, "it is no less notorious, that up to the year 1818, the science of Political Economy was scarcely known or talked of beyond a small circle of philosophers, and that legislation, so far from being in conformity with its principles, was daily receding from them more and more."

Besides the influence of the school of Bentham on political thought, and Ricardo's presence in Parliament, we may find still another reason for the magical effect of his treatise in the circumstances of the time. He lived in an age of economic revolution and anarchy. The complications of industrial phenomena were such as to bewilder the strongest mind. No light had been thrown by Adam Smith on those vital questions, discussed before every Parliamentary committee on industrial distress, as to the relations between rent, profits, wages, and price. Adam Smith had distinctly spoken of rent, profits, and wages as the causes of prices. Not one of those who pored over piles of blue-books, or spent years in minute industrious observation of the actual world, had offered one single suggestion for the solution of these problems. The ordinary business man was simply dazed and helpless. He thought on the whole that a rise or fall in wages was the cause of a rise or fall in prices; but he could not explain himself, and was not sure. "Does a diminution in the prices of the goods generally precede a diminution of wages?" asks a member of a committee. "It has been both ways," answers the manufacturer, "for I have known people decrease the wages before there was a diminution; but it follows the moment the wages are decreased, the goods follow immediately."[1]

To people groping in this darkness, Ricardo's treatise, with its clear-cut answers to their chronic difficulties, was a revelation indeed. But Ricardo's solution of the problem, *i.e.* that the prices of freely produced commodities depend upon cost of production, measured in labour, and that wages, profits, and rent are not the causes but the results of price; this solution was only reached by making certain audacious assumptions which it would have been hardly possible for any economist before his time to make. Adam Smith lived on the eve of an industrial revolution. Ricardo lived in the midst of it. Assumptions which could never have occurred to Adam Smith, because foreign to the quiet world he lived in, a world of restrictions and scarcely perceptible industrial movement, occurred to Ricardo almost as a matter of course. That unceasing, all-penetrating competition—that going to and fro on the earth in search of gold—that rapid migration of men and things, the premises of all his arguments, were but the exaggeration, however wild, of the actual state of the industrial world of Ricardo's time. The steam-engine, the spinning-jenny, the power-loom, had torn up the population by the roots; corporation laws, laws of settlement, acts of apprenticeship, had been swept away by the mere stress of physical circumstances; and with all that visible movement of vast masses of people before his eyes, with that ceaseless tossing and eddying of the liberated industrial stream ever before him, is it to be wondered at that, with the strong native bias of his mind already in this direction, he should make without hesitation that postulate of pure competition on which all the arguments of his treatise depend? It was this assumption, together with its corollaries, which enabled him to pour such a flood of light upon the chaotic controversies of his time, and to appear to his contemporaries like the revealer of a new gospel. But it was this assumption also,

---

[1] Committee on Woollen Petitions, 1808.

wrongly understood, which has led to so much misconception; which has, on the one hand, brought upon Political Economy so much undeserved opprobrium, and, on the other, has led economists themselves into so many mistakes.

Ricardo himself never realised how great were the postulates he was assuming. It is a strange but indubitable and most important fact that he was unconscious of the character of his own logical method. He thought, as has been recently pointed out,[1] that he was talking of actual men and things when he was in fact dealing with abstractions. He makes but one allusion to the great assumption of pure competition. Of his other assumptions, such as private property, perfect mobility of labour, perfect knowledge of wages and profits at all times and in all places, there is no trace of recognition from beginning to end of his treatise. And just as Ricardo remained unconscious of the nature of his method, so he never seems to have realised the scope and effect of his work. His intention was to investigate certain concrete problems which bewildered his contemporaries. His achievement was to create an intensely abstract science—Deductive Political Economy. Of the influences which determined Ricardo to adopt the method of purely abstract reasoning, the intellectual ascendency obtained over him by James Mill was one of the strongest. The method of deduction and abstract analysis was that of the whole school of thinkers, to whom he was so closely related—Bentham, Mill, Austin; and it is significant that Sir H. Maine, who has applied the historical method with so much perseverance to the legal theories of Bentham and Austin, should have turned aside more than once to criticise Ricardo from the same point of view.

But, independently of this influence, it is evident that deduction was natural to Ricardo's mind. The splendid exhibition of logic in his works is alone sufficient proof of this, even if it were not possible to detect signs of the same tendency in his early love of mathematics, and, perhaps, in the extraordinary rapidity with which he made his fortune on the Stock Exchange. Nor is it surprising, when we remember his want of early education, which is visible in the lack of style and arrangement in his book, that Ricardo should never have reflected on the nature of the premises on which he

---

[1] Bagehot's *Economic Studies*, p. 157.

built. His powerful mind, concentrated upon the argument, never stopped to consider the world which the argument implied,—that world of gold-seeking animals, stripped of every human affection, for ever digging, weaving, spinning, watching with keen undeceived eyes each other's movements, passing incessantly and easily from place to place in search of gain, all alert, crafty, mobile—that world less real than the island of Lilliput, which never has had and never can have any existence.

A logical artifice became the accepted picture of the real world. Not that Ricardo himself, a benevolent and kind-hearted man, could have wished or supposed, had he asked himself the question, that the world of his treatise actually was the world he lived in ; but he unconsciously fell into the habit of regarding laws, which were true only of that society which he had created in his study for purposes of analysis, as applicable to the complex society really existing around him. And this confusion was aggravated by some of his followers, and intensified in ignorant popular versions of his doctrines. His hard, clear delineation, with its audacious solutions of hitherto insoluble problems, asserted itself in spite of protests. It was laid as a mask over the living world, and hid its face.

We must not indeed imagine that, rapid and irresistible as was the influence gained by Ricardo over the minds of his contemporaries, his system was allowed to establish itself without objection even on the part of economists. Unavailing protests were repeatedly raised by Ricardo's greatest rival in economic study, Malthus. " I confess to you," writes Malthus to Mr. Napier, with reference to his proposed contribution to the *Encyclopædia Britannica,* " that I think that the general adoption of the new theories of my excellent friend, Mr. Ricardo, into an encyclopædia, while the question was yet *sub judice,* was rather premature. The more I consider the subject, the more I feel convinced that the main part of his structure will not stand." [1] In a second letter on the same point he is still more explicit. " An article of the kind you speak of on Political Economy, would, I think, be very desirable ; but no one occurs to me at this moment with sufficient name and sufficient impartiality to do the subject justice. I am fully aware of the merits of Mr. M'Culloch and Mr. Mill, and have a great respect

---

[1] *Macvey Napier's Correspondence.* Letter from Malthus, September 27, 1821.

for them both; but I certainly am of opinion, after much and repeated consideration, that they have adopted a theory which will not stand the test of experience. It takes a partial view of the subject, like the system of the French economists; and, like that system, after having drawn into its vortex a great number of very clever men, it will be unable to support itself against the testimony of obvious facts, and the weight of those theories which, though less simple and captivating, are more just, on account of their embracing more of the causes which are in actual operation in all economical results."[1]

In these sentences, written four years after the publication of the first edition of Ricardo's work, we find a prediction, curiously exact, of the course taken by Political Economy in England for the last fifty years. But Malthus stood almost alone in England in his opposition to Ricardo. James Mill and M'Culloch were uncompromising disciples. " I think," writes M'Culloch to Mr. Napier, in allusion to the assertion of Malthus that the new theories were still *sub judice*, " I think the *Supplement* will gain credit by being among the first publications which has embodied and given circulation to the new, and, notwithstanding Mr. Malthus's opinion, I will add correct, theories of political economy. Your publication was not intended merely to give a view of the science as it stood forty-five years ago, but to improve it and extend its boundaries. It is, besides, a very odd error in Mr. Malthus to say that the new theories are all *sub judice*. He has himself given his complete and cordial assent to the theory of Rent, which is the most important of the whole; and the rest are assented to by Colonel Torrens, Mr. Mill, Mr. Tooke, and all the best economists in the country."[2]

It is true that M'Culloch, in later days of humility, somewhat abated the confident dogmatism into which his honest zeal had led him. " I believe," he says to Mr. Napier, " I was a little too fond at one time of novel opinions, and defended them with more heat and pertinacity than they deserved; but you will not charge me with anything of the sort at any time during the last seven years."[3] But more than seven years before the date of this letter M'Culloch had expounded the new theories to fashionable audiences

---

[1] *Macvey Napier's Correspondence.* Letter from Malthus, October 8, 1821.
[2] *Ibid.* Letter from M'Culloch, September 30, 1821.
[3] *Ibid.* Letter from M'Culloch, March 6, 1833.

of young Whig statesmen ;[1] and at the time when he wrote it, Miss Martineau was enchanting children and inspiriting discouraged politicians by her dramatic representations of Ricardo. All the world had become political economists of the Ricardian persuasion. The protests of Malthus and his able successor, Richard Jones, were lost in the tumult of applause.

The unbounded ascendency of Ricardo's system was not greatly modified by the labours of his principal successors. They did indeed recognise clearly enough its limitations. If Ricardo himself was unconscious of the logical character of his method, the same cannot be said of his chief disciples of the next generation. Both Mill and Senior state with the utmost plainness the exact character of their abstract science, and the assumptions upon which its conclusions are true. Mill in his *Logic,* published in 1843, and in his essay on the *Method of Political Economy,* written much earlier, and largely quoted in the *Logic,* but not published as a whole till 1844, explains the nature of Ricardo's method with a clearness which leaves nothing to be desired. But what both Mill and Senior ought to have done was not merely to point out what the assumptions were which Ricardo made, but to ascertain from actual observation of the industrial world they lived in how far these assumptions were facts, and from the knowledge thus acquired, to state the laws of prices, profits, wages, rent, in the actual world.

This work they never attempted. Had Mill and Senior completely emancipated themselves from the influence of their master, the history of Political Economy in England would have been a very different one. Endless misunderstanding and hatred would have been avoided, and some great problems would be much nearer their solution. But it was not to be. Ricardo's brilliant deductions destroyed observation. A method so clear, solutions so simple, carried all before them. " Political Economy," said Senior, " is not greedy of facts ; it is independent of facts." Mill, it is true, recognises the opposition to Political Economy caused by its apparent disregard of facts, and does something to meet it. " These sweeping expressions," he says, speaking of the unqualified deductions of Political Economy, " puzzle and mislead, and create an

[1] *Macvey Napier's Correspondence.* Letters from M'Culloch, May 2, 1824, April 23, 1825.

impression unfavourable to Political Economy, as if it disregarded the evidence of facts." But he retained to the end the confidence he had imbibed from early familiarity with the method ; and though he often, by a painful effort, recognised the existence of facts not included in his premises, he failed to see their importance.

For many years every effort made by economists to restore observation to their science, and to institute a new method, met with little encouragement from the general world. The great question of the time was still the removal of restrictions and the establishment of freedom in trade. For the solution of this problem the method of deduction was adequate, and of primary importance. All the most forcible arguments in favour of industrial freedom are deductions from certain familiar facts of human nature. Cobden on the platform was as deductive as Ricardo in the study. But after 1846 the mission of the deductive method was fulfilled. Up to that time economists had seen in the removal of restrictions the solution of every social difficulty. After that time they had no remedy to offer for the difficulties which yet remained. Political Economy, in spite of Mill's great work, published two years after the chief triumph of the old method, became barren. And it was worse than barren. Instead of a healer of differences it became a sower of discord. Instead of an instrument of social union it became an instrument of social division. It might go on its way unshaken by denunciation when tearing down the last remnants of obsolete restrictions imposed in the interest of a class ; it could not remain unshaken by such denunciation when opposing the imposition of new restrictions in the interest of the whole people.

It was the labour question, unsolved by that removal of restrictions which was all Deductive Political Economy had to offer, that revived the method of observation. Political Economy was transformed by the working classes. The pressing desire to find a solution of problems which the abstract science treated as practically insoluble, drew the attention of economists to neglected facts. Mr. Thornton, Professor Cairnes, and Professor Walker restored observation to its place. Mr. Thornton pointed to the existence of reserved prices—a fact patent in every newspaper; and, together with Professor Walker, overthrew the accepted theory of wages. Professor Cairnes showed the bearing of the existence

of non-competing groups of workmen—a fact noticed and then
neglected by Mill—on the theory of value. Professor Walker
explained the function of the employer as distinct from the
capitalist in the economy of industrial life. The step which
might have been taken half a century ago has been taken at last
in the past decade, and Political Economy bids fair to bear fruit
once more. Not that the deductive method, which failed so
lamentably after its first triumphs, will be discarded as useless.
It will take its place as a needful instrument of investigation, but
its conclusions will be generally recognised as hypothetical. Care
will be taken to include in its premises the greatest possible
number of facts, and to apply its results with the utmost
scrupulousness to existing industrial and social relations. It will
no longer be a common error to confuse the abstract science of
Economics with the real science of human life.

II.

The philosophic assumptions of Ricardo—They are derived from Adam Smith
—The worship of individual liberty—It involves freedom of competition and
removal of industrial restrictions—The flaw in this theory—It is confirmed
by the doctrine of the identity of individual and social interests—Criticism
of this doctrine—The idea of invariable law—True nature of economic laws
—Laws and precepts—The great charge brought against Political Economy
—Its truth and its falsehood.

But in examining the system of Ricardo and the causes alike of
its extraordinary success, and the deep repugnance which it has
excited, it is not sufficient to consider only the nature of his logical
method. We must take into account also the general philosophical
conceptions which underlie his treatise. Ricardo's economic
assumptions were of his own making. Not so his philosophical
assumptions. These were derived from his great predecessor, Adam
Smith, whose intellectual position he accepted in the main without question. Two conceptions are woven into every argument
of the *Wealth of Nations*—the belief in the supreme value of individual liberty, and the conviction that Man's self-love is God's
providence, that the individual in pursuing his own interest is promoting the welfare of all. To these conceptions there is not a
single allusion in Ricardo's treatise, but that is simply because,

neither a theologian nor a politician himself, he was not aware of the political and theological elements in his economic inheritance. Though not expressly acknowledged, these two ideas permeate his doctrine, as they do that of all the economists of the old school. The first belief is too familiar to need illustration, but the second, which is the foundation of all the practical precepts of the old economists, it may be worth while once more to exhibit in its most unmistakeable shape. "Private interest," writes James Anderson, the Scotch farmer whose theory of rent was brought to light by his laborious countryman MacCulloch, "is in this, as it ought to be in every case in well-regulated society, the true *primum mobile*, and the great source of public good, which, though operating unseen, never ceases one moment to act with unabating power, if it be not perverted by the futile regulations of some short-sighted politician." [1] But it is in the great work of the clergyman Malthus that the opinion takes its most theological form. "By this wise provision," he says, "*i.e.* by making the passion of self-love beyond comparison stronger than the passion of benevolence, the more ignorant are led to pursue the general happiness, an end which they would have totally failed to attain if the moving principle of their conduct had been benevolence. Benevolence, indeed, as the great and constant source of action, would require the most perfect knowledge of causes and effects, and therefore can only be the attribute of the Deity. In a being so short-sighted as man it would lead to the grossest errors, and soon transform the fair and cultivated soil of human society into a dreary scene of want and confusion." [2] This is the doctrine which, divested of its theological fervour and blended with the political doctrine of individual liberty, constitutes the main philosophical assumption of Ricardo's treatise.

It is necessary to consider the effect of these ideas upon the attitude of the economists, and the reception which was accorded to their doctrines. And first, for the idea of the supreme value of individual liberty.

It was as the gospel of industrial freedom that the *Wealth of Nations* obtained its magical power. The civilised world was

---

[1] *A Comparative View of the Effects of Rent and of Tythe in influencing the Price of Corn*, 1801. In *Recreations in Agriculture*, vol. v. (2d series, vol. i.) p. 408.

[2] Malthus, *Essay on Population*, 1872 (7th edition, Appendix), p. 492.

restless with dreams of political emancipation; it trembled with expectation of a deliverance to come. The principle which was in the mind of every eager politician Adam Smith and the Physiocrats applied to industry and trade. They claimed " as one of the most sacred rights of mankind," not merely liberty of thought and speech, but liberty of production and exchange. Personal, political, and industrial liberty were for them but parts of one great system; and if they dwelt with greater emphasis on industrial liberty it was because they saw in that the most certain and least dangerous remedy for the evils of their time. It was impossible, however, to advocate the one without giving support to the other; and it is interesting to find Adam Smith pointed to in the House of Lords as the real originator of the " French Principles," against which a crusade was contemplated. " With respect to French principles, as they have been denominated," said the Marquis of Lansdowne, three years after Smith's death, " these principles have been exported from us to France, and cannot be said to have originated among the people of the latter country. The new principles of government founded on the abolition of the old feudal system were originally propagated among us by the Dean of Gloucester, Mr. Tucker, and have since been more generally inculcated by Dr. Adam Smith in his work on the *Wealth of Nations*, which has been recommended as a book necessary for the information of youth by Mr. Dugald Stewart in his *Elements of the Philosophy of the Human Mind.*"[1]

Without stopping to comment on this curious statement, we may remark that it is a striking evidence of the impression produced on a cultivated mind by Adam Smith's great work as a treatise of political philosophy. Such in fact it was, as we know from Adam Smith's own words, the statements of his pupil, and the composition of the work itself. Whether he writes as a pamphleteer or a historian; whether he is pursuing a grave investigation into the influence of political institutions on economic progress, or dogging tedious and confused advocates of the mercantile system through all the weary windings of their arguments; whether he is engaged in learned research, fierce denunciation, or dubious refutation, every page of Adam Smith's writings is illumined by one great

---

[1] House of Lords, February 1, 1793.

passion, the passion for freedom. This was the first and last word of his political and industrial philosophy, as it was the first and last word of the political and industrial philosophy of the age. All around were the signs of an obsolete system of restriction, cramping and choking political and industrial life. Every philosopher, every enlightened statesman, every enlightened merchant saw only one remedy. Talking with Turgot in Paris, or with Cochran, "one of the sages of the kingdom," in Glasgow, Adam Smith found the same echo of his own opinions. Turgot in Limousin, Adam Smith in Glasgow, saw in a different form the hateful evils of the ancient system. Whilst Turgot, the governor of a province, was labouring day and night to improve the condition of down-trodden peasants, Adam Smith, the professor, was shielding from the effects of obsolete privileges the greatest mechanical genius of the age. Nothing can be more interesting than that story of James Watt, refused permission to practise his trade by the corporation of hammermen, but admitted by the professor within the walls of the University of Glasgow, and allowed there to set up his workshop. Thus in Glasgow, "a perfect bee-hive of industry," according to Smollett, where people were filled "with a noble spirit of enterprise," where commercial and intellectual activity went hand in hand—many of the principal writings of the mercantile system being reprinted there whilst Adam Smith was giving his lectures—and in Limousin, the oppressed and poverty-stricken French province, the same lesson was being forced into men's minds—the need of liberty; and at the same time great mechanical inventions were preparing the way for a new age.

The *Wealth of Nations* was published on the eve of an industrial revolution. When Adam Smith talked with James Watt in his workshop at Glasgow, he little thought that by the invention of the steam-engine Watt would make possible the realisation of that freedom which Adam Smith looked upon as a dream, a utopia. It is true we see traces in the *Wealth of Nations* of the great changes that were everywhere beginning, but the England described by Adam Smith differed more from the England of to-day than it did from the England of the middle ages. The cotton manufacture is mentioned only once in Smith's book. The staple industries of the country were still wool, tanned leather, and hardware, while silk and linen came next in importance. Iron was still smelted chiefly by charcoal, though smelting by pit-coal had been introduced. It was not, however, produced in such quantities as to supply the greater part of England's demand; much was imported from America, Russia, and Sweden. Wool and silk were woven and spun in scattered villages by families who eked out their subsistence by agriculture. "Manufacturer" meant not the owner of power-looms and steam-engines and factories, buying and selling in the markets of the world, but the actual weaver at his loom, the actual spinner at her wheel. But seven years before the publication of the *Wealth of Nations* Arkwright had patented his water-frame and James Watt his steam-engine. A few years after its publication Cartwright invented the power-loom, Crompton the mule. It was by these discoveries that population was drawn out of cottages in distant valleys by secluded streams and driven together into factories and cities. Old restrictions became obsolete by sheer force of necessity, and the freedom of internal trade to which England, according to Adam Smith, owed so much, was completed under conditions which Adam Smith could not imagine.

In all respects but one the internal trade of England in the time of Adam Smith was completely free. "The inland trade," he says, "is almost perfectly free." And he adds, "this freedom of interior commerce . . . is perhaps one of the principal causes of the prosperity of Great Britain." But there was one great exception to this general freedom, and that was the position of labour, which was entangled in a perfect network of restrictions. Combination was illegal—a strike generally ended in "nothing but the punishment or ruin of the ringleaders." Laws of settlement prevented the emigration of artisans and labourers. "There is scarce a poor man in England of forty years of age, I will venture to say," wrote Adam Smith, "who has not in some part of his life felt himself most cruelly oppressed by this ill-contrived law of settlement." Emigration of labourers was forbidden by statute. Corporation laws and the law of apprenticeship closed innumerable employments. Adam Smith's condemnation of these restrictions is memorable : "The property which every man has in his own labour, as it is the original foundation of all other property, so it is the most sacred and inviolable. The patrimony of a poor man lies in the strength and dexterity of his hands, and to hinder him from employing this strength and dexterity in what manner he thinks proper, without injury to his neighbour, is a plain violation of this most sacred property." Equally memorable is the famous edict of Turgot for the dissolution of the *jurandes*, which adopts almost the same language : " God, when He made man with wants, and rendered labour an indispensable resource, made the right of work the property of every individual in the world, and this property is the first, the most sacred, and the most imprescriptible of all kinds of property. We regard it as one of the first duties of our justice, and as one of the acts most of all worthy of our benevolence, to free our subjects from every infraction of that inalienable right of humanity." It is correctly stated by Malthus that Adam Smith mixes up with one profound subject of his treatise "another still more interesting "—" the causes which affect the happiness and comfort of the lower orders of society, which in every nation form the most numerous class." And the result of his investigation was the demand for free exchange of labour. " Break down," he writes, " the exclusive privilege of corporations, and repeal the statute of apprenticeship, both which are real encroachments on natural liberty, and add to these the repeal of the law of settlement." This was his remedy for the distress of the mass of the people.

Now it is not the doctrine of free exchange of goods that has brought political economists into collision with the feelings of the people—it is the doctrine of free exchange of labour. Yet we see that this doctrine was first popularised by a warm champion of the labourers as the true solution of all the evils of their state. It is impossible to ascertain how far this demand for the abolition of corporation and apprentice laws really represented the opinions of the workmen of that age. Adam Smith's language would lead us to suppose that it did. But whatever may have been their wishes with respect to the removal of particular restrictions then, it is certain that this doctrine of freedom of labour has since then become the principal weapon against the methods by which the labourers have sought to improve their condition. The explanation of this result of the theory of industrial freedom must be sought in the latent assumption which made it possible for Adam Smith to offer it as a complete solution of the labour question. Had he attempted to analyse competition, even under the conditions of his own time, he would have become conscious of the fatal flaw in his doctrine. He would have discovered that what he sought to establish was the *free competition of equal industrial units*, that what he was in fact helping to establish was the *free competition of unequal industrial units*. This was the disastrous oversight. Adam Smith believed in the natural economic equality of men. That being so, it only needed legal equality of rights and all would go well. Liberty was to him the gospel of salvation; he could not imagine that it might become the means of destruction—that legal liberty, where there was no real economic independence, might turn to the disadvantage of the workman. He never dreamed that Freedom, the instrument by which monopoly was to be destroyed, might become the means of establishing monopoly.

It is true that Adam Smith saw that the labourer was not a match for his employer in making a bargain, that he was poorer, weaker, and oppressed by the law. But he did not on that account recognise the necessity of combination. Misled by the observation that all obstacles to industry seemed in the past to have come from associations, all progress from individuals—an observation which partly explains the indifference of the early economists to co-operation—he distinctly condemned every form of association, and though his belief in the limited functions of the State prevented him from suggesting that the State should suppress them, he was of opinion that it should at least give no facilities for them. As soon, however, as the factory system was established, the inequality of women and children in their struggle with employers attracted the attention of even the most careless observers; and, attention once drawn to this circumstance, it was not long before the inequality of adult men was also brought into prominence. The recognition of the first resulted in the Factory Acts; the recognition of the second in the abolition of the combination laws and the acknowledgment of the true function of trades-unions in the settlement of wages.

It is a remarkable fact that Hume, who, at the advice of Ricardo, proposed the repeal of the combination laws, though quoting Adam Smith in favour of free-trade in labour, yet based his argument largely on the inequality of the isolated workman in making his bargain with his employer. "The property of the masters," he said, quoting a particular case, " enabled them to get the better of the men; who were at last obliged to come in unconditionally. When they did this, the masters punished their resistance in a very decided manner; for they actually deducted the loss they had sustained by this cessation of labour from the amount of the men's wages, the men being obliged to pay at the rate of 10 per cent. per week until the masters declared themselves satisfied." Again, in another debate: "If the masters combined to give their men only half a sufficient rate of wages, and had strength enough to starve them into taking it, there was nothing in the bill to prevent their doing so. And how could this danger be met by the workmen, except by counter-combination; for which, short of carrying them to the extent of violence, he still thought they ought to have the fullest permission." This argument of Hume's is the more notice-able, because, nearly ten years afterwards, in a debate on the Factory Acts, he ignored it altogether. He could see the force of the argu-ment when seeking to remove old restrictions on trade: he could not see it when seeking to resist the imposition of new restrictions on trade. In the debate on the Government Factory Bill, 18th August 1833, he declared himself "perfectly satisfied that all legislation of this nature is pernicious and injurious to those whom it is intended to protect; and I have not the slightest doubt that, if this bill should continue in operation five years, it will have produced in-calculable mischief. It must be the interest of masters to protect their workmen; and it is a libel upon human nature to suppose that they will allow persons in their employment to be injured for the want of due caution." A changed estimate this of the masters' humanity from his estimate nine years before.

Very different from Hume's attitude was that of Michael Thomas Sadler, the Tory socialist, who attacked the economists in the House of Commons, questioned their infallibility and, as his followers delighted to assert, endangered their ascendency. Speaking on the same subject in the year before, Sadler used the argument which Hume himself had once employed but now repudiated, only with much greater passion and significance. Dealing with the expected opposition to his bill, he said: "I apprehend the strongest objection that will be offered on this occasion will be grounded upon the pretence that the very principle of the bill is an improper interference between the employer and the employed, and an attempt to regulate by law the market of labour. Were that market supplied by free agents, properly so denominated, I should fully participate in their objections. Theoretically, indeed, such is the case; but practically, I fear the fact is far otherwise, even regarding those who are of mature age; and the boasted freedom of our labourers in many pursuits will, in a just view of their condition, be found to be little more than nominal. Those who argue the question on mere abstract principles seem, in my apprehension, too much to forget the condition of society, the unequal division of property, or rather its total monopoly by the few, leaving the many nothing whatever but what they can obtain by their daily labour; which very labour cannot become available for the purpose of daily subsistence without the consent of those who own the property of the community, all the materials, elements, call them what you please, on which labour is bestowed, being in their possession. Hence it is clear that, excepting in a state of things where the demand for labour fully equals the supply (which it would be absurdly false to say exists in this country), the employer and the employed do not meet on equal terms in the market of labour; on the contrary, the latter, whatever his age, and call him as free as you please, is often almost entirely at the mercy of the former. He would be wholly so were it not for the operation of the poor laws, which are a palpable interference with the market of labour, and condemned as such by their opponents."[1] It was the refusal of the economists to recognise this truth—their absolute disregard of it—which gave the greatest impulse to socialistic speculation in England. Had they acknowledged, instead of seeking to disprove, the industrial inequality of men, the epithets, " cruel, inhuman, infant killer," heaped upon them would have been spared, and the best part of the popular repugnance to Political Economy would have been avoided.

The influence of a recognition of the economic inequality of men on our estimate of competition is immense. Not admitting, with the socialist, the natural right of all men to an equal share in the benefits of civilisation, not proposing, with the socialist, to stamp out competition, and substitute a community of goods, we yet plead for the right of all to equal opportunities of development, according to their nature. Competition we now recognise to be a

---

[1] House of Commons, March 16, 1832.

thing neither good nor bad ; we look upon it as resembling a great physical force which cannot be destroyed, but may be controlled and modified. As the cultivator embanks a stream and distributes its waters to irrigate his fields, so we control competition by positive laws and institutions. These we recognise may be altered and reformed; a better economy of competition may be obtained, and better results may be reached. But just as the cultivator knows that when he has obtained the best system of irrigation, he must have sunlight and rain from heaven to ripen his crops, so we know that when we have done our best with competition, when we have controlled it and modified it, the fullest life will not be reached without the action of religion and morality. The old economists thought competition good in itself. The socialists think it an evil in itself. We think it neither good nor evil, but seek to analyse it, and ascertain when it produces good and when it produces bad results. The old economists thought competition allsufficient to secure the welfare of mankind. The socialists think community of goods and equality of distribution all-sufficient. We accept competition as one means, a force to be used, not to be blindly worshipped ; but assert religion and morality to be the necessary conditions of attaining human welfare.

The conception of individual liberty in Adam Smith was, however, as we have seen, not a merely negative conception. It had a positive side, and received substance and reality from the second idea already referred to—the idea of the desire of the individual to better his condition as the mainspring of progress, of the identity of individual and social interests. It was this idea which lent force to the advocacy of unrestricted competition and absolute freedom of contract, as we see in the words of Hume quoted above. It was this idea which made the economists, in the first instance, so indifferent to association. A long and bitter experience was required to convince them of the insufficiency of individual effort to secure the general good. Their suspicion of trade combinations and reluctant admission of co-operation as a social remedy, are both due to the same cause.

Closely connected with this idea is the principle of *Laissez Faire*. Undoubtedly related to the worship of nature—that great reaction of the eighteenth century against artificial conditions of ife—and in many instances visibly confirmed by experience, this doctrine obtained an extraordinary hold upon the minds of men. It became identified with Political Economy as a practical science. Later economists, like Mill and Cairnes, have indeed modified it; but just as the belief in a natural or divine arrangement of human instincts lent power to it at first, so an elaborate analogy between the individual and social organism, which is the latest product of our philosophy, bids fair to give fresh power to it in our own days. And yet this theory of the sufficiency of individual self-seeking for the salvation of the race, with its practical outcome in the precept of *Laissez Faire*, includes within itself, like other generalisations of the early economists, some unwarrantable assumptions. It assumes not only that the economic interest of the individual is in fact identical with that of the community, but that he knows his own interest and follows it. But it is perfectly clear that, in the case of adulteration, of jerry-building, and of the hundred and one devices of modern trade by which a man may grow rich at the expense of his neighbours, the first of these assumptions breaks down. Whatever may be the case with his higher moral interests, the economic interest of the individual is certainly not always identical with that of the community. Neither can it be said that he always even knows his economic interest, especially under the complex conditions of modern industry and commerce. That he follows his interest, or what he conceives to be his interest, is no doubt a safer assumption, though even this truth lacks the universality attributed to it in this mechanical conception of human action.

The whole theory, indeed, of the identity of individual and common interests is a perfect instance of the reckless abstractness of the old kind of Political Economy. There is a truth underlying it, but it is a truth which the theory overstates. The truth in question is, that under a system of division of labour each man can only live by finding out what other people want. The pressure of competition does undoubtedly tend to the satisfaction of the greatest number of wants at the lowest cost, but not without innumerable evils in the process—evils which, as we now see, the wise regulation of the competitive impulse may, in a number of instances, avert. But as long as the identity of the individual and general interest was preached as a universal truth, every attempt to regulate competition was decried as an unwise and even an impious interference with the providential scheme for making each man's selfishness subservient to the good of all his neighbours.

Another conception which strengthened the belief in individual liberty—the mere freedom from restrictions—as the great economic truth, was the idea of invariable law. This was one of the chief bulwarks of *Laissez Faire.* It is in Malthus that the idea of invariable law in the economic world first makes its appearance. A little later we find in Ricardo the first instance of that comparison of economic laws to the law of gravity which has been echoed with wearisome iteration ever since. Economists have failed to distinguish between laws of physical and laws of social science. They have refused to see that whilst the former are inevitable and eternal, the latter—though some of them too, like that of "diminishing returns," are immutable—express, for the most part, facts of human nature, which is capable of modification by self-conscious human endeavour.

It must be admitted, however, that this idea of law produced one great effect. It made men patient—those men at least who believed in it. To this fact must be attributed the singular confidence exhibited by economists in the result of teaching Political Economy to the working classes. Teach them, it was said, that the rate of wages is not the result of accidental causes within the control of man, but of great natural laws beyond his control, and all will be well. But, so far from having the desired effect, it was just the insistence on this doctrine which brought Political Economy into conflict with the working classes. The wage-fund theory, of which Malthus is the undoubted author, and the consequent denunciation of combinations of workmen as useless, was the great cause of feud. In this case the law, so far from being of universal validity, was not true at all. This is now generally recognised. But the popular expounders of economic principles, especially in the newspapers, were prompt to accept it, and thus Political Economy entered into alliance with the capitalists against the labourers.

But it was not only that Political Economy asserted the existence of laws that did not exist. More misleading still was the failure of ordinary economic writers to distinguish between laws and precepts, between general statements of fact and the practical maxims based upon them. It is true that writers like Cairnes have striven to make it clear that the laws of economics are as distinct as possible from rules of action, that Political Economy is "neutral." But they forget that the laws of Political Economy are converted into rules by sheer force of necessity, and that the maintenance of this neutrality is practically impossible. Some answer must be given to the pressing questions of the day, and if Political Economy did not lay down rules and become a practical science, journalism would. And, as a matter of fact, while affecting the reserved and serious air of students, political economists have all the time been found brawling in the market-place.

By these various influences acting upon them from so many sides was the belief in individual freedom, in the uselessness of industrial restrictions, established and confirmed in the minds of the older economists as the central doctrine of their science. But it was just this doctrine which was the chief cause of the fierce antagonism they aroused. If we would probe to the bottom the cause which excited the liveliest invective against economists we always come back to the charge of individualism. Of that continuous storm of denunciation which has been poured down upon the central doctrine of liberalism, the economists have received the largest share. And this is natural; for the conception of men, not as members of families, associations, and nations, but as isolated individuals connected only by pecuniary interests, is essentially the conception of them which pervaded economic science. And not only was this conception the peculiar characteristic of Political Economy as a theoretical science, but it determined its whole bearing as a practical science. I have alluded to the fatal confusion between laws and precepts which made Political Economy appear as the gospel of self-interest. But though it was not the gospel of self-interest in the sense often supposed, it did without doubt place absolute reliance on individual action; it did without doubt practically assert that pecuniary interest was a sufficient bond between men—the primary bond at any rate in the present age. No wonder, then, that against the economists were arrayed philosophers, moralists, even statesmen. All these saw in the doctrine of individualism a solvent of domestic, political and national union—a great disintegrating element of social life. They all saw in the proclamation of the reign of self-interest the universal abolition of feelings of kindliness and gratitude, of filial reverence and paternal care, of political fidelity and patriotism—in short, of all the sentiments which welded society into a whole. Christian ministers lamented the decay of domestic ties, the refusal of children to support parents, the neglect of parents to educate children. Moralists deplored the growing alienation of masters and workmen—the harsh self-seeking of the employers, the indolence and hatred of the employed. Statesmen lamented the destruction of national life, the subordination of national welfare to individual gain, the advocacy of measures which might enrich individuals, but must, they thought, disintegrate the empire. "If an empire were made of dust," said Napoleon, "it would be pounded to dust by the economists." "The entire tendency of the modern or Malthusian Political Economy is to denationalise," said Coleridge. "At the very outset," he said on another occasion, "what are we to think of the soundness of this modern system of Political Economy, the direct tendency of which is to denationalise, and to make the law of our country a foolish superstition?" "We have profoundly forgotten," wrote Carlyle some years later, "that cash-payment is not the sole relation of human beings; we think, nothing doubting, that it absolves and liquidates all engagements to man. . . . 'My starving workers?' answers the rich mill-owner; 'did not I hire them fairly in the market? did I not pay them to the last sixpence the sum covenanted for? what have I to do with them more?'" "Society," writes his disciple Mr. Froude, "is an aggregate of dust."

Such was the accusation. Political Economy, it was said, destroyed the moral and political relations of men, and dissolved the social union. It is remarkable that this accusation was made not only by philosophers and moralists, but by politicians. And it is still more remarkable that the defects of Political Economy were never more clearly stated than in the days of its greatest influence—in the golden era of economic discussion which preceded free-trade. But for all the force with which the accusation was urged, the opponents of Political Economy were defeated. In one memorable point, and in one alone—the regulation of factories—were they successful. In their general attack upon individualism they were completely beaten. And the reason was because they failed to see that the old economic conditions had to be destroyed before new moral relations could come into existence. Right in their general conception, they were wrong in their particular application of it. For the moral relations which they wished to preserve were based upon the dependence of the labourer, and until that dependence was destroyed no new life could be reached. The historical method, the great enemy of the old Political Economy, is here on the side of the old economists against their assailants. For it shows us how the " cash-nexus," which the latter denounced so vehemently, is essential to the independence of the labourer. And that independence is a necessary condition of the new and higher form of social union, which is based on the voluntary association of free men.[1]

The historical method has revolutionised Political Economy, not by showing its laws to be false, but by proving that they are relative for the most part to a particular stage of civilisation. This destroys their character as eternal laws, and strips them of much of their force and all their sanctity. In this way the historical method has rescued us from intellectual superstitions.

The earlier economists, like Adam Smith, were concerned with production. Increased production was necessary for man as an instrument of social and political progress. And the old economy succeeded in establishing new conditions of production. But when it came to the more delicate task of distribution it failed. A more equitable distribution of wealth is now demanded and required. But this end can only be attained coincidently with moral progress. For such an end a gospel of life is needed, and the old Political Economy had none. This was its great fault, a fault which, now its work is done, has become glaring in the extreme. Such a gospel must now be put forward or all that work will fail. Morality must be united with economics as a practical science. The better distribution which is sought for will then be found in

---

[1] At this point the consecutive MSS., which bears traces of being hastily written in the preceding paragraph, breaks off altogether, and there remain only some fragmentary passages which Toynbee never wove into the thread of his argument.—ED.

the direction of (1) a modification of the idea of private property by (*a*) public opinion and (*b*) legislation, but not so as to destroy individualism, which will itself be modified by duty and the love of man; (2) State action in the interest of the whole people; (3) association not only of producers but of consumers.

.   .   .   .

THE INDUSTRIAL REVOLUTION.[1]

I.

INTRODUCTORY.

Division of the subject—Advantages of combining the study of History and Political Economy—The Deductive Method—The Historical Method—Importance of a discussion of Method—Laws and precepts relative—The Social Problems of the Present to be borne in mind in studying the history of the Past.

THE subject of these lectures is the Industrial and Agrarian Revolution at the end of the eighteenth and beginning of the nineteenth centuries. The course is divided into three parts. The first deals with Adam Smith and the England of his time. It will describe England on the eve of the Industrial Revolution, and the system of regulation and protection of industry as it existed in 1760. It will give also an outline of Adam Smith's book, its aims and character, and especially his theory of free trade. The second part will group itself round the work of Malthus, who dealt not so much with the causes of wealth as with the causes of poverty, with the distribution of wealth rather than with its production. It will describe England in the midst of the Industrial Revolution, and will inquire into the problem of pauperism and the subjects connected with it. The third part will be associated with the name of Ricardo, and will deal with England at the time of the Peace. It will discuss the doctrine of rent and wages together with certain theories of economic progress, *and will cover the questions of currency, so much agitated at that period, and the history of the commercial and financial changes which followed the Peace.*[2]

[1] The fragment of economic history here printed under the title of the "Industrial Revolution," a title that Toynbee had himself selected for a book, of which the following pages contain some of the raw material, consists of notes of lectures delivered by Toynbee in the Hall of Balliol College, Oxford, between October 1881 and Midsummer 1882.

[2] The sequel, as readers will observe, realises very imperfectly the plan here sketched out by Toynbee, and especially fails to deal with those portions of the scheme which are described in the words printed in italics. This is due partly to the fact that Toynbee himself found his subject, as he first conceived it, too large to be dealt with in a single course of lectures, and partly to the imperfection of even the best notes taken by his hearers, especially on the more diffi-

I have chosen the subject because it was in this period that modern Political Economy took its rise. It has been a weakness of the science as pursued in England that it has been too much dissociated from History. Adam Smith and Malthus, indeed, had historical minds ; but the form of modern text-books is due to Ricardo, whose mind was entirely unhistorical. Yet there is a double advantage in combining the two studies. In the first place Political Economy is better understood by this means. Abstract propositions are seen in a new light when studied in relation to the facts which were before the writer at the time when he formulated them. So regarded they are at once more vivid and less likely to mislead. Ricardo becomes painfully interesting when we read the history of his time. And, in the second place, History also is better understood when studied in connection with Political Economy ; for the latter not only teaches us in reading History to look out for the right kind of facts, but enables us to explain many phenomena like those attending the introduction of enclosures and machinery, or the effects of different systems of currency, which without its assistance would remain unintelligible. The careful deductive reasoning, too, which Political Economy teaches, is of great importance to the historian, and the habits of mind acquired from it are even more valuable than the knowledge of principles which it gives, especially to students of facts, who might otherwise be overwhelmed by the mass of their materials.

Of late years, however, there has been a steady sustained attack upon the abstract Deductive Method of Political Economy pursued by Ricardo and Mill, and an attempt to set up historical investigation in its place as the only true method of economic inquiry. This attack rests on a misconception of the function of the Deductive Method. The best exposition of the place of Abstract Political Economy is to be found in Bagehot's *Economic Studies.* Bagehot points out that this abstract science holds good only upon certain assumptions, but though the assumptions are often not entirely correct, the results may yet be approximately true. Thus the economists, firstly, regard only one part of man's nature, and treat him simply as a money-making animal ; secondly, they disregard the influence of custom, and only take account of com-

cult and abstruse, and in particular the purely financial and monetary, topics discussed by him.—Ed.

petition.   Certain laws are laid down under these assumptions;
as, for instance, that the rate of wages always tends to an equality,
the permanent difference obtaining in various employments being
only sufficient to balance the favourable or unfavourable circumstances attending each of them—a law which is only true after a
certain stage of civilisation and in so far as the acquisition of
wealth is the sole object of men.   Such hypothetical laws, though
leading only to rough conclusions, are yet useful in giving us a
point of view from which to observe and indicate the existence of
strong overmastering tendencies.   Advocates of the Historical
Method, like Mr. Cliffe Leslie, therefore go too far when they condemn the Deductive Method as radically false.   There is no real
opposition between the two.   The apparent opposition is due to a
wrong use of deduction; to a neglect on the part of those employing it to examine closely their assumptions and to bring their
conclusions to the test of fact; to arguments based on premises
which are not only not verified but absolutely untrue (as in the
wage-fund theory); and generally to the failure to combine induction with deduction.   But this misuse of the method does not
imply any radical faultiness in it.   The right method in any particular case must be largely determined by the nature of the
problem.   Neither is it fair to make abstract Political Economy
responsible for the confusion in many minds between its laws and
the precepts which are based on them.   It is a pure science, and
its end is knowledge.   But the Political Economy of the press and
the platform is a practical science, that is, a body of rules and
maxims to guide conduct.   Journalists and Members of Parliament confound the laws of the pure science with the maxims of
the practical science.   It was thus that Mr. Gladstone in the
Land Act controversy of 1881 was constantly accused of violating
the laws of Political Economy.   It was impossible for Mr. Gladstone
to do any such thing.   The laws of Political Economy can no more
be violated than those of physical science.   What the journalists
meant was that he had departed from a great economic precept—
that which recommends freedom of contract.

The Historical Method pursues a different line of investigation.
It examines the actual causes of economic development and considers the influence of institutions, such as the mediæval guilds,
our present land-laws, or the political constitution of any given

country, in determining the distribution of wealth. Without the aid of the Historical Method it would be impossible, for instance, to understand why one-half of the land in the United Kingdom is owned by 2512 persons.[1]

And not only does it investigate the stages of economic development in a given country, but it compares them with those which have obtained in other countries and times, and seeks by such comparison to discover laws of universal application. Take, as an instance of the discoveries of this Comparative Political Economy, the tendency which Sir H. Maine and M. de Laveleye have pointed out to pass from collective to individual ownership of land. This is a law which is true of nearly all civilised countries. We must be careful, however, not to generalise too hastily in these matters. A clever pamphlet lately published in Dublin appeals to another generalisation of Sir H. Maine—"Maine's Law," as it is denominated—in condemnation of recent legislation. "Sir H. Maine," says the writer, "in his *Ancient Law* has remarked that the movement of all progressive societies has hitherto been a movement from status to contract. The demand of this agitation is that Ireland should be legislatively declared a retrograde society, and that the social movement should be from contract back again to status."[2] "Is it expedient," asks another, "to reform our laws so as to assimilate them to those in use among nations of an inferior social development?"[3] A deeper study of existing civilisation in England, and of other civilisations, past and present, would have shown that the step was not a retrograde one,—that whilst the sphere of contract has been widening, it has been also narrowing, and that such a condition of things as we see in Ireland has never existed anywhere else without deep social misery, outrage, and disturbance. Custom or law or public opinion, or all three, have intervened in the past, and will intervene in the future. It is true that there is a movement from status to contract; yet if we look closely, we find that the State has over and over again had to in-

[1] The owners of properties over 3000 acres, and yielding a rental of at least £3000 are 2512 ; they own in

England and Wales,	14,287,373	acres out of	34,344,226.
Scotland,	14,118,164	„	18,986,694.
Ireland,	9,120,689	„	20,316,129.

—BATEMAN's *Great Landowners.*

[2] *Confiscation or Contract ?* (Dublin, 1880), p. 23.

[3] Richey, *The Irish Land-Laws,* p. 108.

terfere to restrict the power of individuals in which this movement results. The real course of development has been first from status to contract, then from contract to a new kind of status determined by the law,—or, in other words, from unregulated to regulated contract.

The Historical Method is also of value because it makes us see where economic laws and precepts are relative.[1] The old economists were wont to speak as if these laws and precepts were universal. Free trade, for instance, is a sound policy, no doubt, for England, and for all nations at a certain stage of development; but it is open to any one to say that free trade is only good under certain conditions. No English economist, it is true, has dared to say this. Mr. Jevons, to take an example, would admit restrictions only for considerations of the most paramount importance.[2] But it is an unjustifiable prejudgment of the question to lay down that this policy must be wise at all times and places. I do not mean to assert, however, that there are not some laws which are universally true, such as the law of diminishing returns.

This discussion about method may seem barren, but it is not really so. Take such a question as the functions of the State. Mr. Senior spent much time in attempting to discover an universal formula which should define their proper limit all the world over. Such an attempt must be abandoned. The proper limits of Government interference are relative to the nature of each particular state and the stage of its civilisation. It is a matter of great importance at the present day for us to discover what these limits are in our own case, for administration bids fair to claim a large share of our attention in the future. It would be well if, in studying the past,[3] we could always bear in mind the problems of the present, and go to that past to seek large views of what is of lasting importance to the human race. It is an old complaint that histories leave out of

---

[1] Comte was one of the first to recognise this truth, and it was from him, that Mill learned that "the deductive science of society will not lay down a theorem asserting in an universal manner the effect of any cause, but will rather teach us how to frame the proper theorem for the circumstances of any given case. It will not give the laws of society in general, but the means of determining the phenomena of any given society from the particular elements or data of that society."—*System of Logic*, bk. vi. c. 9, § 2.

[2] As, for instance, to check the exhaustion of our coal supplies.—*The Coal Question*, 247-354.

[3] Toynbee was addressing an audience principally composed of men studying for the History Schools.—Ed.

sight those vital questions which are connected with the condition of the people. The French Revolution has indeed profoundly modified our views of History, but much still remains to be done in that direction. If I could persuade some of those present to study Economic History, to follow out the impulse originally given by Malthus to the study of the history of the mass of the people, I should be indeed glad. Party historians go to the past for party purposes; they seek to read into the past the controversies of the present. You must pursue facts for their own sake, but penetrated with a vivid sense of the problems of your own time. This is not a principle of perversion, but a principle of selection. You must have some principle of selection, and you could not have a better one than to pay special attention to the history of the social problems which are agitating the world now, for you may be sure that they are problems not of temporary but of lasting importance.

II.

ENGLAND IN 1760.

POPULATION.

Numbers of population difficult to determine—Finlayson's estimate—The distribution of population—The growth of the great towns—Rural and urban population—The occupations of the people.

PREVIOUSLY to 1760 the old industrial system obtained in England; none of the great mechanical inventions had been introduced; the agrarian changes were still in the future. It is this industrial England which we have to contrast with the industrial England of to-day. For determining the population of the time we have no accurate materials. There are no official returns before 1801. A census had been proposed in 1753, but rejected as " subversive of the last remains of English liberty." [1]   In this absence

[1] Mr. Thornton, member for the City of York, said: "I did not believe that there was any set of men, or indeed any individual of the human species, so presumptuous and so abandoned as to make the proposal we have just heard. . . . I hold this project to be totally subversive of the last remains of English liberty. . . . The new Bill will direct the imposition of new taxes, and indeed the addition of a very few words will make it the most effective engine of rapacity and

of trustworthy data all sorts of wild estimates were formed. During the American War a great controversy raged on this subject. Dr. Price, an advocate of the Sinking Fund, maintained that population had in the interval between 1690 and 1777 declined from 6,596,075 to 4,763,670.[1] On the other hand, Mr. Howlett, Vicar of Dunmow, in Essex, estimated the population in 1780 at 8,691,000,[2] and Arthur Young, in 1770, at 8,500,000 on the lowest estimate.[3] These, however, are the extremes in either direction. The computations now most generally accepted are those made by Mr. Finlaison (Actuary to the National Debt Office), and published in the Preface to the Census Returns of 1831. These are based on an examination of the registers of baptisms and burials during the eighteenth century. But the data are deficient in three respects : because the number of people existing at the date when the computation begins is a matter of conjecture ; because in some parishes there were no registers ; and because the registration, being voluntary, was incomplete.[4] Mr. Finlaison, however, is stated to have subjected his materials to " every test suggested by the present comparatively advanced state of physical and statistical science." [5]

Now, according to Mr. Finlaison, the population of England and Wales was, in 1700, 5,134,516, in 1750, 6,039,684, an increase of not quite a million, or between 17 and 18 per cent. in the first half of the century.[6] In 1801 the population of England and Wales was 9,187,176, showing an increase of three millions, or

---

oppression which was ever used against an injured people. . . . Moreover, an annual register of our people will acquaint our enemies abroad with our weakness."—*Vide Preface to Preliminary Census Returns,* 1881, p. 1. The Bill was carried in the Commons by large majorities, but thrown out on second reading by the Lords.

[1] *An Essay on the Population of England from the Revolution to the Present Time,* by Richard Price, D.D., F.R.S. (London, 1780).

[2] *An Examination of Dr. Price's Essay on the Population of England and Wales,* by Rev. John Howlett (1781). See M'Culloch's *Literature of Political Economy,* p. 258.

[3] *Northern Tour,* iv. 419 (2d edition, 1771).

[4] Porter's *Progress of the Nation,* p. 5 (2d edition, 1847).

[5] *Ibid.* p. 13.

[6] Slightly different calculations are made by Mr. Rickman (*Introductory Remarks to Census Returns of* 1841, pp. 36, 37), and Mr. Marshall in his *Geographical and Statistical Display* (1833), p. 22. The former gives the population in 1700 at 6,045,008, and in 1750 at 6,517,035, being an increase of nearly 8 per cent. ; the latter gives 5,475,000 and 6,467,000 for the two dates, or an increase of 18·1 per cent. Gregory King, in 1696, estimates, from "the assessments on marriages, births, and burials," the population at 5,500,000.

more than 52 per cent. in the second half.[1] The difference in the rate of increase is significant of the great contrast presented by the two periods. In the former, England, though rapidly increasing in wealth owing to her extended commercial relations, yet retained her old industrial organisation ; the latter is the age of transition to the modern industrial system, and to improved methods of agriculture.

The next point to consider is the distribution of population. A great difference will be found here between the state of things at the beginning of the eighteenth century, or in Adam Smith's time, and that prevailing now. Every one remembers Macaulay's famous description in the beginning of his history of the desolate condition of the northern counties. His picture is borne out by Defoe, who, in his *Tour through the Whole Island* (1725), remarks that " the country south of Trent is by far the largest, as well as the richest and most populous," though the great cities were rivalled by those of the north.[2] If we consider as the counties north of Trent Northumberland, Durham, Yorkshire, Cumberland, Westmoreland, Lancashire, Cheshire, Derbyshire, Nottinghamshire, and Staffordshire (about one-third of the total area of England), we shall find on examination that in 1700 they contained about one-fourth of the population,[3] and in 1750 less than one-third,[4] while, in 1881, they contained more than two-fifths ;[5] or, taking only the six northern counties, we find that in 1700 their population was under one-fifth of that of all England, in 1750 it was about one-fifth, in 1881 it was all but one-third.[6]

In 1700 the most thickly peopled counties (excluding the metropolitan counties of Middlesex and Surrey) were Gloucestershire, Somerset, and Wilts, the manufacturing districts of the west; Worcestershire and Northamptonshire, the seats of the midland manufactures; and the agricultural counties of Herts and Bucks—all of them being south of the Trent. Between 1700 and 1750 the greatest increase of population took place in the following counties :—

---

[1] Mr. Rickman gives the rate of increase at 41 per cent., and Mr. Marshall at 42 per cent.

[2] iii. 57 (7th edition, 1769).

[3] 1,285,300 out of 5,108,500.

[4] 1,740,000 out of 6,017,700. These are Marshall's estimates; they differ a little from those of Mr. Finlaison.

[5] 10,438,705 out of 24,608,391.

[6] In 1700, 902,100 out of 5,108,500 ; in 1750, 1,261,500 out of 6,017,700 ; in 1881, 7,906,760 out of 24,608,391.

Lancashire increased from		166,200	to	297,400,	or	78 per cent.	
Warwickshire	„	96,600	„	140,000,	„	45	„
The West Riding of Yorkshire	„	} 236,700	„	361,500,	„	52	„
Durham	„	95,500	„	135,000,	„	41	„
Staffordshire	„	117,200	„	160,000,	„	36	„
Gloucestershire	„	155,200	„	207,800,	„	34	„

while Cornwall, Kent, Berks, Herts, Worcestershire, Salop, Cheshire, Northumberland, Cumberland, and Westmoreland each increased upwards of 20 per cent.[1]

The change in the distribution of population between the beginning of the eighteenth century and Adam Smith's time, and again between his time and our own, may be further illustrated by the following table. The twelve most densely populated counties and their density to the square mile were in—

1700		1750		1881	
Middlesex, . . .	2221	Middlesex, . .	2283	Middlesex, . . .	. 10,387
Surrey, ...	207	Surrey, . . .	276	Surrey, .	. 1,919
Gloucester, . . .	123	Warwick, . .	159	Lancashire, . .	1,813
Northampton, . .	121	Gloucester, . .	157	Durham, . . .	891
Somerset, . . .	119	Lancashire, . .	156	Stafford, . . .	862
Worcester, . . .	119	Worcester, . .	148	Warwick, . . .	825
Herts, ...	115	Herts, ...	141	West Riding, . .	815
Wilts, ...	113	Stafford, . . .	140	Kent, ...	600
Bucks, ...	110	Durham, . . .	138	Cheshire, . . .	582
Rutland, ...	110	Somerset, . .	137	Worcester, . . .	515
Warwick, . . .	109	West Riding, .	135	Nottingham, . .	475
Oxford, ...	107	Berks, . . .	131	Gloucester, . .	455

The most suggestive fact in the period between 1700 and 1750 is the great increase in Lancashire and the West Riding, the seats of the cotton and coarse woollen manufactures. Staffordshire and Warwickshire, with their potteries and hardware, had also largely grown. So had the two northern counties of Durham and Northumberland, with their coalfields. The West of England woollen districts of Somerset, and Wilts, on the other hand, though they had grown also, showed nothing like so great an increase. The population of the eastern counties, Norfolk, Suffolk, and Essex, had increased very little; though Norwich was still a large manufacturing town, and there were many smaller towns engaged in the woollen trade scattered throughout Norfolk

[1] J. Marshall: *A Geographical and Statistical Display*, etc. (1833), p. 12 ; printed also at the end of his *Analysis of Returns made to Parliament*, 1835.

and Suffolk.   Among the few agricultural counties which showed a decided increase during this period was Kent, the best farmed county in England at that time:

If we turn to the principal towns we shall find in many of them an extraordinary growth between the end of the seventeenth century and the time of Adam Smith.   While the population of Norwich had only increased, according to the best authority, by about one-third, and that of Worcester by one-half, the population of Sheffield had increased seven-fold, that of Liverpool ten-fold, of Manchester five-fold, of Birmingham seven-fold, of Bristol more than three-fold. The latter was still the second city in the kingdom.   Newcastle (including Gateshead and North and South Shields) numbered 40,000 people.

The following are the estimates of population for 1685, 1760, and 1881 in twelve great provincial towns :—

	1685.	*c.* 1760.	1881.[h]
Liverpool,	4,000 [a]	40,000 [c] 30-35,000 [d] 34,000 [e]	552,425
Manchester,	6,000 [a]	30,000 [c] 40-45,000 [d]	393,676
Birmingham,	4,000 [a]	28,000 [b] 30,000 [d]	400,757
Leeds,	7,000 [a]	——	309,126
Sheffield,	4,000 [a]	30,000 [c] 20,000 [d]	284,410
Bristol,	29,000 [a]	100,000 [d]	206,503
Nottingham,	8,000 [a]	17,711 [f]	111,631
Norwich,	28,000 [a]	40,000 [c] 60,000 [d]	87,843
Hull,	——	20,000 [c] 24,000 [d]	161,519
York,	10,000 [a]	——	59,596
Exeter,	10,000 [a]	——	47,098
Worcester,	8,000 [a]	11-12,000 [c]	40,421

Another point to be considered is the relation of rural to urban population.   According to Gregory King, writing in 1696, London contained 530,000 inhabitants, other cities and market-

[a] Macaulay's *History of England*, c. 3.   [b] Defoe's *Tour* (1725).
[c] Arthur Young (1769).   [d] Macpherson's *Annals of Commerce* (1760).
[e] Levi's *History of British Commerce.*
[f] Eden's *State of the Poor* (1797).   [g] Local estimate in Arthur Young.
[h] The returns for 1881 are those of the parliamentary district.

towns, 870,000, while villages and hamlets numbered 4,100,000.[1]
Arthur Young, seventy years later, calculated that London contained one-sixth of the whole population,[2] and remarked that, " in
flourishing countries," as England, " the half of a nation is found
in towns."[3] Both estimates are very unreliable, apart from the
fact that both, and especially that of Arthur Young, over-estimate
the total number of the population, but the contrast between them
justly indicates the tendency of towns even then to grow out of
proportion to the rural districts. That disproportion has, of course,
become even more marked since Arthur Young's day. In 1881
the total urban population was 17,285,026, or 66·6 per cent., while
the rural was 8,683,026, or 33·3 per cent.[4]

The only estimates of occupations with which I am acquainted
are again those of Gregory King in 1696, and Arthur Young in
1769. They are too vague, and too inconsistent with one another,
to be relied on, but I give them for what they are worth. According to the former, freeholders and their families numbered 940,000,
farmers and their families, 750,000, labouring people and out servants, 1,275,000, cottagers and paupers, 1,300,000 ; making a total
agricultural population of 4,265,000, against only 240,000 artisans
and handicraftsmen.[5] Arthur Young estimates the number of
different classes as follows :—

Farmers (whether freeholders or leaseholders), their servants and labourers,	2,800,000
Manufacturers of all kinds,	3,000,000
Landlords and their dependants, fisher-men and miners,	800,000
Persons engaged in commerce,	700,000
Non-industrious poor,	500,000
Clergy and lawyers,	200,000
Civil servants, army and navy,	500,000
Total,	8,500,000 [6]

[1] *Natural and Political Observations upon the State and Condition of England,*
by Gregory King, Lancaster Herald, 1696 (printed in Chalmers's *Estimate,* 1804),
p. 36.
[2] *Southern Tour,* p. 326 (2d edition, 1769).
[3] *Travels in France* (2nd edition), i. 480. He contrasts it with France, where
"less than one-fourth of the people inhabit towns." His estimate is, however,
in all probability exaggerated.
[4] Census Returns. See Preliminary Report, p. vii.
[5] Eden's *State of the Poor,* i. 228, and Chalmers's *Estimate* (1804), p. 203.
[6] *Northern Tour,* iv. 417-19 ; cf. also 364.

But the number set down to manufactures here is probably as much too high, in proportion to the total population, as the total itself is in excess of the fact.

III.

ENGLAND IN 1760.

AGRICULTURE.

Proportion of cultivated land to waste.—Large amount of common land.—Beneficial effect of enclosures upon agriculture.—Comparative progressiveness of different districts.—Improvements in cultivation and in the breed of live stock.—Slowness of agricultural development between 1700 and 1760.

IN describing the agriculture of the time the first point of importance is the proportion of cultivated land to waste. Gregory King, who rather over-estimated the total acreage of England and Wales, put the arable land at 11,000,000 acres, pasture and meadow at 10,000,000, houses, gardens, orchards, etc., at 1,000,000, being a total of 22,000,000 acres of cultivated land, or nearly three-fifths of the whole country.[1] A land-agent in 1727 believed one-half of the country to be waste.[2] Arthur Young, writing fifty years later, puts the cultivated area at a much higher figure. Estimating the total acreage of England alone at 34,000,000 acres, he considered that 32,000,000 of these were in arable and pasture, in equal proportions.[3]

One or other of the two first-mentioned estimates is certainly nearer the truth than the last. The exact proportion is, however, impossible to determine.

There is no respect in which the agricultural England of to-day differs more from that of the period which we are considering, than in the greatly reduced amount of common land. The enclosure of commons had been going on for centuries before 1760, but with nothing like the rapidity with which it has been going on since. It is known that 334,974 acres were enclosed between 1710 and

[1] P. 52 (ed. Chalmers, 1804).
[2] Edward Laurence, *Duty of a Steward to his Lord.* London, 1727.
[3] *Northern Tour*, iv. 340-41. See also *Eastern Tour*, iv. 455-56, for a somewhat different estimate.

1760, while nearly 7,000,000 were enclosed between 1760 and 1843.[1] At the beginning of the latter period a large proportion of this land, since enclosed, was under the primitive tillage of the common-fields. Throughout considerable districts the agrarian system of the middle ages still existed in full force. Some parishes had no common or waste lands belonging to them, but where common lands were cultivated, one and the same plan was generally pursued. The arable land of each village was divided into three great strips sub-divided by " baulks " three yards wide.[2] Every farmer would own at least one piece of land in each field, and all were bound to follow the customary tillage. One strip was left fallow every year ; on the other two were grown wheat and barley ; sometimes oats, pease, or tares were substituted for the latter. The meadows were also held in common. Up to hay harvest, indeed, every man had his own plot, but, while in the arable land the plots rarely changed hands, in the meadows the different shares were apportioned by lot every year. After hay-harvest the fences in the meadow land were thrown down, and all householders had common rights of grazing on it. Similarly the stubbles were grazed, but here the right was rarely open to all. Every farmer had the right of pasture on the waste.

Though these] common fields contained the best soil in the kingdom, they exhibited the most wretched cultivation. " Never," says Arthur Young, " were more miserable crops seen than all the spring ones in the common fields ; absolutely beneath contempt." [3]

---

[1] Shaw Lefevre, *Essays on English and Irish Land Question,* p. 199.

[2] Maine's *Village Communities,* p. 89.

[3] A. Young, *Southern Tour* (3rd ed. 1772), p. 384. See also *Northern Tour,* i. 160-62, where he compares the yields of open and enclosed lands at Risby and the neighbourhood as follows :—

	Open land.	Inclosed.
Wheat	17·18 bushels per acre	26
Barley	36 „	40
Oats	32 „	44
Beans	28 „	32

See also *View of the Agriculture of Oxfordshire,* by A. Young (1809), p. 100 ; Clifford's *Agricultural Lockout in* 1874, p. 121, *n.* ; and Laurence's *Duty of a Steward,* p. 37-8. The latter gives the following preamble for a form of agreement for enclosure :— " Whereas it is found by long experience that common or open fields, wherever they are suffered or continued, are great hindrances to a public good, and the honest improvement which every one might make of his own by diligence and a seasonable charge ; . . . and whereas all or most the inconveniences and misfor-tunes which usually attend the open wastes and common fields have been fatally experienced at ——, to the great discouragement of industry and good husbandry

The causes of this deficient tillage were three in number—(1.) The same course of crops was necessary. No proper rotation was feasible ; the only possible alteration being to vary the proportions of different white-straw crops. There were no turnips or artificial grasses, and consequently no sheep-farming on a large scale. Such sheep as there were were miserably small ; the whole carcase weighed only 28 lbs., and the fleeces 3½ lbs. each, as against 9 lbs. on sheep in enclosed fields.[1]   (2.) Much time was lost by labourers and cattle "in travelling to many dispersed pieces of land from one end of a parish to another."[2]   (3.) Perpetual quarrels arose about rights of pasture in the meadows and stubbles, and respecting boundaries ; in some fields there were no "baulks" to divide the plots, and men would plough by night to steal a furrow from their neighbours.[3]

For these reasons the connection between the practice of enclosing and improved agriculture was very close. The early enclosures, made under the Statutes of Merton (1235), and Westminster (1285), were taken by the lords of the manor from the waste. But in these cases the lord had first to prove that sufficient pasturage had been left for the commoners ; and if rights of common existed independent of the possession of land, no enclosure was permitted. These early enclosures went on steadily, but the enclosures which first attract notice towards the end of the fifteenth century were of a different kind. They were often made on cultivated land, and, if Nasse is correct, they took the form not only of permanent conversions from arable into pasture, but of temporary conversions from arable into pasture, followed by reconversion from pasture into arable. The result was a great increase of produce. The lord having separated his plots from those of his neighbours, and having consolidated them, could pursue any system of tillage which seemed good to

in the Freeholders ; viz., that the poor take their advantage to pilfer and steal and trespass ; that the corn is subject to be spoiled by cattle, that stray out of the common and high-ways adjacent ; that the tenants, or owners, if they would secure the fruits of their labours to themselves, are obliged either to keep exact time in sowing and reaping, or else to be subject to the damage and inconvenience that must attend the lazy practices of those who sow unseasonably, suffering their corn to stand to the beginning of winter, thereby hindering the whole parish from eating the herbage of the common field till the frosts have spoiled the most of it For these reasons," etc. etc.

[1] A. Young, *Northern Tour,* iv. 190.
[2] *View of the Agriculture of Oxfordshire,* p. 100.   [3] *Ib.,* p. 239.

him.   The alternate and convertible husbandry, mentioned above, was introduced; the manure of the cattle enriched the arable land, and " the grass crops on the land ploughed up and manured were much stronger and of a better quality than those on the constant pasture." [1]   Under the old system the manure was spread on the common pasture, while in the enclosures it was used for the benefit of land broken up for tillage.   The great enclosures of the sixteenth century took place in Suffolk, Essex, Kent, and Northamptonshire, which were in consequence the most wealthy counties. [2]   They were frequent also in Oxford, Berks, Warwickshire, Bedfordshire, Bucks, and Leicestershire, and with similar results.   In Arthur Young's time Norfolk, Suffolk, Essex, and Kent were the best cultivated parts of England.

Taking a general view of the state of agriculture in 1760, we find that improvements were confined to a few parts of the country. The first enclosure Bill (1710) was to legalise the enclosure of a parish in Hampshire.   I have looked through twelve of these Bills of the reign of George I., and I find that they applied to parishes in Derbyshire, Lancashire, Yorkshire, Staffordshire, Somersetshire, Gloucestershire, Wilts, Warwickshire, and Norfolk. [3]   But though enclosures were thus widely distributed, certain counties continued to bear a much higher reputation than others, and in some improvements were confined to one or two parishes, and not spread over a wide district.   The best cultivated counties were those which had long been enclosed.   Kent, which was spoken of by William Stafford in 1581 as a county where much of the land was enclosed, is described by Arthur Young as having " long been reckoned the best cultivated in England." . . . " It must astonish strangers," he says, " to East Kent and Thanet, to find such numbers of *common* farmers that have more drilled crops than broadcast ones, and to see them so familiar with drill-ploughs and horsehoes.   The drill culture carried on in so complete a manner is the great peculiarity of this country. . . . Hops are extremely well cultivated." [4]   In another passage he says that Kent and Hertford-

---

[1] Nasse's *Agricultural Community of the Middle Ages,* p. 85.

[2] Cf. Tusser, William Stafford, and Holinshed, quoted by Nasse.

[3] Seven of them were for the enclosure of common fields and waste, five for waste alone.

[4] *Eastern Tour,* iii. 108-9.   The italics are Arthur Young's.

shire "have the reputation of a very accurate cultivation."[1] The Marquis of Rockingham brought a Hertfordshire farmer to teach his tenants in the West Riding to hoe turnips.[2] The husbandry both of that district and of the East Riding was very backward. The courses of crops and the general management of the arable land were very faulty; very few of the farmers hoed turnips, and those who did executed the work in so slovenly a way that neither the crop nor the land was the least the better for it; beans were never hoed at all.[3] The husbandry of Northumberland, on the other hand, was much superior to that of Durham and Yorkshire. Turnips were hoed, manure was better managed, and potatoes were cultivated on a large scale.[4] Essex, held up by Tusser in the reign of Elizabeth as an example of the advantages of enclosures,[5] and described by Young in 1807 as having "for ages been an enclosed country," is mentioned as early as 1694 as a county where " some have their fallow after turnips, which feed their sheep in winter,"[6]—the first mention of turnips as a field crop.

But the greatest progress in the first half of the eighteenth century seems to have taken place in Norfolk. Every one has heard of Townshend growing turnips at Raynham, after his quarrel with Walpole; and Young, writing in 1812, after speaking of the period 1700-1760 as one of stagnation, owing to low prices, ("it is absolutely vain to expect improvements in agriculture unless prices are more disposed to rise than to remain long without variations that give encouragement to the farmer "), admits that the improvements made in Norfolk during that time were an exception. In his *Eastern Tour* (1770), he had spoken of the husbandry " which has rendered the name of this county so famous in the farming world ;"[7] and given seven reasons for the improvements. These were:—(1.) Enclosing without assistance of Parliament. Parliamentary enclosure

[1] *Northern Tour*, i. 292.

[2] *Ib.*, 283. Other novelties introduced by him were improved drains, laying down of pastures level, instead of ridge and furrow, and improved machines and manuring. He kept upwards of 2000 acres in his own hands, on which he experimented, but found great difficulty in inducing " the good common farmers " to imitate his husbandry.

[3] *Northern Tour*, i. 215-221.   [4] *Ib.* iii. 91.

[5] " All these doth enclosures bring,   But only a truth to express.
  Experience teacheth no less ;   Example, if doubt ye do make,
  I speak not to boast of the thing,   By Suffolk and Essex go take."

[6] See Houghton's *Collections in Husbandry and Trade*, quoted in *Encyc. Brit.* sub " Agriculture."   [7] *Eastern Tour*, ii. 150.

" through the knavery of commissioners and attorneys," was very expensive. " Undoubtedly many of the finest loams on the richest marls would at this day have been sheep-walks had there been any right of commonage on them;"[1] (2.) Marling, for there was plenty of marl under the sand everywhere; (3.) An excellent rotation of crops—the famous Norfolk four years' course of turnips, barley, clover (or clover and rye-grass), and wheat; (4.) The culture of turnips well hand-hoed; (5.) The culture of clover and rye-grass; (6.) The granting of long leases;[2] (7.) The division of the county chiefly into large farms. " Great farms," he says, " have been the soul of the Norfolk culture,"[3] though in the eastern part of the county there were little occupiers of £100 a year.[4]

Throughout the whole of the South of England, however, there had been a certain amount of progress. Hoeing turnips, according to Young, was common in many parts of the south of the kingdom,[5] although the extensive use of turnips,—*i.e.* all their uses, for fattening cattle as well as feeding lean sheep—" is known but little of, except in Norfolk, Suffolk, and Essex." [6] Clover husbandry, on the other hand, was " universal from the North of England to the further end of Glamorganshire." Clover, the " great clover," had been introduced into England by Sir Richard Weston about 1645, as had probably been turnips also. Potatoes at the beginning of the century were only garden crops. Hemp and flax were frequently grown, as were also hops, which had been introduced in the beginning of the sixteenth century.

If we turn from the cultivation of the soil to the management and breeding of live stock, we shall find that no great progress had been made in this branch during the years 1700-1760. Davenant in 1700 estimated the net carcase of black cattle at 370 lb., and of a sheep at 28 lb. A century later Eden calculated that " bullocks now killed in London weigh, at an average, 800 lb., sheep 80 lb.,

---

[1] *Eastern Tour*, ii. 152.
[2] " It is a custom growing pretty common," he says, "in several parts of the kingdom to grant no leases. Had the Norfolk landlords conducted themselves on such narrow principles, their estates, which are raised five, six, and ten fold, would yet have been sheep walks."—*Ib.* ii. 160, 161. [3] *Ib.*
[4] *Ib.* Caird, however, asserts that "the present pre-eminence of the county in improved husbandry is due alone to the celebrated Coke of Norfolk, the late Earl of Leicester."—*English Agriculture in* 1850, p. 163.
[5] *Northern Tour*, i. 282.
[6] *Southern Tour*, pp. 280, 281.

and lambs about 50 lb. each;"[1] and Young in 1786 put the weight of bullocks and sheep at 840 lb. and 100 lb. respectively. But this improvement seems to have come about after 1760. It was not until 1760-85 that Bakewell perfected the new breed of sheep —the Leicesters—and improved the breed of long-horned cattle, and that the brothers Colling obtained the short-horn, or Durham cattle, from the breed in the valley of the Tees.[2] Some improvements in the breed of sheep, however, had already been made. " The wool of Warwickshire, Northamptonshire, Lincolnshire, and Rutland, with some parts of Huntingdon, Bedford, Buckinghamshire, Cambridgeshire, and Norfolk has been accounted the longest and finest combing wool. But of late years " (this was written in 1739) " there have been improvements made in the breed of sheep by changing of rams and sowing of turnips and grass seeds, and now there is some large fine combing wool to be found in most counties in England, which is fine, long, and soft, fit to make all sorts of fine stuff and hose of."[3] Still improvements in feeding sheep were by no means universally adopted for half a century later.[4] Agricultural implements, too, were still very primitive, wooden ploughs being commonly in use,[5] while the small, narrow-wheeled waggon of the North held 40 or 50 bushels with difficulty.

Arthur Young constantly attributes much of the bad agriculture to the low rentals prevalent. " Of so little encouragement to them," he writes of the farmers of Cleveland, " is the lowness of their rents, that many large tracts of land that yielded good crops of corn within thirty years are now overrun with whins, brakes,

---

[1] Eden's *State of the Poor* (1797), i. 334. Tooke thought that Eden's estimate was rather too high.—*High and Low Prices* (1823), p. 184.

[2] *Ency. Brit.*—" Agriculture;" *Northern Tour*, ii. 127; *Eastern Tour*, i. 111.

[3] *Pamphlet by a Woollen Manufacturer of Northampton*, in Smith's *Memoirs of Wool*, ii. 320. The woollen manufacturers complained that enclosures lessened the number of sheep, but Young denies this.—*Eastern Tour*, ii. 5.

[4] An old Norfolk shepherd, who was drawn for the Militia in 1811 (when he was probably about eighteen years old), described how the sheep lived when he was a boy:—" As for the sheep, they hadn't such food provided for them as they have now. In winter there was little to eat, except what God Almighty sent for them, and when the snow was thick on the ground, they ate the ling, or died off. Sheep were not of much account then. I have known lambs sold at 1s. 6d. apiece."—Clifford's *Agricultural Lockout*, p. 266.

[5] " The plough in many parts of England differs but little from the description we have of the Roman plough. Agricultural machinery has of all others received the least improvement."—Eden, i. 442. n.

and other trumpery. . . If I be demanded how such ill courses are
to be stopped, I answer, Raise their rents. First with moderation,
and if that does not bring forth industry, double them."[1] At the
same time Young strongly advocated long leases. But it must be
remembered that besides tenant-farmers there were still a large
number of freeholders and still more copyholders either for life or
by inheritance.

On the whole, though the evidence on some points is somewhat
contradictory, the progress of agriculture between 1700 and 1760
may be said to have been slow. Writing in 1770 Arthur Young
ascribes to the last ten years " more experiments, more discoveries,
and more general good sense displayed in the walk of agriculture
than in an hundred preceding ones." Though drill-husbandry was
practised by Jethro Tull, " a gentleman of Berkshire," as early as
1701, and his book was published in 1731, " he seems to have had
few followers in England for more than thirty years,"[2] and Young
in 1770 speaks of "the new husbandry" as having sunk with
Tull, and " not again put in motion till within a few years."[3] On
the other hand, we have as early as 1687 Petty's notice of " the
draining of fens, watering of dry grounds, and improving of forests
and commons." Macpherson in the year 1729 speaks of the great
sums lately expended in the enclosing and improving of lands ;[4]
and Laurence in 1727 asserts that " it is an undoubted truth that
the Art of Husbandry is of late years greatly improved, and
accordingly many estates have already admitted their utmost
improvement, but," he adds, " much the greater number still
remains of such as are so far from being brought to that perfection
that they have felt few or none of the effects of modern arts and
experiments."[5]

Still, in spite of the ignorance and stupidity of the farmers and
their use of wretched implements, the average produce of wheat
was large. In 1770 it was twenty-five bushels to the acre, when

[1] *Northern Tour,* ii. 80-83.
[2] For Tull see *Encyclopædia Britannica*—" Agriculture," Rev. Mr. Smith's
Word in Season, and Day's Lecture before the Royal Agricultural Society.
[3] *Rural Economy* (1770), p. 315.
[4] *Annals of Commerce,* iii. 147. According to Defoe agriculture had much
improved in the north. Davenant, in 1698, speaks of the great improvement
since 1666, *Works* (Whitworth's edition, 1771), i. 359. See also Rogers, *Notes
to Adam Smith,* ii. 81.
[5] *Duty of a Steward,* p. 2.

in France it was only eighteen.[1] At the beginning of the century some of our colonies imported wheat from the mother country. The average export of grain from 1697 to 1765 was nearly 500,000 quarters, while the imports came to a very small figure. The exports were sent to Russia, Holland, and America.

IV.

ENGLAND IN 1760.

MANUFACTURES AND TRADE.

Great importance of the Woollen Manufacture—Its introduction into England—
   Its chief centres : 1. In the eastern counties. 2. In Wilts, Gloucester, and
   Somerset. 3. In Yorkshire—The Iron, Cotton, Hardware, and Hosiery
   Trades—Tendency to concentration—State of the mechanical arts—Imper-
   fect division of labour—Means of communication—Organisation of industry
   —Simple system of exchange—Growth of Foreign Trade and its effects.

AMONG the manufactures of the time the woollen business was by far the most important. "All our measures," wrote Bishop Berkeley in 1737, "should tend towards the immediate encourage- ment of our woollen manufactures, which must be looked upon as the basis of our wealth." In 1701 our woollen exports were worth £2,000,000, or "above a fourth part of the whole export trade."[2] In 1770 they were worth £4,000,000, or between a third and a fourth of the whole.[3] The territorial distribution of the manufac- ture was much the same as now. This industry had probably existed in England from an early date. It is mentioned in a law of 1224.[4] In 1331 John Kennedy brought the art of weaving woollen cloth from Flanders into England, and received the pro- tection of the king, who at the same time invited over fullers and

---

[1] *Travels in France*, i. 354.   The average yield in England now is 28 bushels, but of course we raise part of our present crops from a non-natural soil.

[2] Baines's *History of the Cotton Manufacture* (1835), p. 112.

[3] Macpherson's *Annals of Commerce* (1805), iii. 506.   That book, together with the *Gazetteer* of the same author, has been largely drawn from in this account of the woollen industry.

[4] 9 H. III. c. 27.   Coke's comment is—"True it is that broad cloths were made, though in small number, at this time and long before it."   See Smith, *Memoirs of Wool* (1747), i. 17.

dyers. There is extant a petition of the worsted-weavers and merchants of Norwich to Edward III. in 1348. The coarse cloths of Kendal and the fine cloths of Somerset, Dorset, Bristol, and Gloucester are mentioned in the statutes of the same century. In 1391 we hear of Guildford cloths, and in 1467 of the woollen manufacture in Devonshire—at Lifton, Tavistock, and Rowburgh. In 1402 the manufacture was settled to a great extent in and near London, but it gradually shifted, owing to the high price of labour and provisions, to Surrey, Kent, Essex, Berkshire, and Oxfordshire, and afterwards still further, into the counties of Dorset, Wilts, Somerset, Gloucester, and Worcester, and even as far as Yorkshire.

There were three chief districts in which the woollen trade was carried on about 1760. One of these owed its manufacture to the wars in the Netherlands. In consequence of Alva's persecutions (1567-8) many Flemings settled in Norwich (which had been desolate since Ket's rebellion in 1549), Colchester, Sandwich, Canterbury, Maidstone, and Southampton. The two former towns seem to have benefited most from the skill of these settlers so far as the woollen manufacture was concerned. It was at this time, according to Macpherson, that Norwich "learned the making of those fine and slight stuffs which have ever since gone by its name," such as crapes, bombazines, and camblets ; while the baize-makers settled at Colchester and its neighbourhood. The stuffs thus introduced into England were known as the "new drapery," and included baize, serges, and other slight woollen goods as distinguished from the "old drapery," a term applied to broad cloth, kersies, etc.

The chief seats of the West of England manufacture were Bradford in Wilts, the centre of the manufacture of superfine cloth ; Devizes, famous for its serges ; Warminster and Frome, with their fine cloth ; Trowbridge ; Stroud, the centre of the dyed-cloth manufactures ; and Taunton, which in Defoe's time possessed 1100 looms.[1] The district reached from Cirencester in the north to Sherborne in the south, and from Witney in the east to Bristol in the west, being about fifty miles in length where longest, and twenty in breadth where narrowest,—"a rich enclosed country," as Defoe says, "full of rivers and towns, and infinitely

[1] Defoe's *Tour* (7th edition, 1769), ii. 19.

populous, insomuch that some of the market towns are equal to cities in bigness, and superior to many of them in numbers of people." It was a "prodigy of a trade," and the "fine Spanish medley cloths" which this district produced were worn by "all the persons of fashion in England."[1] It was no doubt the presence of streams and the Cotswold wool which formed the attractions of the district. A branch of the industry extended into Devon, where the merchants of Exeter bought in a rough state the serges made in the country round, to dye and finish them for home consumption or export.

The third chief seat of the manufacture was the West Riding of Yorkshire, where the worsted trade centred round Halifax, which, according to Camden, began to manufacture about 1537; and where Leeds and its neighbourhood manufactured a coarse cloth of English wool. In 1574 the manufacturers of the West Riding made 56,000 pieces of broad cloth and 72,000 of narrow. It will be seen from this short survey that, however greatly the production of these different districts may have changed in proportion since 1760, the several branches of the trade are even now distributed very much as they were then, the West Riding being the headquarters of the worsted and coarse cloth trade, while Norwich still keeps the crape industry, and the West manufactures fine cloth.

The increased demand for English wool consequent upon the extension of this industry led to large enclosures of land, especially in Northamptonshire, Rutlandshire, Leicestershire, and Warwickshire, which counties supplied most of the combing wools used for worsted stuffs and stockings; but parts of Huntingdon, Bedford, Bucks, Cambridgeshire, Romney Marsh, and Norfolk competed with them, and by 1739 most counties produced the fine combing wool. Defoe mentions the sale of wool from Lincolnshire, "where the longest staple is found, the sheep of those parts being of the largest breed;"[2] and in Arthur Young's time Lincolnshire and Leicestershire wools were still used at Norwich.[3] The Cotswold and Isle of Wight sheep yielded clothing or short wools, "but they were inferior to the best Spanish wools," and could not "enter into the composition without spoiling and degrading in

---

[1] Defoe's *Tour*, ii. 26, 37, 38. [2] *Ibid.* i. 94.
[3] *Eastern Tour*, ii. 74, 75.

some degree the fabric of the cloth."[1] Consequently in the West of England, occupied as it was with the production of the finest cloths, Spanish wool was largely used, though shortly before Young's time it was discovered that "Norfolk sheep yielded a wool about their necks equal to the best from Spain."[2]

Next in importance was the iron trade, which was largely carried on, though by this time a decaying industry, in the Weald of Sussex, where in 1740 there were ten furnaces, producing annually 1400 tons. The trade had reached its chief extent in the seventeenth century, but in 1724 was still the principal manufacturing interest of the county. The balustrades which surround St. Paul's were cast at Lamberhurst, and their weight, including the seven gates, is above 200 tons. They cost £11,000. Gloucestershire, Shropshire, and Yorkshire had each six furnaces. In the latter county, which boasted an annual produce of 1400[3] tons, the most famous works were at Rotherham. There were also great ironworks at Newcastle.[4]

In 1755 an ironmaster named Anthony Bacon had got a lease for ninety-nine years of a district eight miles in length, by five in breadth, at Merthyr-Tydvil, upon which he erected iron and coal works.[5] In 1709 the Coalbrookdale works in Shropshire were founded, and in 1760 Carron iron was first manufactured in Scotland.[6] Altogether, there were about 1737 fifty-nine furnaces in eighteen different counties, producing 17,350 tons annually. It has been computed that we imported 20,000 tons.[7] In 1881 we exported 3,820,315 tons of iron and steel, valued at £27,590,908, and imported to the value of £3,705,332.

The cotton trade was still so insignificant as to be mentioned only once, and that incidentally, by Adam Smith. It was confined to Lancashire, where its headquarters were Manchester and Bolton. In 1760 not more than 40,000 persons were engaged in it, and the annual value of the manufactures was estimated at £600,000.

---

[1] Smith, *Memoirs of Wool*, ii. 542, 543, 1st edition, London, 1747. Adam Smith, *Wealth of Nations*, book iv. ch. viii. (ii. 235).

[2] *Eastern Tour*, loc. cit.

[3] Scrivenor's *History of the Iron Trade* (1841), p. 57.

[4] *Northern Tour*, iii. 9-11.

[5] Scrivenor's *History of the Iron Trade*, p. 121.

[6] Smiles's *Industrial Biography*, pp. 82, 136.

[7] Scrivenor, pp. 57, 71.

The exports, however, were steadily growing; in 1701 they amounted to £23,253, in 1751 to £45,986, in 1764 to £200,354. Burke about this time spoke of "that infinite variety of admirable manufactures that grow and extend every year among the spirited, inventive, and enterprising traders of Manchester." But even in 1764 our exports of cotton were still only one-twentieth of the value of the wool exports.

The hardware trade then as now was located chiefly in Sheffield and Birmingham, the latter town employing over 50,000 people in that industry in 1727.[1] The business, however, was not so much concentrated as now, and there were small workshops scattered about the kingdom. "Polished steel," for instance, was manufactured at Woodstock, locks in South Staffordshire, pins at Warrington, Bristol, and Gloucester, where they were "the staple of the city."[2]

The hosiery trade, too, was as yet only in process of concentration. By 1800 the manufacture of silk hosiery had centred in Derby, that of woollen hosiery in Leicester, though Nottingham had not yet absorbed the cotton hosiery. But at the beginning of the century there were still many looms round London, and in other parts of the South of England. In 1750 London had 1000 frames, Surrey 350, Nottingham 1500, Leicester 1000, Derby 200, other places in the Midlands, 7300; other English and Scotch towns, 1850; Ireland, 800; Total, 14,000.[3] Most of the silk was woven in Spitalfields, but first spun in the North at Stockport, Knutsford, Congleton, and Derby.[4] In 1770 there was a silk-mill at Sheffield on the model of Derby, and a manufactory of waste silk at Kendal.[5] Coventry had already, in Defoe's time, attracted the ribbon business.[6] In 1721 the silk manufacture was said to be worth £700,000 a year more than at the Revolution.[7]

Linen was an ancient manufacture in England, and had been introduced into Dundee at the beginning of the seventeenth century. In 1746 the British Linen Company was incorporated to

[1] Anderson, *On Commerce*, iii. 144.
[2] *Southern Tour*, p. 141 (2d edition, 1769).
[3] Felkin's *History of the Hosiery and Lace Manufactures* (1867), p. 76.
[4] Defoe's *Tour*, ii. 397 ; iii. 73. The Derby mill was unique of its kind.
[5] *Northern Tour*, i. 124 ; iii. 135.
[6] Defoe's *Tour*, ii. 421.
[7] *British Merchant*, quoted in Smith's *Memoirs of Wool*.

supply Africa and the American plantations with linen made at home,[1] and Adam Smith considered it a growing manufacture. It was, of course, the chief manufacture of Ireland, where it had been further developed by French Protestants, who settled there at the end of the seventeenth century.

The mechanical arts were still in a very backward state. In spite of the fact that the woollen trade was the staple industry of the country, the division of labour in it was in Adam Smith's time "nearly the same as it was a century before, and the machinery employed not very different." According to the same author there had been only three inventions of importance since Edward IV.'s reign: the exchange of the rock and spindle for the spinning-wheel; the use of machines for facilitating the proper arrangement of the warp and woof before being put into the loom; and the employment of fulling mills for thickening cloth instead of treading it in water. In this enumeration, however, he forgot to mention the fly-shuttle, invented in 1738 by Kay, a native of Bury, in Lancashire, the first of the great inventions which revolutionised the woollen industry. Its utility consisted in its enabling a weaver to do his work in half the time, and making it possible for one man instead of two to weave the widest cloth.[2]

"The machines used in the cotton manufacture," says Baines, "were, up to the year 1760, nearly as simple as those of India; though the loom was more strongly and perfectly constructed, and cards for combing the cotton had been adapted from the woollen manufacture. None but the strong cottons, such as fustians and dimities, were as yet made in England, and for these the demand must always have been limited."[3] In 1738 John Wyatt invented spinning by rollers, but the discovery never proved profitable. In 1760 the manufacturers of Lancashire began to use the fly-shuttle. Calico printing was already largely developed.[4]

The reason why division of labour was carried out to so small an extent, and invention so rare and so little regarded, is given by

[1] Anderson, iii. 252.
[2] Fox Bourne's *Romance of Trade*, p. 183.
[3] Baines's *History of the Cotton Manufacture*, p. 115.
[4] In 1719 "all the mean people, the maid servants, and indifferently poor persons, who would otherwise clothe themselves, and were usually clothed, in thin women's stuffs made at Norwich and London, are now clothed in calico or printed linen."—Pamphlet in Smith's *Memoirs*, ii. 195.

Adam Smith himself.   Division of labour, as he points out, is limited by the extent of the market, and, owing chiefly to bad means of communication, the market for English manufactures was still a very narrow one.   Yet England, however slow the development of her manufactures, advanced nevertheless more rapidly in this respect than other nations.   One great secret of her progress lay in the facilities for water-carriage afforded by her rivers, for all communication by land was still in the most neglected condition. A second cause was the absence of internal customs barriers, such as existed in France, and in Prussia until Stein's time.   The home trade of England was absolutely free.

Arthur Young gives abundant evidence of the execrable state of the roads.   It took a week or more for a coach to go from London to Edinburgh.   On "that infernal" road between Preston and Wigan the ruts were four feet deep, and he saw three carts break down in a mile of road.   At Warrington the turnpike was "most infamously bad," and apparently "made with a view to immediate destruction."   "Very shabby," "execrable," "vile," "most execrably vile," are Young's ordinary comments on the highways.   But the water routes for traffic largely made up for the deficiencies of the land routes.

Attempts to improve water communication began with deepening the river beds.   In 1635 there was a project for rendering the Avon navigable from its junction with the Severn at Tewkesbury through Gloucestershire, Worcestershire, and Warwickshire, but it was abandoned owing to the civil war.   From 1660 to 1755 various Acts were passed for deepening the beds of rivers.   In 1720 there was an Act for making the Mersey and Irwell navigable between Liverpool and Manchester.   About the same time the navigation of the Aire and Calder was opened out.   In 1755 the first canal was made, eleven miles in length, near Liverpool.   Three years later the Duke of Bridgewater had another constructed from his coal mines at Worsley to Manchester, seven miles distant.   Between 1761 and 1766 a still longer one of twenty-nine miles was completed from Manchester through Chester to the Mersey above Liverpool. From this time onwards the canal system spread with great rapidity.

When we turn to investigate the industrial organisation of the time, we find that the class of capitalist employers was as yet but in its infancy.   A large part of our goods were still produced on the domestic system.   Manufactures were little concentrated in towns, and only partially separated from agriculture.   The "manufacturer" was, literally, the man who worked with his own hands in his own cottage.   Nearly the whole cloth trade of the West Riding, for instance, was organised on this system at the beginning of the century.

An important feature in the industrial organisation of the time was the existence of a number of small master-manufacturers, who were entirely independent, having capital and land of their own, for they combined the culture of small freehold pasture-farms with their handicraft.   Defoe has left an interesting picture of their life. The land near Halifax, he says, was " divided into small Enclosures from two Acres to six or seven each, seldom more, every three or four Pieces of Land had an House belonging to them ; . . . hardly an House standing out of a Speaking-distance from another ; . . . we could see at every House a Tenter, and on almost every Tenter a piece of Cloth or Kersie or Shalloon. . . . At every considerable house was a manufactory. . . . Every clothier keeps one horse, at least, to carry his Manufactures to the Market ; and every one, generally, keeps a Cow or two or more for his Family.   By this means the small Pieces of enclosed Land about each house are occupied, for they scarce sow Corn enough to feed their Poultry. . . . The houses are full of lusty Fellows, some at the Dye-vat, some at the looms, others dressing the Cloths ; the women and children carding or spinning ; being all employed from the youngest to the oldest. . . . Not a Beggar to be seen nor an idle person." [1]

This system, however, was no longer universal in Arthur Young's time.   That writer found at Sheffield a silk-mill employing 152 hands, including women and children ; at Darlington " one master-manufacturer employed above fifty looms ;" at Boynton there were 150 hands in one factory.[2]   So, too, in the West of England cloth-trade the germs of the capitalist system were visible.   The rich merchant gave out work to labourers in the surrounding villages, who were his employés, and were not independent.   In the Nottingham hosiery trade there were, in 1750, fifty manufacturers, known as " putters out," who employed 1200

[1] Defoe's *Tour*, iii. 144-6.
[2] *Northern Tour*, i. 124 ; ii. 6, 427.   See Smith's *Memoirs*, ii. 313.

frames; in Leicestershire 1800 frames were so employed.[1]　In the hand-made nail business of Staffordshire and Worcestershire, the merchant had warehouses in different parts of the district, and gave out nail-rod iron to the nail-master, sufficient for a week's work for him and his family.[2]　In Lancashire we can trace, step by step, the growth of the capitalist employer.　At first we see, as in Yorkshire, the weaver furnishing himself with warp and weft, which he worked up in his own house and brought himself to market.　By degrees he found it difficult to get yarn from the spinners;[3] so the merchants at Manchester gave him out linen warp and raw cotton, and the weaver became dependent on them.[4] Finally, the merchant would get together thirty or forty looms in a town.　This was the nearest approach to the capitalist system before the great mechanical inventions.

Coming to the system of exchange, we find it based on several different principles, which existed side by side, but which were all, as we should think, very simple and primitive.　Each trade had its centre in a provincial town.　Leeds, for instance, had its market twice a week, first on the bridge over the Aire, afterwards in the High Street, where, at a later time, two halls were built.　Every clothier had his stall, to which he would bring his cloth (seldom more than one piece at a time, owing to the frequency of the markets).　At six or seven o'clock a bell rang, and the market began; the merchants and factors came in and made their bargains with the clothiers, and in little more than an hour the whole business was over.　By nine the benches were cleared and the hall empty.[5]　There was a similar hall at Halifax for the worsted trade. But a large portion of the inland traffic was carried on at fairs, which were still almost as important as in the Middle Ages.　The most famous of all was the great fair of Sturbridge,[6] which lasted from the middle of August to the middle of September.　Hither came representatives of all the great trades.　The merchants of

---

[1] Felkin's *History of Hosiery*, etc., p. 83.

[2] Timmins's *Resources, Products, etc., of Birmingham* (1866), pp. 110, 111.

[3] Baines, p. 115.　Ure's *Cotton Manufacture* (1836), i. 192, 193.　The weaver would walk three or four miles in a morning, and call on many spinners, before he could get work enough for the day.—Compare Young's *Northern Tour*, iii. 189.

[4] Baines, p. 104 n.

[5] Defoe's *Tour*, iii. 124-126.　　　　　[6] Near Chesterton, in Cambridgeshire.

Lancashire brought their goods on a thousand pack-horses; the Eastern Counties sent their worsteds, and Birmingham its hardware. An immense quantity of wool was sold, orders being taken by the wholesale dealers of London. In fact, a large part of the home trade found its way to this market.[1] There were also the four great annual fairs, which retained the ancient title of " marts," at Lynn, Boston, Gainsborough, and Beverley.[2]

The link between these fairs and the chief industrial centres was furnished by travelling merchants. Some would go from Leeds with droves of pack-horses to all the fairs and market-towns throughout England.[3] In the market-towns they sold to the shops; elsewhere they would deal directly with the consumer, like the Manchester merchants, who sent their pack-horses the round of the farm-houses, buying wool or other commodities in exchange for their finished goods. Sometimes the London merchants would come to the manufacturers, paying their guineas down at once, and taking away the purchases themselves. So too in the Birmingham lock trade, chapmen would go round with pack-horses to buy from manufacturers; in the brass trade likewise the manufacturer stayed at home, and the merchant came round with cash in his saddle-bags, and put the brasswork which he purchased into them, though in some cases he would order it to be sent by carrier.[4]

Ready cash was essential, for banking was very little developed. The Bank of England existed, but before 1759 issued no notes of less value than £20. By a law of 1709 no other bank of more than six partners was allowed; and in 1750, according to Burke, there were not more than " twelve bankers' shops out of London."[5] The Clearing-House was not established till 1775.

Hampered as the inland trade was by imperfect communications, extraordinary efforts were made to promote exchange. It is striking to find waste silk from London made into silk-yarn at Kendal and sent back again,[6] or cattle brought from Scotland to Norfolk to be fed.[7] Many districts, however, still remained completely excluded, so that foreign products never reached them at

---

[1] Defoe's *Tour,* i. 91-96.   [2] *Ibid.* iii. 16, 17.   [3] *Ibid.* iii. 126.
[4] Timmins, p. 241.
[5] *Letter on a Regicide Peace,* Burke's *Works* (Bohn's edition), v. 197.
[6] *Northern Tour,* iii. 135.
[7] Defoe's *Tour,* i. 61; 40,000 were fed in Norfolk every year.

all.   Even at the beginning of this century the Yorkshire yeoman,
as described by Southey,[1] was ignorant of sugar, potatoes, and
cotton ; the Cumberland dalesman, as he appears in Wordsworth's
Guide to the Lakes,[2] lived entirely on the produce of his farm.   It
was this domestic system which the great socialist writers Sismondi
and Lassalle had in their minds when they inveighed against the
modern organisation of industry.   Those who lived under it, they
pointed out, though poor, were on the whole prosperous ; over-production was absolutely impossible.[3]   Yet at the time of which I
am speaking, many of the evils which modern Socialists lament
were already visible, especially in those industries which produced
for the foreign market.   Already there were complaints of the
competition of men who pushed themselves into the market to
take advantage of high prices; already we hear of fluctuations of
trade and irregularity of employment.[4]   The old simple conditions
of production and exchange were on the eve of disappearance
before the all-corroding force of foreign trade.

The home trade was still indeed much greater in proportion
than now; but the exports had grown from about £7,000,000 at
the beginning of the century[5] to £14,500,000 in 1760.   During
that interval great changes had taken place in the channels of
foreign commerce.   In 1700 Holland was our great market, taking
more than one-third of all our exports, but in 1760 the proportion
was reduced to about one-seventh.   Portugal, which in 1703 took

---

[1] *The Doctor,* c. iv.   [2] *Prose Works,* ii. 262, 263.

[3] " Le paysan qui fait avec ses enfants tout l'ouvrage de son petit héritage, qui
ne paie de fermage à personne au dessus de lui, ni de salaire à personne au
dessous, qui règle sa production sur sa consommation, qui mange son propre blé,
boit son propre vin, se revêt de son chanvre et de ses laines, se soucie peu de
connaître les prix du marché, car il a peu à vendre et peu a acheter."—Sismondi,
Économie Politique, Essai iii.   But see Young's *Northern Tour,* iii. 189.

[4] In 1719 it is first asserted that "the grand cause of the weavers wanting
work is the covetousness of both masters and journeymen in taking so many
prentices for the sake of the money they have with them, not considering
whether they shall have employment for them or not."   In 1737 we find a
writer lamenting that the factors "set up people to act as master-clothiers, on
their stock, during any little glut of business," to the great disadvantage of those
who "employ the poor in good and bad times alike." . . . "And hence more
people are admitted into trade than the trade can possibly maintain ; which
opens a new door to the tumults and riots so lately felt."—Smith's *Memoirs,*
ii. 186, 313.

[5] The *British Merchant* calculated that the export trade was one-sixth of the
home-trade, or £7,000,000.—Smith's *Memoirs,* ii. 112.   Burke possessed a MS. of
Davenant, which gave the exports in 1703 at £6,552,019.—*Works,* i. 221.

one-seventh, now took only about one-twelfth. The trade with France was quite insignificant. On the other hand, the Colonies were now our chief markets, and a third of our exports went there. In 1770 America took three-fourths of all the manufactures of Manchester.[1] In 1767 the exports to Jamaica were nearly as great as they had been to all the English plantations together in 1704.[2] The shipping trade had doubled,[3] and the ships themselves were larger. In 1732 ships of 750 tons were considered remarkable; in 1770 there were many in Liverpool of 900 tons; but in this as in other branches of business progress was still slow, partial, local, thus presenting a striking contrast to the rapid and general advance of the next half-century.

V.

ENGLAND IN 1760.

THE DECAY OF THE YEOMANRY.[4]

The historical method not always conservative—Changes commonly attributed to natural law are sometimes shown by it to be due to human injustice—The decay of the Yeomanry a case in point—The position of the Yeomanry in the seventeenth century—Their want of political initiative—Effect of the Revolution upon them—The aristocracy and the moneyed class absorb the land—Pressure put upon small owners to sell—The custom of settlement and primogeniture—The effect of enclosures upon small properties.

IT is a reflection that must have occurred to every one that the popular philosophy of the day, while in the region of speculation it has undermined ancient beliefs, has exerted in the practical world a distinctly conservative influence. The conception of slow development, according to definite laws, undoubtedly tends to strengthen the position of those who offer resistance to radical changes. It may, however, well be doubted whether the theory of evolution is really such a support as it seems to be to those who

---

[1] *Northern Tour*, iii. 194.   [2] Burke's *Works*, i. 278.
[3] The capacity of British shipping in 1762 was nearly 560,000 tons.—*Ib.* i. 201.
[4] The greater part of this chapter is taken from an essay in Toynbee's own handwriting.—ED.

would uphold the existing framework of society. It is certainly remarkable that the most recent legislation has been at once revolutionary in its character and justified by appeals to historical experience. I do not forget that the most distinguished exponent of the doctrine of evolution as applied to politics has developed a theory of government opposed to recent legislative reforms, but that theory is an *a priori* one. Those, on the other hand, who have applied the historical method to political economy and the science of society, have shown an unmistakeable disposition to lay bare the injustice to which the humbler classes of the community have been exposed, and to defend methods and institutions adopted for their protection which have never received scientific defence before.

The fact is, that the more we examine the actual course of affairs, the more we are amazed at the unnecessary suffering that has been inflicted upon the people. No generalities about natural law or inevitable development can blind us to the fact, that the progress in which we believe has been won at the expense of much injustice and wrong, which was not inevitable. Perhaps this is most conspicuous in our land system, and we shall find with regard to it, as with regard to some other matters, that the more we accept the method of historical inquiry, the more revolutionary shall we tend to become in practice. For while the modern historical school of economists appear to be only exploring the monuments of the past, they are really shaking the foundations of many of our institutions in the present. The historical method is often deemed conservative, because it traces the gradual and stately growth of our venerable institutions; but it may exercise a precisely opposite influence by showing the gross injustice which was blindly perpetrated during this growth. The historical method is supposed to prove that economic changes have been the inevitable outcome of natural laws. It just as often proves them to have been brought about by the self-seeking action of dominant classes.

It is a singular thing that no historian has attempted an adequate explanation of the disappearance of the small freeholders who, down to the close of the seventeenth century, formed with their families one-sixth of the population of England, and whose stubborn determination enabled Cromwell and Fairfax to bring the Civil War to a successful close. This neglect is the more remarkable, as economists have so emphatically dwelt upon the extraordinary difference between the distribution of landed property in England and in countries like Germany and France. The modern reformer is content to explain the facts by the existence in England of a law of primogeniture and a system of strict settlement, but the explanation is obviously a superficial one. To show why in England the small landed proprietors have vanished, whilst in Germany and France they have increased and thriven, it is necessary to carry our inquiries far back into the history of law, politics, and commerce. The result of a closer examination of the question is a little startling, for we find that the present distribution of landed property in England is in the main due to the existence of the system of political government which has made us a free people. And on the other hand, the distribution of landed property in France and Germany, which writer after writer points to as the great bulwark against revolution, is in the main due to a form of government that destroyed political liberty and placed the people in subjection to the throne.

Evidence in support of this conclusion is not difficult to adduce. The first fact which arouses our interest is that at the conclusion of the seventeenth century it was estimated by Gregory King that there were 180,000 freeholders in England,[1] and that, less than a hundred years later, the pamphleteers of the time, and even careful writers like Arthur Young, speak of the small freeholders as practically gone. The bare statement of this contrast is in itself most impressive. A person ignorant of our history during the intervening period might surmise that a great exterminatory war had taken place, or a violent social revolution, which had caused a transfer of the property of one class to another. But though the surmise in this particular form would be incorrect, we are nevertheless justified in saying that a revolution of incalculable importance had taken place,—a revolution, though so silent, of as great importance as the political revolution of 1831. " The able and substantial freeholders," described by Whitelock, " the freeholders and freeholders' sons, well armed within with the satisfaction of their own good consciences, and without by iron arms, who stood firmly and charged desperately,"—this devoted class, who had

---

[1] Macaulay, following Davenant, thinks this too high, and puts them at 160,000.—*History of England*, c. iii.

broken the power of the king and the squires in the Civil Wars, were themselves, within a hundred years from that time, being broken, dispersed, and driven off the land.   Numerous and prosperous in the fifteenth century, they had suffered something by the enclosures of the sixteenth; but though complaints are from time to time made in the seventeenth of the laying together of farms, there is no evidence to show that their number underwent any great diminution during that time.   In the picture of country life which we find in the literature of the first years of the eighteenth century, the small freeholder is still a prominent figure.   Sir Roger de Coverley, in riding to Quarter Sessions, points to the two yeomen who are riding in front of him, and Defoe, in his admirable *Tour through England*, first published a few years later, describes with satisfaction the number and prosperity of the Grey-coats of Kent (as they were called from their home-spun garments), whose political power forced the gentlemen to treat them with circumspection and deference.[1]   " Of the freeholders of England," says Chamberlayne, in the *State of Great Britain*,[2] first published towards the close of the seventeenth century, "there are more in extent and richer than in any other country in Europe.   £40 or £50 a year is very ordinary, £100 or £200 in some counties is not rare; sometimes in Kent, and in the Weald of Sussex, £500 or £600 per annum, and £3000 to £4000 stock."   The evidence is conclusive that up to the Revolution of 1688 the freeholders were in most parts of the country an important feature in social life.

If, however, we ask whether they had possessed, as a class, any political initiative, we must answer in the negative.   In the lists of the Eastern Counties' Association, formed in the Civil War (the eastern counties were the districts, perhaps, where the freeholders were strongest), we find no name which has not appended to it the title of gentleman or esquire.   The small landed proprietor, though courageous and independent in personal character, was ignorant, and incapable himself of taking the lead.   There was little to stimulate his mind in his country life; in agriculture he pursued the same methods as his forefathers, was full of prejudices, and difficult to move.   The majority of this class had never travelled beyond their native village or homestead and the neighbouring

[1] *Tour*, i. pp. 159, 60.   At election times 1400 or 1500 would troop into Maidstone to give their votes.   [2] Part i. Book iii. p. 176, ed. 1737.

market town. In some districts those freeholders were also artisans, especially in the eastern counties, which were still the richest
part of the country, and the most subject to foreign influence.
But, on the whole, if we may judge from the accounts of rather
later times, the yeomen, though thriving in good seasons, often
lived very hard lives, and remained stationary in their habits and
ways of thinking from generation to generation.   They were capable
in the Civil War, under good leadership, of proving themselves
the most powerful body in the kingdom ; but, after constitutional
government had been secured, and the great landowners were independent of their support, they sank into political insignificance.
The Revolution of 1688, which brought to a conclusion the constitutional struggle of the seventeenth century, was accomplished
without their aid, and paved the way for their extinction. A revolution in agricultural life was the price paid for political liberty.

At first, however, the absorption of the small freeholders went
on slowly. The process of disappearance has been continuous from
about 1700 to the present day, but it is not true to say, as Karl
Marx does,[1] that the yeomanry had disappeared by the middle of
the eighteenth century. It was not till the very period which we
are considering, that is to say about 1760, that the process of
extinction became rapid. There is conclusive evidence that many
were still to be found about 1770. There were at that time still
9000 freeholders in Kent.[2]

Even as late as 1807, estates in Essex, if divided, were bought
by farmers at high prices, and there was some prospect of landed
property coming back to the conditions of a century before, " when
our inferior gentry resided upon their estates in the country;" and
about the same date there were in Oxfordshire " many proprietors
of a middling size, and many small proprietors, particularly in the
open fields."[3] They were especially strong in Cumberland, the
West Riding, and parts of the East Riding.   In the Vale of Pickering in 1788 nearly the whole district belonged to them, and no
great landowner had been able to get a footing.[4] But in 1788 this

---

[1] *Le Capital* (French translation), p. 319.
[2] Kenny's *History of Primogeniture* (1878), p. 52.
[3] Howlett in Young's *General View of the Agriculture of Essex* (1807), i. 40 ;
View of the Agriculture of Oxfordshire (1809), p. 16.
[4] " The major part of the lands of the district are the property, and in general are in the occupation, of yeomanry ; a circumstance this which it would be

was already an exceptional case, and in other writers of that period we find a general lament at the disappearance of the yeomen. Arthur Young " sincerely regrets the loss of that set of men who are called yeomen . . . who really kept up the independence of the nation," and is "loth to see their lands now in the hands of monopolising lords;"[1] and in 1787 he admits that they had practically disappeared from most parts of the country.[2] And with the yeomen went the small squires, victims of the same causes.[3]

These causes, as I stated above, are to be sought less in economical than in social and political facts. The chief of them was our peculiar form of government. After the Revolution the landed gentry were practically supreme. Not only national but local administration was entirely in their hands, and, as a natural consequence, land, being the foundation of social and political influence, was eagerly sought after. We may contrast France and Prussia, where the landowners had no political power as such, and where, in consequence, small properties remained unassailed. The second fact is the enormous development of the mercantile and moneyed interest. The merchants could only obtain political power and social position by becoming landowners. It is true that Swift says that "the power which used to follow land had gone over to money," and that the great Turkey merchants, like Addison's Sir Andrew Freeport, occupied a good position; but few mere merchants were in Parliament,[4] and Dr. Johnson made the significant remark that "an English merchant is a new species of gentleman."[5] To make himself a gentleman, therefore, the merchant who had accumulated his wealth in the cities, which, as we

difficult to equal in so large a district. The township of Pickering is a singular instance. It contains about 300 freeholders, principally occupying their own small estates, many of which have fallen down by lineal descent from the original purchasers. No great man, nor scarcely an esquire, has yet been able to get a footing in the parish ; or, if any one has, the custom of portioning younger sons and daughters by a division of lands has reduced to its original atoms the estates which may have been accumulated."—Marshall's *Rural Economy of Yorkshire* (1788), i. 20.

[1] *Inquiry into the present Price of Provisions and the Size of Farms* (1773), pp. 126, 139 *et seq.*

[2] *Travels in France* (Dublin edition 1793), i. 86, ii. 262.

[3] See extracts from Howlett, referred to above.

[4] Thrale, the brewer, father of Johnson's friend, was one of the exceptions. He was Member for Southwark and High Sheriff of Surrey in 1733. He died in 1758.—Boswell's *Life of Johnson* (7th edition), ii. 106, 107.

[5] *Ibid.* p. 108, *n.*

have seen, were growing rapidly during the first half of the eighteenth century with an expanding commerce, bought land as a matter of course.   Hence the mercantile origin of much of our nobility.   James Lowther, created Earl of Lonsdale in 1784, was great-grandson of a Turkey merchant; the ancestor of the Barings was a clothier in Devonshire; Anthony Petty, father of Sir W. Petty, and the ancestor on the female side of the Petty-Fitz-maurices, was a clothier at Romsey, in Hampshire; Sir Josiah Child's son became Earl of Tilney.[1] The landowners in the West of England, " who now," in Defoe's words, " carry their heads so high," made their fortunes in the clothing trade.   And not only did a new race of landowners thus spring up, but the old families enriched themselves, and so were enabled to buy more land by intermarriage with the commercial magnates.   The Fitzmaurices, for instance, inherited the wealth of the Pettys; Child's daughter married the Marquis of Worcester, and, by a second marriage, Lord Grenville of Potheridge; Lord Conway and Walpole married daughters of John Shorter, merchant of London.   " I think I remember," said Sir R. Temple between 1675 and 1700, " the first noble families that married into the City for money." [2]   " Trade," said Defoe, " is so far here from being inconsistent with a gentle-man, that, in short, trade in England makes gentlemen ; for, after a generation or two, the tradesmen's children, or at least their grandchildren, come to be as good gentlemen, statesmen, parlia-ment-men, privy-councillors, judges, bishops, and noblemen, as those of the highest birth, and the most ancient families." [3]   Contrast this fusion of classes with the French society of the last century, with its impoverished nobility, living often on the seignorial rights and rent-charges of their alienated estates, but hardly ever inter-marrying with the commercial classes ; or that of Prussia, where the two classes remained entirely separate, and could not even purchase one another's land.

I have established two facts: the special reason for desiring land after the Revolution as a condition of political power and social prestige, and the means of buying land on the part of the wealthy merchants or of the nobility and greater gentry enriched by

[1] Defoe's *Complete Tradesman* (ed. Chambers, 1839), p. 74.
[2] Temple's *Miscellanies*, quoted in Lecky's *History of England*, i. 193, 194.
[3] Defoe's *Tradesman*, loc. cit.

matrimonial alliances with the great commercial class. Now here is a piece of evidence to show that it was the accepted policy of the large landowners to buy out the yeomen. The land agent, whom I have so often quoted, lays downs as a maxim for the model steward, that he " should not forget to make the best inquiry into the disposition of the freeholders, within or near any of his lord's manors, to sell their lands, that he may use his best endeavours to purchase them at as reasonable a price as may be for his lord's advantage and convenience."[1]

On the other hand, as a result of the supremacy of the great landowners in Parliament, their own estates were artificially protected. The system of strict settlements, introduced by Sir Orlando Bridgman in 1666, though not so important as it is often made out to be, prevented much land from coming into the market, though it did not prevent merchants from buying when they wished. The custom of primogeniture checked the division of estates by leading to the disuse of inheritance by gavelkind, and similar customs. In Cumberland primogeniture was introduced among the freeholders in the sixteenth century; in Kent there was, in 1740, nearly as much gavelkind as before the disgavelling Acts began, but thirty years later it was being superseded by primogeniture. It was during these thirty years that the process of concentration in that county first assumed formidable proportions. In Pickering, on the other hand, where the law of equal division still held its own, small landowners also, as we have seen, survived after their extinction in most parts of England.

A third result of landlord supremacy was the manner in which the common-field system was broken up. Allusion has already been made to enclosures, and enclosures meant a break-up of the old system of agriculture and a redistribution of the land. This is a problem which involves delicate questions of justice. In Prussia, the change was effected by impartial legislation; in England, the work was done by the strong at the expense of the weak. The change from common to individual ownership, which was economically advantageous, was carried out in an iniquitous manner, and thereby became socially harmful. Great injury was thus done to the poor and ignorant freeholders, who lost their rights in the

---

[1] Laurence's *Duty of a Steward* (1727), p. 36.

common lands. In Pickering, in one instance, the lessee of the tithes applied for an enclosure of the waste. The small freeholders did their best to oppose him, but, having little money to carry on the suit, they were overruled, and the lessee, who had bought the support of the landless " house-owners " of the parish, took the land from the freeholders and shared the spoil with the cottagers.[1] It was always easy for the steward to harass the small owners till he forced them to sell, like Addison's Touchy, whose income had been reduced by law-suits from £80 to £30, though in this case it is true he had only himself to blame.[2] The enclosure of waste land, too, did great damage to the small freeholders, who, without the right of grazing, naturally found it so much the more difficult to pay their way.

Though the economical causes of the disappearance of the yeomen were comparatively unimportant, they served to accelerate the change. Small arable farms would not pay, and must, in any case, have been thrown together. The little farmers, according to Arthur Young, worked harder and were to all intents and purposes as low in the comforts of life as the day-labourers. But their wretchedness was entirely owing to their occupying arable instead of grass lands.[3] And apart from this, undoubtedly, the new class of large farmers were superior, in some respects, to the too unprogressive yeomen,—" quite a different sort of men . . . in point of knowledge and ideas," [4] with whose improved methods of agriculture the yeomen found it difficult to compete. A further economic cause which tended to depress many of the yeomen was the gradual destruction of domestic industries, which injured them as it injures the German peasant at the present day. In Cumberland the yeomen began to disappear when the spinning-wheel was silenced.[5] The decay of the home manufacture of cloth seems to have considerably affected the Grey-coats of Kent. And finally, as the small towns and villages decayed, owing to the consolidation of farms and of industry, the small freeholders lost their market, for the badness of the roads made it difficult for them to send their

[1] Marshall's *Yorkshire*, p. 54.   [2] *Spectator*, No. 122.

[3] *Travels in France* (Dublin ed. 1793), ii. 262. *Rural Economy*, Essays 3 and 4.

[4] *View of the Agriculture of Oxfordshire*, p. 269. Cf. Howlett, i. 65 : "his understanding and his conversation are not at all superior to those of the common labourers, if even equal to them."

[5] See Wordsworth's *Guide to the Lakes*, p. 268.

E

produce far.   Hence the small freeholders survived longest where they owned dairy-farms, as in Cumberland and the West Riding, and where domestic industry flourished, and they had a market for their products in their own neighbourhood.

When once the ranks of the yeomanry had been appreciably thinned, the process of extinction went on with ever-growing rapidity.   The survivors became isolated.   They would have no one of their own station to whom they could marry their daughters, and would become more and more willing to sell their lands, however strong the passion of possession might be in some places.[1] The more enterprising, too, would move off to the towns to make their fortunes there, just as at the present day the French peasants are attracted to the more interesting and exciting life of the town. Thus Sir Robert Peel's grandfather was originally a yeoman farming his own estate, but being of an inventive turn of mind he took to cotton manufacturing and printing.[2]   This was particularly the case with the small squires, who grew comparatively poorer and poorer, and found it increasingly difficult to keep pace with the rise in the standard of comfort.   Already, at the end of the seventeenth century, the complaint had been raised that the landowners were beginning to live in the county towns.   Afterwards, the more wealthy came up to London; Sir Roger de Coverley had a house in Soho Square.   The small country gentleman felt the contrast between him and his richer neighbours more and more; and as he had none of the political power attaching to land—for the great landowners had the whole administration in their hands—there was every inducement for him to sell and invest his money in a more profitable manner.

To summarise the movement : it is probable that the yeomen would in any case have partly disappeared, owing to the inevitable working of economic causes.   But these alone would not have led to their disappearance on so large a scale.   It was the political conditions of the age, the overwhelming importance of land, which made it impossible for the yeoman to keep his grip upon the soil.

---

[1] See Wordsworth's story of the freeholder and his tree, in Harriet Martineau's *Autobiography*, ii. 233.
[2] Baines, pp. 262, 263.

VI.

ENGLAND IN 1760.

THE CONDITION OF THE WAGE-EARNERS.

The Agricultural Labourer—Improvement in his condition since the beginning of the century—Comparison of his position in 1750 and 1850—Contrast between North and South—Inequality of wages and its cause—The position of the artisans—Great rise in their wages since 1760—Certain disadvantages of their condition now, as compared with that existing then.

THE condition of the agricultural labourer had very much improved since the beginning of the century. In the seventeenth century his average daily wage had been 10¼d., while the average price of corn had been 38s. 2d. During the first sixty years of the eighteenth century his average wages were 1s., the price of corn 32s.[1] Thus, while the price of corn had, thanks to a succession of good seasons, fallen 16 per. cent., wages had risen to about an equal extent, and the labourer was thus doubly benefited. Adam Smith attributes this advance in prosperity to " an increase in the demand for labour, arising from the great and almost universal prosperity of the country ;"[2] but at the same time he allows that wealth had only advanced gradually, and with no great rapidity. The real solution is to be found in the slow rate of increase in the numbers of the people. Wealth had indeed grown slowly, but its growth had nevertheless been more rapid than that of population.

The improvement in the condition of the labourer was thus due to an increase in real and not only in nominal wages. It is true that certain articles, such as soap, salt, candles, leather, fermented liquors, had, chiefly owing to the taxes laid on them, become a good deal dearer, and were consumed in very small quantities ; but the enhanced prices of these things were more than counterbalanced by the greater cheapness of grain, potatoes, turnips, carrots, cabbages, apples, onions, linen and woollen cloth, instru-

[1] Nicholls, *History of the Poor Laws* (1854), ii. 54, 55, quoting from Arthur Young.
[2] *Wealth of Nations*, Book I. ch. xi. (vol. i. 211.)

ments made of the coarser metals, and household furniture.[1] Wheaten bread had largely superseded rye and barley bread, which were "looked upon with a sort of horror," wheat being as cheap as rye and barley had been in former times.[2] Every poor family drank tea once a day at least—a "pernicious commodity," a "vile superfluity," in Arthur Young's eyes.[3] Their consumption of meat was "pretty considerable;" that of cheese was "immense."[4] In 1737 the day-labourers of England, "by their large wages and cheapness of all necessaries," enjoyed better dwellings, diet, and apparel in England, than the husbandmen or farmers did in other countries."[5] The middle of the eighteenth century was indeed about his best time, though a decline soon set in. By 1771 his condition had already been somewhat affected by the dear years immediately preceding, when prices had risen much faster than wages, although the change had as yet, according to Young, merely cut off his superfluous expenditure.[6] By the end of the century men had begun to look back with regret upon this epoch in the history of the agricultural labourer as one of a vanished prosperity. At no time since the passing of the 43d of Elizabeth, wrote Eden in 1796, "could the labouring classes acquire such a portion of the necessaries and conveniences of life by a day's work, as they could before the late unparalleled advance in the price of the necessaries of life."[7]

Nor were high wages and cheap food their only advantages. Their cottages were often rent-free, being built upon the waste. Each cottage had its piece of ground attached,[8] though the piece was often a very small one, for the Act of Elizabeth, providing that

---

[1] *Wealth of Nations*, Book I. ch. viii. (vol. i. 82.)

[2] Harte's *Essays on Husbandry*, pp. 176, 177, quoted by A. Young, *Farmer's Letters* (3rd edition, 1771), i. 207, 208. In the north, rye and barley bread alone were still consumed. [Wheaten bread was certainly unknown among the Norfolk labourers at the beginning of this century.]

[3] *Ibid.*, pp. 200, 297. Much of the tea was very bad, and smuggled. A family at Epsom made a quarter of a pound last them for a fortnight.—Eden, iii. 710. Still the imports had increased enormously, from 141,995 lbs. in 1711, to 2,515,875 lbs. in 1759-1760.—Nicholls, ii. 59.

[4] *Travels in France* (Dublin edition, 1793), ii. 313.

[5] Chamberlayne, *State of Great Britain* (1737), p. 177. He says that "the meanest mechanics and husbandmen want not silver spoons and some silver cups in their houses.

[6] *Farmer's Letters*, i. 203-205 ; *cf.* also Howlett, quoted in Eden's *State of the Poor*, i. 384-385.　　　　　　　　　　　　[7] Eden, i. 478.

[8] *Farmer's Letters*, i. 205.

every cottage should have four acres of land, was doubtless unob-
served, and was repealed in 1775. Their common rights, besides
providing fuel, enabled them to keep cows and pigs and poultry on
the waste, and sheep on the fallows and stubbles. But these rights
were already being steadily curtailed, and there was " an open war
against cottages," [1] consequent on the tendency to consolidate holdings into large sheep-farms. It was becoming customary, too, for
unmarried labourers to be boarded in the farmers' houses.

On the whole, the agricultural labourer, at any rate in the south
of England, was much better off in the middle of the eighteenth
century than his descendants were in the middle of the nineteenth.
At the later date wages were actually lower in Suffolk, Essex, and
perhaps parts of Wilts, than they were at the former ; in Berks they
were exactly the same ; in Norfolk, Bucks, Gloucestershire, and South
Wilts, there had been a very trifling rise ; with the exception of
Sussex and Oxfordshire, there was no county south of the Trent in
which they had risen more than one-fourth.[2] Meanwhile rent and
most necessaries, except bread, had increased enormously in cost,
while most of the labourer's old privileges were lost, so that his
real wages had actually diminished. But in the manufacturing
districts of the north his condition had improved. While nominal
wages in the south had risen on the average 14 per cent., here
they had risen on the average 66 per cent. In some districts the
rise had been as great as 200 per cent. In Arthur Young's time
the agricultural wages of Lancashire were 4s. 6d.—the lowest rate
in England ; in 1821 they had risen to 14s. It may be roughly
said that the relative positions of the labourer north and south of
the Trent had been exactly reversed in the course of a century.

In Arthur Young's time the highest wages were to be found in
Lincolnshire, the East Riding, and, following close upon these, the
metropolitan and eastern counties. At first sight the high rate of
wages in the first two counties seems to contradict the general law
about their relative condition in north and south. But on investigation we find it to be due to exceptional circumstances.
Arguing on the deductive method, we should conjecture a large
demand for or a small supply of labour ; and, in fact, we find both
these influences in operation. The population had actually dimi-

1 *Farmer's Letters*, i. 301.
2 Caird, *English Agriculture*, p. 513.

nished, in Lincolnshire from 64 to 58 to the square mile, in the
East Riding, from 80 to 71 ; this was partly due to the enclosures
and the conversion of arable to pasture, partly to the increase of
manufactures in the West Riding. Thus the labourers had been
drawn off to the latter at the same time that they were being
driven out of the agricultural districts. And for the remaining
labourers there was a great demand in public works, such as turn-
pike-roads and agricultural improvements on a large scale.[1]

But there were many local variations of wages which are far
less easy to bring under the ordinary rules of Political Economy.
There was often the greatest inequality in the same county. In
Lincolnshire, for instance, wages varied from 12s. 3d. to 7s., and
even 6s.[2] It was at this very time that Adam Smith, arguing
deductively from his primary axiom that men follow their pecuniary interest, enunciated the law that wages tend to an equality in
the same neighbourhood and the same occupation. Why then these
variations ? Adam Smith himself partly supplies the answer.
His law pretends to exactness only "when society is left to the
natural course of things."[3] Now this was impossible when natural
tendencies were diverted by legal restrictions on the movement
of labour, such as the law of settlement, which resulted in confining every labourer to his own parish. But we must not seek the
cause of these irregularities of wages merely in legal restrictions.
Apart from disturbing influences such as this, men do not always
act in accordance with their pecuniary interest ; there are other
influences at work affecting their conduct. One of the strongest of
these is attachment to locality. It was this influence which partly
frustrated the recent efforts of the Labourers' Union to remove the
surplus labour of the east and south to the north. Again, there
are apathy and ignorance, factors of immense importance in determining the action of the uneducated majority of men. In 1872
there were labourers in Devon who had never heard of Lancashire,
where they might have been earning double their own wages.[4]
Human beings, as Adam Smith says, are " of all baggage the most

---

[1] Young's *Northern Tour*, i. 172 ; Eden, i. 329.
[2] Young's *Eastern Tour*, iv. 312-313.
[3] *Wealth of Nations*, Book I. ch. x. (vol. i. 104).
[4] See Heath's *Peasant Life in the West*, p. 94, and Clifford's *Agricultural Lockout in* 1874.

difficult to be transported,"[1] though their comparative mobility depends upon the degree of their education, the state of communications, and the industrial conditions of any particular time. The English labourer to-day is far more easy to move than he was a hundred years ago. In a stirring new country like America there is much more mobility of labour than in England.

Turning from the agricultural wage-earners to those engaged in manufactures, we find their condition at this period on the whole much inferior to what it is now. In spite of the widening gulf between capitalist and labourer, the status of the artisan has distinctly improved since Adam Smith's time. His nominal wages have doubled or trebled. A carpenter then earned 2s. 6d. a day; he now earns 5s. 6d. A cotton weaver then earned 5s.[2] a week, he now earns 20s., and so on. But it is difficult to compare the condition of the artisan as a whole at the two periods, because so many entirely new classes of workmen have come into existence during the past century; for instance, the engineers, whose Union now includes 50,000 men earning from 25s. to 40s. a week. And if wages have on the whole very greatly increased, there were, on the other hand, some obvious advantages which the artisan possessed in those days, but has since lost. For the manufacturing population still lived to a very great extent in the country. The artisan often had his small piece of land, which supplied him with wholesome food and healthy recreation. His wages and employment too were more regular. He was not subject to the uncertainties and knew nothing of the fearful sufferings which his descendants were to endure from commercial fluctuations, especially before the introduction of free trade. For the whole inner life of industry was, as we have seen, entirely different from what it now is. The relation between the workmen and their employers was much closer, so that in many industries they were not two classes, but one. As among the agriculturists the farmer and labourer lived much the same life—for the capitalist farmers as a class were not yet in existence—and ate at the same board, so in manufacturing industries the journeyman was often on his way to become a master. The distribution of wealth was, indeed, in all respects more equal. Landed property, though gradually being

[1] *Wealth of Nations*, Book I. ch. viii. (vol. i. 79).
[2] Baines, p. 361.

concentrated, was still in a far larger number of hands, and even the great landlords possessed nothing like their present riches. They had no vast mineral wealth, or rapidly developing town property. A great number of the trading industries, too, were still in the hands of small capitalists. Great trades, like the iron trade, requiring large capital, had hardly come into existence.

VII.

THE MERCANTILE SYSTEM AND ADAM SMITH.

Change in the spirit of commercial policy—The mediæval idea of the State—
The regulation of internal trade and industry—Restrictions upon the
movement of labour—The law of apprentices—Wages and prices fixed
by authority—The regulation of Foreign Trade—Chartered companies—
The Mercantile System and Protection—Evils of that system—The struggle
of interests—Injustice to Ireland and the Colonies—Characteristics of the
Wealth of Nations—Its arrangement—Adam Smith's cosmopolitanism and
belief in self-interest.

THE contrast between the industrial England of 1760 and the industrial England of to-day is not only one of external conditions. Side by side with the revolution which the intervening century has effected in the methods and organisation of production, there has taken place a change no less radical in men's economic principles, and in the attitude of the State to individual enterprise. England in 1760 was still to a great extent under the mediæval system of minute and manifold industrial regulations. That system was indeed decaying, but it had not yet been superseded by the modern principle of industrial freedom. To understand the origin of the mediæval system we must go back to a time when the State was still conceived of as a religious institution with ends that embraced the whole of human life. In an age when it was deemed the duty of the State to watch over the individual citizen in all his relations, and provide not only for his protection from force and fraud, but for his eternal welfare, it was but natural that it should attempt to insure a legal rate of interest, fair wages, honest wares. Things of vital importance to man's life were not to be left to chance or self-interest to settle. For no philosophy had as yet identified God and Nature; no optimistic theory of the world had reconciled public and private interest. And at the same time, the smallness of the world and the community, and the comparative simplicity of the social system made the attempt to regulate the industrial relations of men less absurd than it would appear to us in the present day.

This theory of the State, and the policy of regulation and restriction which sprang from it, still largely affected English industry at the time when Adam Smith wrote. There was, indeed, great freedom of internal trade ; there were no provincial customs-barriers as in contemporary France and Prussia. Adam Smith singled out this fact as one of the main causes of English prosperity, and to Colbert and Stein, and other admirers of the English system, such freedom appeared as an ideal to be constantly striven after. But though internal trade was free for the passage of commodities, yet there still existed a network of restrictions on the mobility of labour and capital. By the law of apprenticeship[1] no person could follow any trade till he had served his seven years. The operation of the law was limited, it is true, to trades already established in the fifth year of Elizabeth, and obtained only in market towns and cities. But wherever there was a municipal corporation, the restrictions which they imposed made it generally impossible for a man to work unless he was a freeman of the town, and this he could as a rule become only by serving his apprenticeship. Moreover, the corporations supervised the prices and qualities of wares. In the halls, where the smaller manufacturers sold their goods, all articles exposed for sale were inspected. The mediæval idea still obtained that the State should guarantee the genuineness of wares ; it was not left to the consumer to discover their quality. And in the Middle Ages, no doubt, when men used the same things from year to year, a proper supervision did secure good work. But with the expansion of trade it ceased to be effective. Sir Josiah Child already recognised that changes of fashion must prove fatal to it, and that a nation which intended to have the trade of the world must make articles of every quality.[2] Yet the belief in the necessity of regulation was slow in dying out, and fresh Acts to secure it were passed as late as George II.'s reign.

It is not clear how far the restrictions on the mobility of capital

[1] 5 Eliz., c. 4.
[2] *On Trade*, p. 131 (ed. 1692).

and labour were operative.   No doubt they succeeded to a large extent; but when Adam Smith wrote his bitter criticism of the corporations,[1] he was probably thinking of the particular instance of Glasgow, where Watt was not allowed to set up trade.   There were, however, even at that time, many free towns, like Birmingham and Manchester, which flourished greatly from the fact of their freedom.   And even in the chartered towns, if Eden is to be trusted, the restrictions were far less stringent than we should gather from Adam Smith.[2]   " I am persuaded," he says, " that a shoemaker, who had not served an apprenticeship, might exercise his industry at Bristol or Liverpool, with as little hazard of being molested by the corporation of either place, as of being disturbed by the borough-reve of Manchester or the head-constable at Birmingham."   Then after quoting and criticising Adam Smith, he adds : " I confess, I very much doubt whether there is a single corporation in England, the exercise of whose rights does at present operate in this manner. . . . In this instance, as in many others, the insensible progress of society has reduced chartered rights to a state of inactivity." [3]   We may probably conclude that non-freemen were often unmolested, but that, when trade was bad, they were liable to be expelled.

Another relic of Mediævalism was the regulation of wages by Justices of the Peace, a practice enjoined by the Act of Elizabeth already referred to.   Adam Smith speaks of it as part of a general system of oppression of the poor by the rich.   Whatever may have been the case in some instances this was not generally true.   The country gentry were, on the whole, anxious to do justice to the working classes.   Combinations of labourers were forbidden by law, because it was thought to be the wrong way of obtaining the object in view, not from any desire to keep down wages.   The Justices often ordained a rise in wages, and the workmen themselves were strongly in favour of this method of fixing them.   The employers on their part also often approved of it.   In fact we have an exactly similar system at the present day

---

[1] *Wealth of Nations*, Book i. ch. x., pt. ii. (vol. i. 125).

[2] The maintenance of restrictions in the chartered towns was largely due to the fact that the dissenters, who, perhaps, comprised the richest of the commercial classes, were legally altogether, and in practice to a considerable degree, excluded from office in the chartered towns.

[3] *State of the Poor*, i. 436, 437.

in boards of arbitration. The Justice was an arbitrator, appointed by law; and it is a mistaken assumption that such authoritative regulation may not have been good in its day.

The principle of regulation was applied much more thoroughly to our external than to our internal trade. The former was entirely carried on by great chartered companies, whether they were on a joint-stock footing, like the East India Company, or were " regulated " like the Turkey Company, in which every man traded on his own capital.[1] Here, again, Adam Smith carried too far his revolt against the restrictive system, which led him to denounce corporate trading as vicious in principle. " The directors of such companies," he says, " being the managers rather of other people's money than of their own, it cannot well be expected that they should watch over it with the same anxious vigilance with which the partners in a private copartnery frequently watch over their own. . . . Negligence and profusion must always prevail, more or less, in the management of the affairs of such a company." [2] This is an instance of pure *a priori* reasoning, but Smith's main argument is derived from the history of Joint-Stock Companies. He sought to show that, as a matter of fact, unless they had had a monopoly, they had failed; that is, he proceeded inductively, and wound up with an empirical law: " it seems *contrary to all experience* that a Joint-Stock Company should be able to carry on successfully any branch of foreign trade, when private adventurers can come into any sort of open and fair competition with them." [3] But he was too honest not to admit exceptions to his rule, as in the instance of banking, which he explained by the fact that it could be reduced to routine.

Smith's empirical law is, as we all now know, far from being universally true, though it was a reasonable induction enough at the time when it was made. Since then a large number of Joint-Stock companies have succeeded, as for instance in the iron trade. Nor is it difficult to see the reason of this change. The habit of combination is stronger than it was, and we have discovered how to interest paid servants by giving them a share in the results of the enterprises they direct. Experience has shown also that a big company can buy the best

[1] *Wealth of Nations*, Book v. ch. i., pt. iii. sec. i. (vol. ii. 317, *et seq.*).
[2] *Ibid.* vol. ii. 326, 329.   [3] *Ibid.* p. 331.

brains. In the recent depression of trade the ironworks of Dowlais, which are managed on the Joint-Stock system, alone remained successful amid many surrounding failures, and that because they had the ablest man in the district as manager.

In Adam Smith's time, however, the existence of Joint-Stock Companies was due not to any notion of their economical superiority, but to the tendency to place restrictions upon individual enterprise, based upon that belief in the antagonism of public and private interests which was characteristic of the time. The same idea of opposition obtained equally in international relations. The prosperity of one country was thought to be incompatible with that of another. If one profited by trade, it seemed to do so at the expense of its neighbours. This theory was the foundation of the mercantile system. It had its origin in the spirit of Nationalism—the idea of self-sustained and complete national life —which came in with the Renaissance and the Reformation.

But how came this Nationalism to be connected with a belief in the special importance of gold and silver, which is generally regarded as the essence of the mercantile system? The object of that system was national greatness, but national greatness depends on national riches generally, not on one particular kind of riches only, such as coin. The explanation must be sought in the fact that, owing to the simultaneous development of trade and the money system, gold and silver became peculiarly essential to the machinery of commerce. With the growth of standing armies, moreover, State finance acquired a new importance, and the object of State finance was to secure a ready supply of the precious metals. Thus the theory sprang up that gold and silver were the most solid and durable parts of the moveable wealth of a nation, and that, as they had more value in use than any other commodities, every state should do all in its power to acquire a great store of them. At first the Government tried to attain this object by accumulating a hoard; but this policy soon proved too wasteful and difficult. It then turned its attention to increasing the quantity of bullion in the hands of the people, for it came to see that if there was plenty of bullion in the country it could always draw upon it in case of need. The export of gold and silver was accordingly forbidden; but if hoarding had proved impracticable, this new method of securing the desired end was soon found to be useless, as the prohibition could be easily evaded. In the last resort, therefore, it was sought to insure a continuous influx of the precious metals through the ordinary channels of trade. If we bought less than we sold, it was argued, the balance of trade must be paid in coin. To accomplish this end every encouragement was given to the importation of raw materials and the necessaries of life, but the purchase of foreign manufactures was, for the most part, prohibited, and individuals were entreated not to buy imported luxuries. The result was retaliation abroad, and a deadlock in the commercial machine. Wars of tariff were common; for instance, we prohibited the importation of gold-lace from Flanders, and the Flemings in return excluded our wool. The system, however, resisted the teaching of experience, despite the fact that in abolishing the prohibition of the export of gold and silver, the Government acknowledged the true principle of free trade put forward by the East Indian Company. The latter contended that the law forbidding the export of bullion was not only useless, since it was easily stultified by smuggling, but even, if enforced, was hurtful, since the Orientals would only sell their valuable goods for silver. The success of this contention marks the transition from the Mercantile System proper to modern Protection. The advocates of that system had shifted their ground, and instead of seeking merely to prohibit the export of the precious metals, they established a general protection of native industries.

Their measures were not all alike bad. The Navigation Acts, for instance, were defended by Adam Smith, and Mill has indorsed his defence, on the ground that national defence is more important than national opulence.[1]

The most famous of these Acts was the law of 1651,[2] by which no goods of the growth or manufacture of Asia, Africa, or America were to be imported into England, Ireland, or the Plantations, except in ships belonging to English subjects, and manned by a crew three-fourths of whom were English; while no goods of any country in Europe were to be imported except in English ships, or ships belonging to the country from

---

[1] *Wealth of Nations*, Bk. iv. ch. ii. (vol. ii. 38) ; Mill's *Principles* (first edition), Bk. v. ch. x. (vol. ii. 485).

[2] There had been earlier Navigation Acts, of more or less stringency, from the time of Henry VII. onwards.

which the goods came. The argument used by the promoters of the law was that by excluding the Dutch from the carrying trade to this country we should throw it into the hands of English shipowners, and there would be an increase of English ships. It was admitted, indeed, that this would be giving a monopoly to English shipowners and English sailors, and that therefore freights would be dearer, and a check given to the growth of commerce. It was further admitted that owing to their higher charges English ships might be driven out of neutral ports; but the contention was, that we should secure to ourselves the whole of the carrying trade between America and the West Indies and England, and that this would amply compensate for our expulsion from other branches of commerce.

These anticipations were on the whole fulfilled. The price of freights was raised, because English ships cost more to build and man than Dutch ships, and thus the total amount of our trade was diminished.[1] We were driven out of neutral ports, and lost the Russian and the Baltic trades, because the English shipowners, to whom we had given a monopoly, raised their charge.[2] But on the other hand, we monopolised the trade to ports coming within the scope of the Act, the main object of which was " the preservation of our plantation trade entire." [3] Our shipping received a great stimulus, and our maritime supremacy grew with it. At the time when the Navigation Act was passed our colonial trade was insignificant; New York and Jersey were Dutch; Georgia, the Carolinas, Pennsylvania, Nova Scotia were not yet planted; Virginia, Maryland, New England were in their infancy.[4] At the end of the century the Barbadoes alone employed 400 vessels; while with the growth of the colonies the English power at sea had increased, until it rivalled the Dutch. In the next century the continuous development of the American and East Indian trades gave us a position of unquestionable maritime superiority.[5]

There is another argument in favour of Protection, at any rate in its early days. Its stimulus helped to overcome the apathy

---

[1] Anderson, ii. 443-4 ; *Wealth of Nations*, Bk. iv. ch. vii. (vol. ii. 179) ; Child *On Trade*, p. 93 (ed. 1692) ; *Britannia Languens* (1680), 66 ; Richardson (1750), 52.

[2] Child, p. 98 (ed. 1692).   [3] Anderson, ii. 416.

[4] *Wealth of Nations*, loc. cit.   [5] Payne's *History of the Colonies*, 78.

and dulness of a purely agricultural population, and draw a part of the people into trade.[1] But here, as everywhere, Protection involves this great disadvantage, that, once given, it is difficult to withdraw, and thus in the end more harm is done than good. English industries would not have advanced so rapidly without Protection, but the system, once established, led to perpetual wrangling on the part of rival industries, and sacrificed India and the colonies to our great manufacturers. And our national dislike to Protection deepens into repugnance when we examine the details of the system. Looking at its results during the period from 1688 to 1776, when it was in full force, we are forced to acknowledge that Adam Smith's invectives against the merchants, violent as they were, were not stronger than the facts demanded.

But the maintenance of Protection cannot be entirely set down to the merchants. Though the trading classes acquired much influence at the Revolution, the landed gentry were still supreme in Parliament; and the question arises, why they should have lent themselves to a policy which in many cases, as in the prohibition of the export of wool, was distinctly opposed to the interests of agriculture. Adam Smith's explanation is very simple. The country gentleman, who was naturally " least subject of all people to the wretched spirit of monopoly," was imposed upon by the " clamours and sophistry of merchants and manufacturers," and " the sneaking arts of underling tradesmen," who persuaded him into a simple but honest conviction that their interest and not his was the interest of the public.[2] Now this is true, but it is not the whole truth. The landowners, no doubt, thought it their duty to protect trade, and, not understanding its details, they implicitly followed the teaching of the merchants. But, besides this, there was the close connection, already referred to, between them and the commercial classes. Their younger sons often went into trade; they themselves, in many cases, married merchants' daughters. Nor did they give their support gratuitously; they wanted Protection for themselves, and if they acquiesced in the prohibition of the wool export, they persuaded the merchants to allow them in return bounty of 5s. a quarter on the export of corn.

---

[1] Mill's *Principles of Political Economy*, i. ch. 8, 2, p. 141.
[2] *Wealth of Nations*, Bk. i. ch. x ; Bk. iv. ch. iii. (vol. i. 134 ; ii. 34, 68).

One of the worst features of the system was the struggle of rival interests at home. A great instance of this was the war between the woollen and cotton trades, in which the former, supported by the landed interest,[1] for a long time had the upper hand, so that an excise duty was placed on printed calicoes, and in 1721 they were forbidden altogether. It was not till 1774 that they were allowed again, and the excise duty was not repealed till 1831. To take another instance : it was proposed in Parliament in 1750 to allow the importation of pig and bar iron from the colonies. The tanners at once petitioned against it, on the ground that if American iron was imported, less iron would be smelted in England, fewer trees would be cut down, and therefore their own industry would suffer ; and the owners of woodland tracts supported the tanners, lest the value of their timber should be affected.[2] These are typical examples of the way in which, under a protective system, politics are complicated and degraded by the intermixture of commercial interests. And the freer a government is, and the more exposed to pressure on the part of its subjects, the worse will be the result. As an American observer has lately said, Protection may be well enough under a despotism, but in a republic it can never be successful.

We find still stronger illustration of the evils of Protection in our policy towards Ireland and the Colonies. After the Cromwellian settlement, there had been an export of Irish cattle into England ; " but for the pacifying of our landed gentlemen,"[3] after the Restoration the import of Irish live-stock, meat, and dairy produce was prohibited from 1660 to 1685. As cattle-farming then became unprofitable, the Irish turned their lands into sheep-walks, and not only exported wool, but started woollen manufactures at home. Immediately a law was passed (1699) confining the export of Irish wool to the English market ; and this was followed by the imposition of prohibitive duties on their woollen manufactures. The English manufacturers argued that as Ireland was protected by England, and its prosperity was due to English capital, the

---

[1] In the *True Representation of the Manufacture of the Combing and Spinning of Wool* (Bib. Bodl. : N.D.), the author remarks that the importation of Indian yarn " will hinder the consumption of great quantities of wool, by which the gentlemen's tenants, whose lands are used in the growth of wool, will be necessitated to sell their wool for a low price."

[2] Scrivenor, pp. 73-4.   [3] Anderson, vol. ii. p. 507.

Irish ought to reconcile themselves to restrictions on their trade, in the interests of Englishmen. Besides, the joint interests of both kingdoms would be best considered, if England and Ireland respectively monopolised the woollen and linen industries, and the two nations thus became dependent on one another. If we turn to the colonies, we find them regarded simply as markets and farms of the mother country. The same argument was used : that they owed everything to England, and therefore it was no tyranny to exploit them in her interests. They were, therefore, not allowed to export or import in any but British vessels ; they might not export such commodities as Englishmen wanted to any part of Europe other than Great Britain ; while those of their raw materials in which our landowners feared competition were excluded from the English markets. All imports into the colonies from other parts of Europe, except Great Britain, were forbidden, in order that our manufacturers might monopolise the American market. Moreover, every attempt was made to prevent them from starting any manufactures at home. At the end of the seventeenth century some Americans had set on foot a woollen industry ; in 1719 it was suppressed ; all iron manufactures—even nail-making—were forbidden ; a flourishing hat manufacture had sprung up, but at the petition of English hatters, these competitors were not allowed to export to England, or even from one colony to another. Adam Smith might well say, that " to found a great empire, for the sole purpose of raising up a people of customers, may at first sight appear a project fit only for a nation of shopkeepers." [1] Nothing contributed more than this commercial system to the Declaration of Independence, and it is significant that the same year which saw its promulgation saw also the publication of the *Wealth of Nations.*

Many people on first reading the *Wealth of Nations* are disappointed. They come to it, expecting lucid arguments, the clear exposition of universal laws ; they find much tedious and confused reasoning and a mass of facts of only temporary interest. But these very defects contributed to its immediate success. It was because Adam Smith examined in detail the actual conditions of the age, and wrote a handbook for the statesman, and not merely, as Turgot did, a systematised treatise for the philosopher, that he

[1] *Wealth of Nations,* Bk. iv. ch. vii. pt. iii. (vol. ii. p. 196.)

appealed so strongly to the practical men of his time, who, with Pitt, praised his "extensive knowledge of detail," as well as "the depth of his philosophical research." It was the combination of the two which gave him his power. He was the first great writer on the subject; with him political economy passed from the exchange and the market-place to the professor's study; but he was only groping his way, and we cannot expect to meet with neat arrangement and scientific precision of treatment in his book. His language is tentative, he sometimes makes distinctions which he forgets elsewhere, as was inevitable before the language of economics had been fixed by endless verbal discussions. He had none of Ricardo's power of abstract reasoning. His gift lay in the extent and quickness of his observation, and in his wonderful felicity of illustration. We study him, because in him, as in Plato, we come into contact with a great original mind, which teaches us how to think and work. Original people always are confused because they are feeling their way.

If we look for the fundamental ideas of Adam Smith, those which distinguish him most clearly from earlier writers, we are first struck by his cosmopolitanism. He was the precursor of Cobden in his belief that commerce is not of one nation, but that all the nations of the world should be considered as one great community. We may see how widely he had departed from the old national system of economy, by contrasting the mere title of his book, *The Wealth of Nations*, with that of Muir's treatise, *England's Treasure in Foreign Trade.* This cosmopolitanism necessitated a detailed refutation of the mercantile system. He had to prove that gold and silver were not more important than other forms of wealth; and that if we wanted to buy them, we could always do so, if we had other consumable goods to offer in exchange. But it might be objected : "What if a nation refuses to take your other goods, and wants your gold?" Adam Smith replied : "In that case, gold will leave your country and go abroad ; as a consequence, prices will fall at home, foreigners will be attracted by the low prices to buy in your markets, and thus the gold will return." I can give you an actual example from recent history to prove the truth of his deduction. During the potato famine of 1847, we had to import enormous quantities of grain from America, and as a consequence had to send there £16,000,000 worth of bullion. Immediately prices rose in

America and fell in England, English merchants discontinued buying in America, while American merchants bought largely in England, so that in the following year all the gold came back again.

Equally prominent in Adam Smith is his individualism, his complete and unhesitating trust in individual self-interest. He was the first to appeal to self-interest as a great bond of society. As a keen observer, he could point to certain facts, which seemed to bear out his creed. If we once grant the principle of the division of labour, then it follows that one man can live only by finding out what other men want; it is on this fact, for instance, that the food supply of London depends. This is the basis of the doctrine of *laisser faire*. It implies competition, which would result, so Adam Smith believed, in men's wants being supplied at a minimum of cost. In upholding competition he was radically opposed to the older writers, who thought it a hateful thing; but his conclusion was quite true. Again it implies the best possible distribution of industry; for under a system of free competition, every man will carry on his trade in the locality most suitable for it.

But the principle of *laisser faire* breaks down in certain points not recognised by Adam Smith. It fails, for instance, in assuming that it is the interest of the producer to supply the wants of the consumer in the best possible manner, that it is the interest of the producer to manufacture honest wares. It is quite true that this is his interest, where the trade is an old-established one and has a reputation to maintain, or where the consumer is intelligent enough to discover whether a commodity is genuine or not. But these conditions exist only to a small extent in modern commerce. The trade of the present day is principally carried on with borrowed capital; and it may be a clever man's interest to sell as large a quantity of goods as possible in a few years and then throw up his business. Thus the interests of producer and consumer conflict, and it has been found necessary to pass Adulteration Acts, which recognise the non-identity of interest of seller and buyer. It was argued, indeed, in Parliament, when these acts were proposed, that consumers ought to take care of themselves, but the consumers are far too ignorant to do so, especially the poor who are the great consumers of the articles protected against adulteration. Adam Smith, moreover, could not foresee that internal free trade might result in *natural* monopolies. A conspicuous feature of our times is the concentration of certain industries in the hands of a few great capitalists, especially in America, where such rings actually dictate the prices of the market. Eighty-five per cent. of the Pennsylvanian coal-mines, for instance, are in the hands of six or seven companies who act in combination. The easiest remedy for such monopolies would be international free-trade; with international competition few could be maintained. Finally, in the distribution of wealth there must necessarily be a permanent antagonism of interests. Adam Smith himself saw this, when he said that the rate of wages depended on contracts between two parties whose interests were not identical. This being granted, we see that in distribution the "harmony" of the individual and the public good is a figment. At the present day each class of workmen cares only for the wages of its own members. Hence the complete breakdown of the *laisser faire* system in the question of wages. We have been driven to attempt the establishment of Boards of Conciliation all over the country, thus virtually surrendering the principle. Nor is it true that self-interest tends to supply all our wants; some of our best institutions, such as hospitals, owe their existence to altruistic sentiment.[1] These antagonisms were to come out more strongly than ever after Adam Smith's time. There were dark patches even in his age, but we now approach a darker period,—a period as disastrous and as terrible as any through which a nation ever passed; disastrous and terrible, because, side by side with a great increase of wealth was seen an enormous increase of pauperism; and production on a vast scale, the result of free competition, led to a rapid alienation of classes and to the degradation of a large body of producers.

[1] On the whole subject see H. Spencer's Essays on *Specialised Administration and the Social Organism*, and Professor Huxley's Essay on *Administrative Nihilism*.

VIII.

THE CHIEF FEATURES OF THE REVOLUTION.

Growth of Economic Science—Competition—Its uses and abuses—The symptoms of the Industrial Revolution—Rapid growth of population—Its relative density in North and South—The agrarian revolution—Enclosures—Consolidation of farms and agricultural improvements—The revolution in manufactures—The factory system—Expansion of trade—Rise in rents—Change in the relative position of classes.

THE essence of the Industrial Revolution is the substitution of competition for the mediæval regulations which had previously controlled the production and distribution of wealth. On this account it is not only one of the most important facts of English history, but Europe owes to it the growth of two great systems of thought—Economic Science, and its antithesis, Socialism. The development of Economic Science in England has four chief landmarks, each connected with the name of one of the four great English economists. The first is the publication of Adam Smith's *Wealth of Nations* in 1776, in which he investigated the causes of wealth and aimed at the substitution of industrial freedom for a system of restriction. The production of wealth, not the welfare of man, was what Adam Smith had primarily before his mind's eye; in his own words, " the great object of the Political Economy of every country is to increase the riches and power of that country."[1] His great book appeared on the eve of the Industrial Revolution. A second stage in the growth of the science is marked by Malthus's *Essay on Population*, published in 1798, which may be considered the product of that revolution, then already in full swing. Adam Smith had concentrated all his attention on a large production; Malthus directed his inquiries, not to the causes of wealth but to the causes of poverty, and found them in his theory of population. A third stage is marked by Ricardo's *Principles of Political Economy and Taxation*, which appeared in 1817, and in which Ricardo sought to ascertain the laws of the distribution of wealth. Adam Smith had shown how wealth could be produced under a system of industrial freedom,

[1] Vol. i. Bk. ii. ch. v. p. 377.

Ricardo showed how wealth is distributed under such a system, a problem which could not have occurred to any one before his time. The fourth stage is marked by John Stuart Mill's *Principles of Political Economy,* published in 1848. Mill himself asserted that "the chief merit of his treatise" was the distinction drawn between the laws of production and those of distribution, and the problem he tried to solve was, how wealth *ought to be* distributed. A great advance was made by Mill's attempt to show what was and what was not inevitable under a system of free competition. In it we see the influence which the rival system of Socialism was already beginning to exercise upon the economists. The whole spirit of Mill's book is quite different from that of any economic works which had up to his time been written in England. Though a re-statement of Ricardo's system, it contained the admission that the distribution of wealth is the result of "particular social arrangements," and it recognised that competition alone is not a satisfactory basis of society.

Competition, heralded by Adam Smith, and taken for granted by Ricardo and Mill, is still the dominant idea of our time; though since the publication of the *Origin of Species,* we hear more of it under the name of the "struggle for existence." I wish here to notice the fallacies involved in the current arguments on this subject. In the first place it is assumed that all competition is a competition for existence. This is not true. There is a great difference between a struggle for mere existence and a struggle for a particular kind of existence. For instance, twelve men are struggling for employment in a trade where there is only room for eight; four are driven out of that trade, but they are not trampled out of existence. A good deal of competition merely decides what kind of work a man is to do;[1] though of course when a man can only do one kind of work, it may easily become a struggle for bare life. It is next assumed that this struggle for existence is a law of nature, and that therefore all human interference with it is wrong. To that I answer that the whole meaning of civilisation is interference with this brute struggle. We intend to modify the violence of the fight, and to prevent the weak being trampled under foot.

Competition, no doubt, has its uses. Without competition no

[1] Inability to see this fact is the source of the Protectionist fallacy.

progress would be possible, for progress comes chiefly from without; it is external pressure which forces men to exert themselves. Socialists, however, maintain that this advantage is gained at the expense of an enormous waste of human life and labour, which might be avoided by regulation. But here we must distinguish between competition in production and competition in distribution, a difference recognised in modern legislation, which has widened the sphere of contract in the one direction, while it has narrowed it in the other. For the struggle of men to outvie one another in production is beneficial to the community; their struggle over the division of the joint produce is not. The stronger side will dictate its own terms; and as a matter of fact, in the early days of competition the capitalists used all their power to oppress the labourers, and drove down wages to starvation point. This kind of competition has to be checked; there is no historical instance of its having lasted long without being modified either by combination or legislation, or both. In England both remedies are in operation, the former through Trades-Unions, the latter through factory legislation. In the past other remedies were applied. It is this desire to prevent the evils of competition that affords the true explanation of the fixing of wages by Justices of the Peace, which seemed to Ricardo a remnant of the old system of tyranny in the interests of the strong. Competition, we have now learnt, is neither good nor evil in itself; it is a force which has to be studied and controlled; it may be compared to a stream whose strength and direction have to be observed, that embankments may be thrown up within which it may do its work harmlessly and beneficially. But at the period we are considering it came to be believed in as a gospel, and, the idea of necessity being superadded, economic laws deduced from the assumption of universal unrestricted competition were converted into practical precepts, from which it was regarded as little short of immoral to depart.

Coming to the facts of the Industrial Revolution, the first thing that strikes us is the far greater rapidity which marks the growth of population. Before 1751 the largest decennial increase, so far as we can calculate from our imperfect materials, was 3 per cent. For each of the next three decennial periods the increase was 6 per cent.; then between 1781 and 1791 it was 9 per cent.; between 1791 and 1801, 11 per cent.; between 1801 and 1811, 14 per cent.;

between 1811 and 1821, 18 per cent.[1] This is the highest figure ever reached in England, for since 1815 a vast emigration has been always tending to moderate it; between 1815 and 1880 over eight millions (including Irish) have left our shores. But for this our normal rate of increase would be 16 or 18 instead of 12 per cent. in every decade.[2]

Next we notice the relative and positive decline in the agricultural population. In 1811 it constituted 35 per cent. of the whole population of Great Britain; in 1821, 33 per cent.; in 1831, 28 per cent.[3] And at the same time its actual numbers have decreased. In 1831 there were 1,243,057 adult males employed in agriculture in Great Britain; in 1841 there were 1,207,989. In 1851 the whole number of persons engaged in agriculture in England was 2,084,153; in 1861 it was 2,010,454, and in 1871 it was 1,657,138.[4] Contemporaneously with this change, the centre of density of population has shifted from the Midlands to the North; there are at the present day 458 persons to the square mile in the counties north of the Trent, as against 312 south of the Trent. And we have lastly to remark the change in the relative population of England and Ireland. Of the total population of the three kingdoms, Ireland had in 1821 32 per cent., in 1881 only 14·6 per cent.

An agrarian revolution plays as large part in the great industrial change of the end of the eighteenth century as does the revolution in manufacturing industries, to which attention is more usually directed. Our next inquiry must therefore be: What were the agricultural changes which led to this noticeable decrease in the rural population? The three most effective causes were: the destruction of the common-field system of cultivation; the enclosure, on a large scale, of commons and waste lands; and the consolidation of small farms into large. We have already seen that while between 1710 and 1760 some 300,000 acres were enclosed,

---

[1] "In the cotton trade," said Sir R. Peel in 1806, "machinery has given birth to a new population; it has promoted the comforts of the population to such a degree that early marriages have been resorted to, and a great increase of numbers has been occasioned by it, and I may say that they have given rise to an additional race of men."—Parl. Report, p. 440.

[2] See Jevons on *The Coal Question*, p. 170; Census Returns for 1881, pp. iii, xi.

[3] Porter's *Progress of the Nation* (2d edition, 1847), p. 52.

[4] *Ib.* pp. 61, 65. Kolb's *Condition of Nations*, translated by Mrs. Brewer, p. 73.

between 1760 and 1843 nearly 7,000,000 underwent the same process. Closely connected with the enclosure system was the substitution of large for small farms. In the first half of the century Laurence, though approving of consolidation from an economic point of view, had thought that the odium attaching to an evicting landlord would operate as a strong check upon it.[1] But these scruples had now disappeared. Eden in 1795 notices how constantly the change was effected, often accompanied by the conversion of arable to pasture; and relates how in a certain Dorsetshire village he found two farms where twenty years ago there had been thirty.[2] The process went on uninterruptedly into the present century. Cobbett, writing in 1826, says: " In the parish of Burghclere one single farmer holds, under Lord Carnarvon, as one farm, the lands that those now living remember to have formed fourteen farms, bringing up in a respectable way fourteen families."[3] The consolidation of farms reduced the number of farmers, while the enclosures drove the labourers off the land, as it became impossible for them to exist without their rights of pasturage for sheep and geese on common lands.

Severely, however, as these changes bore upon the rural population, they wrought, without doubt, distinct improvement from an agricultural point of view. They meant the substitution of scientific for unscientific culture. " It has been found," says Laurence, " by long experience, that common or open fields are great hindrances to the public good, and to the honest improvement which every one might make of his own." Enclosures brought an extension of arable cultivation and the tillage of inferior soils; and in small farms of 40 to 100 acres, where the land was exhausted by repeated corn crops, the farm buildings of clay and mud walls and three-fourths of the estate often saturated with water,[4] consolidation into farms of 100 to 500 acres meant rotation of crops, leases of nineteen years, and good farm buildings. The period was one of great agricultural advance; the breed of cattle was improved, rotation of crops was generally introduced, the steam-plough was

---

[1] *Duty of a Steward*, pp. 3, 4.
[2] *State of the Poor*, ii. pp. 147-8.   Cf. also p. 621.
[3] *Rural Rides*, ed. 1830, p. 579.
[4] Kebbel's *Agricultural Labourer*, pp. 207-8.

invented, agricultural societies were instituted.[1]　In one respect alone the change was injurious.　In consequence of the high prices of corn which prevailed during the French war, some of the finest permanent pastures were broken up.　Still, in spite of this, it was said in 1813 that during the previous ten years agricultural produce had increased by one-fourth, and this was an increase upon a great increase in the preceding generation.[2]

Passing to manufactures, we find here the all-prominent fact to be the substitution of the factory for the domestic system, the consequence of the mechanical discoveries of the time.　Four great inventions altered the character of the cotton manufacture; the spinning-jenny, patented by Hargreaves in 1770 ; the water-frame, invented by Arkwright the year before ; Crompton's mule introduced in 1779, and the self-acting mule, first invented by Kelly in 1792, but not brought into use till Roberts improved it in 1825.[3]　None of these by themselves would have revolutionised the industry.　But in 1769—the year in which Napoleon and Wellington were born—James Watt took out his patent for the steam-engine.　Sixteen years later it was applied to the cotton manufacture.　In 1785 Boulton and Watt made an engine for a cotton-mill at Papplewick in Notts, and in the same year Arkwright's patent expired.　These two facts taken together mark the introduction of the factory system.　But the most famous invention of all, and the most fatal to domestic industry, the power-loom, though also patented by Cartwright in 1785, did not come into use for several years,[4] and till the power-loom was introduced the workman was hardly injured.　At first, in fact, machinery raised the wages of spinners and weavers owing to the great prosperity it brought to the trade.　In fifteen years the cotton trade trebled itself; from 1788 to 1803 has been called " its golden age;" for, before the power-loom but after the introduction of the mule and other mechanical improvements by which for the first time yarn sufficiently fine for muslin and a variety of other fabrics was spun, the demand became such that " old barns, cart-

---

[1] The North and West of England in 1777; the Highland Society in 1784 ; the Board of Agriculture in 1793.

[2] Committee on the Corn Trade (1813).　See Porter, p. 149.

[3] Baines, *passim.*

[4] In 1813 there were only 2400 in use: in 1820 there were 14,150 ; and in 1833, over 100,000.　Baines, pp. 235-7.

houses, out-buildings of all descriptions were repaired, windows broke through the old blank walls, and all fitted up for loom-shops; new weavers' cottages with loom-shops arose in every direction, every family bringing home weekly from 40 to 120 shillings per week." [1] At a later date, the condition of the workman was very different. Meanwhile, the iron industry had been equally revolutionised by the invention of smelting by pit-coal brought into use between 1740 and 1750, and by the application in 1788 of the steam-engine to blast furnaces. In the eight years which followed this latter date, the amount of iron manufactured nearly doubled itself.[2]

A further growth of the factory system took place independent of machinery, and owed its origin to the expansion of trade, an expansion which was itself due to the great advance made at this time in the means of communication. The canal system was being rapidly developed throughout the country. In 1777 the Grand Trunk canal, 96 miles in length, connecting the Trent and Mersey, was finished; Hull and Liverpool were connected by one canal while another connected them both with Bristol; and in 1792, the Grand Junction canal, 90 miles in length, made a waterway from London through Oxford to the chief midland towns.[3] Some years afterwards, the roads were greatly improved under Telford and Macadam; between 1818 and 1829 more than a thousand additional miles of turnpike road were constructed;[4] and the next year, 1830, saw the opening of the first railroad. These improved means of communication caused an extraordinary increase in commerce, and to secure a sufficient supply of goods it became the interest of the merchants to collect weavers around them in great numbers, to get looms together in a workshop, and to give out the warp themselves to the workpeople. To these latter this system meant a change from independence to dependence; at the beginning of the century the report of a committee asserts that the essential difference between the domestic and the factory system is, that in the latter the work is done " by persons who have no property in the goods they manufacture." Another direct consequence of this expansion of trade was the regular recurrence

---

[1] Radcliffe, quoted by Baines, pp. 338-339.   [2] Scrivenor, pp. 83, 87, 93.
[3] Macculloch's *Commercial Dictionary*, pp. 233, 234.
[4] Porter, p. 293.

of periods of over-production and of depression, a phenomenon quite unknown under the old system, and due to this new form of production on a large scale for a distant market.

These altered conditions in the production of wealth necessarily involved an equal revolution in its distribution. In agriculture the prominent fact is an enormous rise in rents. Up to 1795, though they had risen in some places, in others they had been stationary since the Revolution.[1] But between 1790 and 1833, according to Porter, they at least doubled.[2] In Scotland, the rental of land, which in 1795 had amounted to £2,000,000, had risen in 1815 to £5,278,685.[3] A farm in Essex, which before 1793 had been rented at 10s. an acre, was let in 1812 at 50s., though, six years after, this had fallen again to 35s. In Berks and Wilts, farms which in 1790 were let at 14s., were let in 1810 at 70s., and in 1820 at 50s. Much of this rise, doubtless, was due to money invested in improvements—the first Lord Leicester is said to have expended £400,000 on his property [4]—but it was far more largely the effect of the enclosure system, of the consolidation of farms, and of the high price of corn during the French war. Whatever may have been its causes, however, it represented a great social revolution, a change in the balance of political power and in the relative position of classes. The farmers shared in the prosperity of the landlords; for many of them held their farms under beneficial leases, and made large profits by them. In consequence, their character completely changed; they ceased to work and live with their labourers, and became a distinct class. The high prices of the war time thoroughly demoralised them, for their wealth then increased so fast, that they were at a loss what to do with it. Cobbett has described the change in their habits, the new food and furniture, the luxury and drinking, which were the consequences of more money coming into their hands than they knew how to spend.[5] Meanwhile, the effect of all these agrarian changes upon the condition of the labourer was an exactly opposite and most disastrous one. He felt all the burden of high prices, while

---

[1] Eden, ii. 292.   [2] Porter, pp. 151, 165.

[3] *Encyclopædia Britannica*, sub " Agriculture."

[4] The stock-jobbers, *e.g.* Ricardo, bought up estates, and property very much changed hands. The new landlords were probably more capable of developing the resources of their properties.

[5] Cobbett's *Rural Rides*, Reigate, October 20, 1825, p. 241 (ed. 1830). Cf. Martineau's *History of England from* 1800 *to* 1815 (1878), p. 18.

his wages were steadily falling, and he had lost his common-rights. It is from this period, viz., the beginning of the present century, that the alienation between farmer and labourer may be dated.[1]

Exactly analogous phenomena appeared in the manufacturing world. The new class of great capitalist employers made enormous fortunes, they took little or no part personally in the work of their factories, their hundreds of workmen were individually unknown to them; and as a consequence, the old relations between masters and men disappeared, and a "cash nexus" was substituted for the human tie. The workmen on their side resorted to combination, and Trades-Unions began a fight which looked as if it were between mortal enemies rather than joint producers. The misery which came upon large sections of the working people at this epoch was often, though not always, due to a fall in wages, for, as I said above, in some industries they rose. But they suffered likewise from the conditions of labour under the factory system, from the rise of prices, especially from the high price of bread before the repeal of the corn-laws, and from those sudden fluctuations of trade, which, ever since production has been on a large scale, have exposed them to recurrent periods of bitter distress. The effects of the Industrial Revolution prove that free competition may produce wealth without producing wellbeing. We all know the horrors that ensued in England before it was restrained by legislation and combination.[2]

IX.

THE GROWTH OF PAUPERISM.

Political Economy and the instinct of benevolence—The History of the Poor Laws—Pauperism in the sixteenth century—The Poor Law of 1601 and its modifications—Slow growth of pauperism during the seventeenth and eighteenth centuries—Its rapid increase at the end of the latter—The causes of this development of pauperism : consolidation of farms, enclosures, rise of prices, introduction of machinery—Remedies which might have been applied—Vicious principle of the old Poor Law.

MALTHUS tells us that his book was suggested by Godwin's *Inquiry,* but it was really prompted by the rapid growth of pau-

---

[1] Report of Committee on labourers' wages (1824), p. 57.
[2] This period and its sufferings are further treated of in the address entitled *Industry and Democracy.*—ED.

perism which Malthus saw around him, and the book proved the main influence which determined the reform of the English Poor Laws. The problem of pauperism came upon men in its most terrible form between 1795 and 1834. The following statistics will illustrate its growth:—

Year.	Population.	Poor-rate.	Per head of Population.
1760	7,000,000	£1,250,000	or 3s. 7d.
1784	8,000,000	2,000,000	or 5s. 0d.
1803	9,216,000	4,077,000	or 8s. 11d.
1818	11,876,000	7,870,000	or 13s. 3d.

This was the highest rate ever reached. But really to understand the nature of the problem we must examine the previous history of pauperism, its causes in different periods, and the main influences which determined its increase.

Prejudices have arisen against Political Economy because it seemed to tell men to follow their self-interest and to repress their instincts of benevolence. Individual self-interest makes no provision for the poor, and to do so other motives and ideas must take its place; hence the idea that Political Economy taught that no such provision should be made. Some of the old economists did actually say that people should be allowed to die in the street. Yet Malthus, with all his hatred of the Poor Law, thought that "the evil was now so deeply seated, and relief given by the Poor Laws so widely extended, that no man of humanity could venture to propose their immediate abolition."[1] The assumed cruelty of political economy arises from a mistaken conception of its province, and from that confusion of ideas to which I have before alluded, which turned economic laws into practical precepts, and refused to allow for the action of other motives by their side. What we now see to be required is not the repression of the instincts of benevolence, but their organisation. To make benevolence scientific is the great problem of the present age. Men formerly thought that the simple direct action of the benevolent instincts by means of self-denying gifts was enough to remedy the misery they deplored; now we see that not only thought but historical study is also necessary. Both to understand the nature of pauperism and to discover its effectual remedies, we must investi-

[1] *Essay on Population*, 7th edition, p. 429.

gate its earlier history. But in doing this we should take to heart two warnings: first, not to interpret mediæval statutes by modern ideas; and secondly, not to assume that the causes of pauperism have always been the same.

The history of the Poor Laws divides itself into three epochs: from 1349 to 1601, from 1601 to 1782, and from 1782 to 1834. Now, what was the nature of pauperism in mediæval society, and what were then the means of relieving it? Certain characteristics are permanent in all society, and thus in mediæval life as elsewhere there was a class of impotent poor, who were neither able to support themselves nor had relatives to support them. This was the only form of pauperism in the early beginnings of mediæval society, and it was provided for as follows. The community was then broken up into groups—the manor, the guild, the family, the Church with its hospitals, and each group was responsible for the maintenance of all its members; by these means all classes of poor were relieved. In the towns the craft and religious guilds provided for their own members; large estates in land were given to the guilds, which " down to the Reformation formed an organised administration of relief;" (" the religious guilds were organised for the relief of distress as well as for conjoint and mutual prayer;")[1]—while outside the guilds there were the churches, the hospitals, and the monasteries. The " settled poor" in towns were relieved by the guilds, in the country by the lords of the manor and the beneficed clergy. "Every manor had its constitution,"[2] says Professor Stubbs, and, referring to manumission, he adds, "the native lost the privilege of maintenance which he could claim of his lord."[3] Among what were called "the vagrant poor" there were the professional beggars, who were scarcely then considered what we should now call paupers, and "the valiant labourers" wandering only in search of work. Who then were the paupers? In the towns there were the craftsmen, who could not procure admission into a guild. In the country there was the small class of landless labourers nominally free. It is a great law of social development that the movement from slavery to freedom is also a movement from security to insecurity of maintenance. There is a close connection between the growth of freedom

[1] Stubbs's *Constitutional History*, vol. iii. p. 600.
[2] *Ibid.* p. 599.   [3] *Ibid.* p. 604.

and the growth of pauperism; it is scarcely too much to say that the latter is the price we pay for the former. The first Statute, which is in any sense a Poor Law, was enacted at a time when the emancipation of the serfs was proceeding rapidly. This is the Statute of Labourers, made in 1349; it has nothing to do with the maintenance of the poor; its object was to repress their vagrancy.[1]

This statute has been variously interpreted. According to some,[2] it was simply an attempt of the landowners to force the labourers to take the old wages of the times before the Plague. Others object, with Brentano, to this interpretation, and believe that it was not an instance of class legislation, but merely expressed the mediæval idea that prices should be determined by what was thought reasonable and not by competition; for this same Statute regulates the prices of provisions and almost everything which was sold at the time. Probably Brentano is in the main right. It is true that the landowners did legislate with the knowledge that the Statute would be to their own advantage; but the law is none the less in harmony with all the ideas of the age. The Statute affected the labourer in two directions: it fixed his wages, and it prevented him from migrating. It was followed by the Statute of 1388, which is sometimes called the beginning of the English Poor Law. We here find the first distinction between the impotent and the able-bodied poor. This law decreed that if their neighbours would not provide for the poor, they were to seek maintenance elsewhere in the hundred; no one is considered responsible for them; it is assumed that the people of the parish will support them. Here too we catch the first glimpse of a law of settlement, in the provision that no labourer or pauper shall wander out of his hundred unless he carry a letter-patent with him.

No exact date can be assigned to the growth of able-bodied pauperism. It was the result of gradual social changes, and of the inability to understand them. Mediæval legislators could not grasp the necessity for the mobility of labour, nor could they see that compulsory provision for the poor was essential, though the Statute of 1388 shows that the bond between lord and dependant was snapped, and security for their maintenance in this way already at

---

[1] Nicholls's *History of the Poor Law*, i. 36.
[2] *e.g.* Seebohm in *Fortnightly Review*, ii. 270. See Cunningham's *Growth of English Industry and Commerce*, p. 191.

an end. The Church and private charity were deemed sufficient; though it is true that laws were passed to prevent the alienation of funds destined for the poor.[1] And with regard to the mobility of labour, we must remember that the vagrancy of the times did not imply the distress of the labourers, but their prosperity. The scarcity of labour allowed of high wages, and the vagrant labourer of the time seems never to have been satisfied, but always wandering in search of still higher wages. The stability of mediæval society depended on the fixity of all its parts, as that of modern society is founded on their mobility. The Statutes afford evidence that high wages and the destruction of old ties did in fact lead to disorder, robbery, and violence; and by and by we find the condition of the labourer reversed; in the next period he is a vagrant, because he cannot find work.

In the sixteenth century pauperism was becoming a really serious matter. If we ask, What were its causes then, and what the remedies proposed, we shall find that at the beginning of the century a great agrarian revolution was going on, during which pauperism largely increased. Farms were consolidated, and arable converted into pasture;[2] in consequence, where two hundred men had lived there were now only two or three herdsmen. There was no employment for the dispossessed farmers, who became simple vagabonds, "valiant beggars," until later they were absorbed into the towns by the increase of trade. A main cause of the agrarian changes was the dissolution of monasteries, though it was one that acted only indirectly, by the monastic properties passing into the hands of new men who did not hesitate to evict without scruple. About the same time the prices of provisions rose through the influx of the precious metals and the debasement of the coinage. And while the prices of corn in 1541-82 rose 240 per cent. as compared with the past one hundred and forty years, wages rose only 160 per cent.[3] In this fact we discover a second great cause of the pauperism of the time; just as at the end of the eighteenth century we find wages the last to rise, and the labouring man the

---

[1] A law of 15 Richard II. (c. 15) enacts that if "a parish church is appropriated," the "diocesan shall ordain a convenient sum of money to be distributed yearly of the fruits and profits of the same to the poor parishioners, in aid of their living and sustenance, for ever."

[2] More's *Utopia* (Arber's Reprints), p. 41.

[3] Rogers's *History of Agriculture and Prices*, vol. iv. pp. 718-9.

greatest sufferer from increased prices. As regards the growth of pauperism in towns, the main cause may be found in the confiscation of the estates of the guilds by the Protector Somerset.[1] These guilds had been practically friendly societies, and depended for their funds upon their landed properties.

And how did statesmen then deal with these phenomena? The legislation of the age about "vagabonds" is written in blood. The only remedy suggested was to punish the vagrant by cruel tortures—by whipping and branding. Even death was resorted to after a second or third offence; and though these penalties proved very ineffectual, the system was not abandoned till the law of 43 Elizabeth recognised that punishment had failed as a remedy. The other class of paupers, the impotent poor, had been directed by a Statute of Richard II. to beg within a certain limited area; in the reigns of Edward VI. and Elizabeth the necessity of compulsory provision for this class of poor slowly dawned upon men's minds. At first the churchwardens were ordered to summon meetings for the purpose of collecting alms, and overseers were appointed who "shall gently ask and demand" of every man and woman what they of their charity will give weekly towards the relief of the poor. Mayors, head-officers, and church-wardens were to collect money in boxes "every Sunday and holyday." The parsons, vicar and curate, were to reason with those who would not give, and if they were not successful, the obstinate person was to be sent to the bishop, who was to "induce and persuade him;" or by the provisions of a later law, he was to be assessed at Quarter Sessions (1562). Such was the first recognition of the principle of compulsory support, of the fact that there are men in the community whom no one will relieve. There appears upon the scene for the first time the isolated individual, a figure unknown to mediæval society, but who constitutes so striking a phenomenon in the modern world. And hence springs up a new relation between the State and the individual. Since the latter is no longer a member of a compact group, the State itself has to enter into direct connection with him. Thus, by the growth at once of freedom and of poverty, the whole status of the working classes had been changed, and the problem of modern legislation came to be this: to discover how we can

---

[1] Stubbs, iii. p. 600.

have a working class of free men, who shall yet find it easy to obtain sustenance; in other words, how to combine political and material freedom.

All the principles of our modern Poor Laws are found in the next Statute we have to notice, the great law of the 43d year of Elizabeth, which drew the sharp distinction, ever since preserved, between the able-bodied and the impotent poor. The latter were to be relieved by a compulsory rate collected by the overseers, the former were to be set to work upon materials provided out of the rates; children and orphans were to be apprenticed. From this date 1601, there were no fundamental changes in the law till the end of the eighteenth century. The law of settlement, however, which sprang directly out of the Act of Elizabeth, was added; it was the first attempt to prevent the migration of labourers by other means than punishment. It began with the Statute of 1662, which allowed a pauper to obtain relief only from that parish where he had his settlement, and defined settlement as forty days' residence without interruption; but after this Statute there were constant changes in the law, leading to endless complications; and more litigation took place on this question of settlement than on any other point of the Poor Law. It was not till 1795 that the hardship of former enactments was mitigated by an Act under which no new settler could be removed until he became actually chargeable to the parish.[1]

Two other modifications of the Act of Elizabeth require to be noticed. In 1691 the administration of relief was partially taken out of the hands of the overseers and given to the Justices of the Peace, the alleged reason being that the overseers had abused their power. Henceforth they were not allowed to relieve except by order of a Justice of the Peace, and this provision was construed into a power conferred upon the Justices to give relief independently of any application on the part of the overseers, and led, in fact, to Justices ordering relief at their own discretion. The other important change in the Poor Law was the introduction of the workhouse test in 1722. It is clear that pauperism had grown since the reign of Charles II. There are many pamphlets of the

---

[1] See Adam Smith's sketch of the Law of Settlement in his chapter on Wages; and on the Poor Laws generally, Fowle's *History of the Poor Law*, in the *English Citizen* Series.

period full of suggestions as to a remedy, but the only successful idea was this of the workhouse test. Parishes were now empowered to unite and build a workhouse, and refuse relief to all who would not enter it; but the clauses for building workhouses remained inoperative, as very few parishes would adopt them.

The question remains to be asked: Why was pauperism still slowly increasing in the course of the seventeenth and eighteenth centuries in spite of a rise in wages, and, during the first half of the eighteenth century, a low price of corn? Enclosures and the consolidation of farms, though as yet these had been on a comparatively small scale, were partly responsible for it, as they were in an earlier century. Already, in 1727, it was said that some owners were much too eager to evict farmers and cottagers, and were punished by an increase of rates consequent on the evicted tenants sinking into pauperism.[1] By Eden's time the practice of eviction had become general, and the connection between eviction and pauperism is an indisputable fact, though it has been overlooked by most writers. Eden's evidence again shows that pauperism was greatest where enclosures had taken place. At Winslow, for instance, enclosed in 1744 and 1766, "the rise of the rates was chiefly ascribed to the enclosure of the common fields, which, it was said, had lessened the number of farms, and from the conversion of arable into pasture had much reduced the demand for labourers." Again, at Kilworth-Beauchamp in Leicestershire, "the fields being now in pasturage, the farmers had little occasion for labourers, and the poor being thereby thrown out of employment had, of course, to be supported by the parish."[2] Here too the evil was aggravated by the fate of the ejected farmers, who sank into the condition of labourers, and swelled the numbers of the unemployed. "Living in a state of servile dependence on the large farmers, and having no prospect to which their hopes could reasonably look forward, their industry was checked, economy was deprived of its greatest stimulation, and their only thought was to enjoy the present moment." Again, at Blandford, where the same consolidation of farms had been going on, Eden remarks that "its effects, it is said, oblige small industrious farmers to turn labourers

---

[1] Laurence, pp. 3, 4.
[2] *State of the Poor*, ii. 30, 384. See also pamphlet by James Massie (1758) quoted *ibid.* i. 329.

or servants, who, seeing no opening towards advancement, become regardless of futurity, spend their little wages as they receive them without reserving a pension for their old age ; and, if incapacitated from working by a sickness which lasts a very short time, inevitably fall upon the parish."[1]

Besides the enclosure of the common-fields, and the consolidation of farms, the enclosure of the commons and wastes likewise contributed to the growth of pauperism. Arthur Young and Eden thought that commons were a cause of idleness; the labourers wasted their time in gathering sticks or grubbing furze; their pigs and cows involved perpetual disputes with their neighbours, and were a constant temptation to trespass.[2] No doubt this was true where the common was large enough to support the poor without other occupation. But on the other hand, where the labourer was regularly employed, a small common was a great extra resource to him. Arthur Young himself mentions a case at Snettisham in Norfolk, where, when the waste was enclosed, the common rights had been preserved, and as a result of this, combined with the increased labour due to the enclosure, the poor-rates fell from 1s. 6d. to 1s. or 9d., while population grew from five to six hundred. He goes on to say that enclosures had generally been carried out with an utter disregard for the rights of the poor. According to Thornton, the formation of parks contributed to the general result, but I know of no evidence on this head.

A further cause of pauperism, when we come to the end of the century, was the great rise in prices as compared with that in wages. In 1782 the price of corn was 53s. 9¼d., which was considerably higher than the average of the preceding fifty years ; but in 1795 it had risen to 81s. 6d., and in the next year it was even more. The corn average from 1795 to 1805 was 81s. 2½d., and from 1805 to 1815 97s. 6d. In 1800 and 1801 it reached the maximum of 127s. and 128s. 6d., which brought us nearer to a famine than we had been since the fourteenth century. Many other articles had risen too. The taxes necessitated by the debt contracted during the American war raised the prices of soap,

---

[1] *State of the Poor*, ii. 550, 147.

[2] *Ibid.* i. xviii. Eden himself was in favour of enclosures, thinking that the increased demand for regular labour consequent upon them would more than compensate the labourer, but wished each labourer to have "a garden and a little croft" reserved.

leather, candles, etc., by one-fifth; butter and cheese rose 1½d. a pound, meat 1d. And meanwhile, "what advance during the last ten or twelve years," asks a writer in 1788, "has been made in the wages of labourers? Very little indeed; in their daily labour nothing at all, either in husbandry or manufactures." Only by piece-work could they obtain more in nominal wages.[1] Lastly, in the towns there had come the introduction of machinery, the final establishment of the cash-nexus, and the beginning of great fluctuations in trade. In the old days the employer maintained his men when out of work, now he repudiated the responsibility; and the decline in the position of the artisan could be attributed by contemporary writers to "the iniquitous oppressive practices of those who have the direction of them."[2]

Such seem to have been the causes of the growth of pauperism and of the degradation of the labourer; the single effective remedy attempted was the workhouse test, and this was abandoned in 1782. But might not landlords and farmers have done something more to check the downward course? Were there no possible remedies? One cannot help thinking the problem might have been solved by common justice in the matter of enclosures. Those who were most in favour of enclosing for the sake of agricultural improvements, like Eden and Young, yet held that, in place of his common field and pasture rights, the labourer should have had an acre, or two acres, or half an acre, as the case might be, attached to his cottage. By such compensation much misery would have been prevented. A more difficult question is, whether anything could have been done directly to relieve the stress of high prices? Burke contended that nothing could be done, that there was no necessary connection between wages and prices; and he would have left the evil to natural remedies.[3] And, as a matter of fact, in the North where there was no artificial interference with

---

[1] Howlett, quoted in Eden, i. 380 *et seq.*

[2] Howlett, *loc. cit.*

[3] "It is not true that the rate of wages has not increased with the nominal price of provisions. I allow it has not fluctuated with that price, nor ought it; and the squires of Norfolk had dined, when they gave it as their opinion, that it might or it ought to rise with the market of provisions. The rate of wages has in truth no *direct* relation to that price. Labour is a commodity like any other, and rises or falls according to the demand. This is in the nature of things; however, the nature of things has provided for their necessities. Wages have been twice raised in my time; and they bear a full proportion or

wages, the development of mining and manufactures saved the labourer.

In the Midlands and South, where this needful stimulus was absent, the case was different; some increase in the labourer's means of subsistence was absolutely necessary here, in order that he might exist. It would have been dangerous to let things alone; and the true way to meet the difficulty would have been for the farmers to have raised wages—a course of action which they have at times adopted. But an absence alike of intelligence and generosity, and the vicious working of the Poor Laws in the midland and southern counties, prevented this. The farmers refused to recognise the claims alike of humanity and self-interest, so the justices and country gentlemen took the matter into their own hands, while the labourers threw themselves upon the Poor Law, and demanded that the parish should do what the farmers refused to do, and should supplement insufficient wages by an allowance. This was the principle which radically vitiated the old Poor Law. The farmers supported the system; they wished every man to have an allowance according to his family, and declared that "high wages and free labour would overwhelm them." A change had also come over the minds of the landowners as to their relation to the people. In addition to unthinking and ignorant benevolence, we can trace the growth of a sentiment which admitted an unconditional right on the part of the poor to an indefinite share in the national wealth; but the right was granted in such a way as to keep them in dependence and diminish their self-respect. Though it was increased by the panic of the French revolution, this idea of bribing the people into passiveness was not absolutely new; it had prompted Gilbert's Act in 1782, which abolished the workhouse test, and provided work for those who were willing near their homes. It was this Tory Socialism,[1] this principle of protection of the poor by the rich, which gave birth to the frequent use of the term "labouring poor," so common in the

even a greater than formerly to the medium of provision during the last bad cycle of twenty years."—*Thoughts and Details on Scarcity*, Burke's Works, vol. v. p. 85.

[1] There has always been more practical Socialism in England than elsewhere owing to our ruling landed aristocracy. The Factory Act of 1847 was carried by the Conservatives in the teeth of the Radical manufacturers. [See, *Are Radicals Socialists?*—ED.]

Statutes and in Adam Smith, an expression which Burke attacked as a detestable canting phrase.[1]

The war with Napoleon gave a new impulse to this pauperising policy. Pitt and the country gentlemen wanted strong armies to fight the French and reversed the old policy as regards checks upon population. Hitherto they had exercised control over the numbers of the labourers by refusing to build cottages; in 1771, "an open war against cottages" had been carried on, and landlords often pulled down cottages, says Arthur Young, "that they may never become the nests, as they are called, of beggar brats."[2] But now by giving extra allowance to large families, they put a premium on early marriages, and labourers were paid according to the number of their children. Further extension of the allowance system came from actual panic at home. Farmers and landowners were intimidated by the labourers: the landowners had themselves according to Malthus at once inflamed the minds of their labourers and preached to them submission.[3] Rick-burning was frequent; at Swallowfield, in Wiltshire, the justices, "under the influence of the panic struck by the fires, so far yielded to the importunity of the farmers as to adopt the allowance-system during the winter months." In 1795 some Berkshire justices "and other discreet persons" issued a proclamation, which came to be considered as a guide to all the magistrates of the South of England.[4] They declared it to be their unanimous opinion that the state of the poor required further assistance than had been generally given them; and with this view they held it inexpedient to regulate wages according to the statutes of Elizabeth and James; they would earnestly recommend farmers and others to increase the pay of their labourers in proportion to the present price of provisions; but if the farmers refused, they would make an allowance to every

[1] Burke's Works, vol. v. p. 84.

[2] *Farmer's Letters*, vol. i. p. 302.

[3] During the late dearth half of the gentlemen and clergymen in the kingdom richly deserved to have been prosecuted for sedition. After inflaming the minds of the common people against the farmers and corn-dealers by the manner in which they talked of them or preached about them, it was a feeble antidote to the poison which they had infused, coldly to observe that however the poor might be oppressed or cheated it was their duty to keep the peace."—Malthus, *Principle of Population*, 7th ed. p. 438, note.

[4] This was the famous " Speenhamland Act of Parliament," so called because the Magistrates met at Speenhamland, near Newbury.

poor family in proportion to its numbers. They stated what they thought necessary for a man and his wife and children, which was to be produced " either by his own and his family's labour or an allowance from the poor-rates." [1] These were the beginnings of the allowance system, which under its many forms ended in thoroughly demoralising the people; it had not been long in operation before we hear the labourers described as lazy, mutinous, and imperious to the overseers. When grants in aid of wages were deemed insufficient, the men would go to a magistrate to complain, the magistrate would appeal to the humanity of the overseer, the men would add threats, and the overseer would give in. In the parish of Bancliffe " a man was employed to look after the paupers, but they threatened to drown him, and he was obliged to withdraw." The whole character of the people was lowered by the admission that they had a right to relief independent of work.

X.

MALTHUS AND THE LAW OF POPULATION.

Malthus and Godwin—Malthus's two propositions—The Law of Diminishing Returns certainly true—The Law of Population not universally true— Henry George on Malthus—The causes of the growth of population in rural districts and in towns in the Eighteenth Century—Malthus's remedies: Abolition of the Poor Law, Moral Restraints—Actual remedies since his time: Reform of the Poor Law, Emigration, Importation of Food, Moral Restraint in the middle and artisan Classes—Artificial checks on population considered—The problem not a purely economic one.

IT was during this state of things, with population rapidly increasing, that Malthus wrote. Yet he was not thinking directly of the Poor Law, but of Godwin, who, under the influence of Rousseau, had in his *Inquirer* ascribed all human ills to human government and institutions, and drawn bright pictures of what might be in a reformed society. Malthus denied their possibility. Under no system, he contended, could such happiness be insured; human

---

[1] Nicholl's *History of the Poor Law*, vol. ii. p. 137.

misery was not the result of human injustice and of bad institutions, but of an inexorable law of nature, viz., that population tends to outstrip the means of subsistence. This law would in a few generations counteract the effects of the best institutions that human wisdom could conceive. It is remarkable that though in his first edition he gave a conclusive answer to Godwin, Malthus afterwards made an admission which deducted a good deal from the force of his argument. To the "positive check" of misery and vice, he added the "preventive check" of moral restraint, namely, abstinence from marriage.[1] To this Godwin made the obvious reply that such a qualification virtually conceded the perfectibility of society. But Malthus still thought his argument conclusive as against Godwin's Communism.[2] If private property was abolished, he said, all inducements to moral restraint would be taken away. His prophecy has, however, since his time, been refuted by the experience of the communistic societies in America, which proves that the absence of private property is not incompatible with moral restraint.[3]

Is Malthus's law really true? We see that it rests on two premisses. The first is, that the potential rate of increase of the human race is such that population, if unchecked, would double itself in twenty-five years; and Malthus assumes that this rate is constant in every race and at all times. His second premiss is the law of diminishing returns, *i.e.* that after a certain stage of cultivation a given piece of land will, despite any agricultural improvements, yield a less proportionate return to human labour; and this law is true. Malthus did not deny that food might, for a time, increase faster than population; but land could not be increased, and if the area which supplied a people were restricted, the total quantity of food which it produced per head must be at

---

[1] "Throughout the whole of the present work I have so far differed in principle from the former as to suppose the action of another check to population, which does not come under the head of either vice or misery ; and in the latter part I have endeavoured to soften some of the harsher conclusions of the first essay."—Preface to 2d edition, p. vii. Cf. Bagehot's *Economic Studies*, p. 137 : "In its first form the *Essay on Population* was conclusive as an argument, but it was based on untrue facts ; in its second form it was based on true facts, but it was inconclusive as an argument."

[2] *Essay on Population* (7th edition), pp. 271-80.

[3] See Nordhoff's *Communistic Societies of the United States ;* and *Essay on Population*, p. 286.

length diminished, though this result might be long deferred. Malthus himself regarded both his conclusions as equally self-evident. "The first of these propositions," he says, "I considered as proved the moment the American increase was related; and the second proposition as soon as it was enunciated." Why then did he write so long a book? "The chief object of my work," he goes on to say, "was to inquire what effects these laws, which I con-sidered as established in the first six pages, had produced, and were likely to produce, on society;—a subject not very readily exhausted."[1] The greater part of his essay is an historical examination of the growth of population and the checks on it which have obtained in different ages and countries; and he applies his conclusion to the administration of the Poor Laws in England.

Now there are grave doubts as to the universal truth of his first premiss. Some of his earlier opponents, as Doubleday, laid down the proposition that fecundity varies inversely to nutriment.[2] Thus baldly stated their assertion is not true; but it is an observed fact, as Adam Smith noticed long ago, that the luxurious classes have few children, while a "half-starved Highland woman" may have a family of twenty.[3] Mr. Herbert Spencer again has asserted that fecundity varies inversely to nervous organisation, and this statement has been accepted by Carey and Bagehot.[4] But it is not so much the increase of brain power as the worry and exhaustion of modern life which tends to bring about this result. Some statistics quoted by Mr. Amasa Walker tend to prove this. He has shown that in Massachusetts, while there are about 980,000 persons of native birth as against only 260,000 immigrants, the number of births in the two classes is almost exactly the same, the number of marriages double as many in the latter, as in the former, and longevity less and mortality greater among the Americans. Mr. Cliffe-Leslie attributes this fact to a decline in fecundity on the part of American citizens. The whole question, however, is veiled in great obscurity, and is rather for physiologists and biologists to decide; but there do seem to be causes at work which pre-

---

[1] *Essay on Population*, 491, note.
[2] Doubleday's *True Law of Population* (1842), p. 5.
[3] *Wealth of Nations*, bk. i. ch. viii.
[4] Bagehot's *Economic Studies*, 141 *et seq.*

clude us from assuming with Malthus that the rate of increase is invariable.[1]

Another American writer, Mr. Henry George,[2] has recently argued that Malthus was wrong and Godwin right, that poverty is due to human injustice, to an unequal distribution of wealth, the result of private property in land, and not to Malthus's law of the increase of population or to the law of diminishing returns, both of which he altogether rejects. With regard to the latter he urges with truth that in certain communities, for instance California, where the law of diminishing returns evidently does not come into operation, the same phenomenon of pauperism appears. Now against Mr. George it can be proved by facts that there are cases where his contention is not true. It is noticeable that he makes no reference to France, Norway, and Switzerland,—all countries of peasant proprietors, and where consequently the land is not monopolised by a few. But it is certain that in all these countries, at any rate in the present state of agricultural knowledge and skill, the law of diminishing returns does obtain; and it is useless to argue that in these cases it is the injustice of man, and not the niggardliness of nature, that is the cause of poverty, and necessitates baneful checks on population. Still I admit that Mr. George's argument is partially true,—a large portion of pauperism and misery is really attributable to bad government and injustice; but this does not touch the main issue, or disprove the law of diminishing returns.

To return to Malthus's first proposition. The phrase that "population tends to outstrip the means of subsistence" is vague and ambiguous. It may mean that population, if unchecked, *would* outstrip the means of subsistence; or it may mean that population *does* increase faster than the means of subsistence. It is quite clear that, in its second sense, it is not true of England at the present day. The average quantity of food consumed per head is yearly greater; and capital increases more than twice as fast as population.[3] But the earlier writers on population invariably use

---

[1] *Science of Wealth*, 462-4.

[2] *Progress and Poverty*, book ii. ch. i. These lectures were given before the book had acquired general notoriety.—ED.

[3] Since 1860 the population of the United Kingdom has increased from 29,070,932 to 35,003,789, or 20 per cent.; while its wealth has grown in the same time from £5,200,000,000 to £8,420,000,000, or 62 per cent. See Mul-

the phrase in the latter sense, and apply it to the England of their time. At the present day it can only be true in this latter sense of a very few countries. It has been said to be true in the case of India, but even there the assertion can only apply to certain districts. Mr. George, however, is not content to refute Malthus's proposition in this sense; he denies it altogether, denies the statement in the sense that population, if unchecked, *would* outstrip the means of subsistence, and lays down as a general law that there need be no fear of over-population if wealth were justly distributed. The experience of countries like Norway and Switzerland, however, where over-population does exist, although the distribution of wealth is tolerably even, shows that this doctrine is not universally true. Another criticism of Mr. George's, however, is certainly good, as far as it goes. Malthus's proposition was supposed to be strengthened by Darwin's theory, and Darwin himself says that it was the study of Malthus's book which suggested it to him;[1] but Mr. George rightly objects to the analogy between man and animals and plants. It is true that animals, in their struggle for existence, have a strictly limited amount of subsistence, but man can, by his ingenuity and energy, enormously increase his supply.[2] The objection is valid, though it can hardly be said to touch the main issue.

I have spoken of the rapid growth of population in the period we are studying. We have to consider how Malthus accounted for it, and how far his explanation is satisfactory, as well as what practical conclusions he came to. In the rural districts he thought the excessive increase was the consequence of the bad administration of the Poor Laws, and of the premium which they put on early marriages. This was true, but not the whole truth; there are other points to be taken into account. In the old days the younger labourers boarded in the farm-houses, and were of course single men; no man could marry till there was a cottage vacant, and it was the

hall in *Contemporary Review*, Dec. 1881. The consumption of tea per head has increased from 2·66 lbs. to 4·66 lbs., of sugar from 34·61 lbs. to 62·33, of rice from 5·94 lbs. to 14·31, and many other articles in like proportion.

[1] *Origin of Species* (Pop. Ed.), 50.

[2] "While all through the vegetable and animal kingdoms the limit of subsistence is independent of the thing subsisted, with man the limit of subsistence is, within the final limits of earth, air, water, and sunshine, dependent upon man himself."—*Progress and Poverty*, book ii. c. iii. p. 117. Cf. *Unto this Last* (3d edition), p. 157-8.

policy of the landlords in the "close villages" to destroy cottages, in order to lessen the rates.[1] But now the farmers had risen in social position and refused to board the labourers in their houses. The ejected labourers, encouraged by the allowance system, married recklessly,[2] and though some emigrated into the towns, a great evil arose. The rural population kept increasing while the cottage accommodation as steadily diminished, and terrible over-crowding was the result. Owing to the recklessness and demoralisation of the labourer the lack of cottages no longer operated as any check on population.[3] The change in the social habits of the farmers had thus a considerable effect on the increase of rural population and tended to aggravate the effects of the allowance system.

In the towns the greatest stimulus came from the extension of trade due to the introduction of machinery. The artisan's horizon became indistinct; there was no visible limit to subsistence. In a country like Norway, with a stationary society built up of small local units, the labourer knows exactly what openings for employment there are in his community; and it is well known that the Norwegian peasant hesitates about marriage till he is sure of a position which will enable him to support a family.[4] But in a great town, among "the unavoidable variations of manufacturing labour,"[5] all these definite limits were removed. The artisan could always hope that the growth of industry would afford employment for any number of children—an expectation which the enormously rapid growth of the woollen and cotton manufactures justified to a large extent. And the great demand for children's labour in towns increased a man's income in proportion to the number of his family, just as the allowance system did in the country.[6]

---

[1] Eden, i. 361.—"I know several parishes, in which the greatest difficulty the poor labour under is the impossibility of procuring habitations."

[2] *Commission on Labourers' Wages* (1824), p. 60. The number of cottages in rural districts went on decreasing as late as 1860, but the Union Chargeability Act is now said to have "completely cured the practice of clearing away cottages."—Evidence of Right Hon. Sclater-Booth before Agricultural Commission of 1881. Qu. 9090.

[3] Its action has not ceased, however, altogether. See Heath, *English Peasantry*, p. 36, for an instance as late as 1872.

[4] *Essay on Population*, p. 129, 7th ed.   [5] *Ibid.* p. 315.

[6] Children were migrated wholesale into the towns from the country districts. So in Switzerland the introduction of manufactures into some of the smaller cantons, at the end of the last century, gave a great stimulus to early marriages.—*Ibid.* p. 174.

What remedies did Malthus propose? The first was the abolition of the Poor Law; and he was not singular in this opinion. Many eminent writers of the time believed it to be intrinsically bad. He suggested that at a given date it should be announced that no child born after the lapse of a year should be entitled to relief; the improvident were to be left to "the punishment of nature" and "the uncertain support of private charity."[1] Others saw that such treatment would be too hard; that a Poor Law of some sort was necessary, and that the problem was how to secure to the respectable poor the means of support without demoralising them. His second remedy was moral restraint,— abstention from marriage till a man had means to support a family, accompanied by perfectly moral conduct during the period of celibacy.[2]

Let us now see what have been the actual remedies. The chief is the reform of the Poor Laws in 1834, perhaps the most beneficent Act of Parliament which has been passed since the Reform Bill. Its principles were (*a*) the application of the workhouse test and the gradual abolition of out-door relief to able-bodied labourers; (*b*) the formation of unions of parishes to promote economy and efficiency, these unions to be governed by Boards of Guardians elected by the ratepayers, thus putting an end to the mischievous reign of the Justices of the Peace; (*c*) a central Board of Poor Law Commissioners, with very large powers to deal with the Boards of Guardians and control their action; (*d*) a new bastardy law; (*e*) a mitigation of the laws of settlement. The effect of the new law was very remarkable. As an example, take the case of Sussex. Before 1834 there were in that county over 6000 able-bodied paupers; two years later there were 124.[3] A similar change took place in almost all the rural districts, and the riots and rick-burning which had been so rife began to grow less frequent. Equally remarkable was the effect upon the rates. In 1818 they were nearly £8,000,000 in England and Wales; in 1837 they had sunk to a little over £4,000,000, and are now only £7,500,000 in spite of the enormous growth of population. The number of paupers, which in 1849 was 930,000, has dwindled in 1881 to 800,000, though the population has meanwhile increased by more than

[1] *Essay on Population*, p. 430.   [2] *Ibid.* p. 403.
[3] Molesworth, *History of England*, vol. i. p. 319.

8,000,000. Notwithstanding this improvement the Poor Laws are by no means perfect, and great reforms are still needed.

Next in importance as an actual remedy we must place emigration. Malthus despised it. He thought that " from the natural unwillingness of people to desert their native country, and the difficulty of clearing and cultivating fresh soil, it never is or can be adequately adopted;" that, even if effectual for the time, the relief it afforded would only be temporary, " and the disorders would return with increased virulence."[1] He could not of course foresee the enormous development which would be given to it by steam navigation, and the close connection established thereby between England and America. Since 1815 eight and a quarter millions of people have emigrated from the United Kingdom; since 1847 three and a half millions have gone from England and Wales alone; and this large emigration has of course materially lightened the labour market. Nor could Malthus any more foresee the great importation of food which would take place in later times. In his day England was insulated by war and the corn laws; now, we import one half of our food, and pay for it with our manufactures.

As to moral restraint, it is very doubtful, whether it has been largely operative. According to Professor Jevons, writing fifteen years ago, it has been so only to a very small extent.[2] Up to 1860 the number of marriages was rather on the increase; but if among the masses, owing to cheap food, marriages have become more frequent, restraint has on the other hand certainly grown among the middle classes and the best of the artisan class.

I wish to speak of one more remedy, which Malthus himself repudiated,[3] namely, that of artificial checks on the number of children. It has been said that such questions should only be discussed " under the decent veil of a dead language." Reticence on them is necessary to wholesomeness of mind; but we ought nevertheless to face the problem, for it is a vital one. These preventive checks on births excite our strong moral repugnance. Men may call such repugnance prejudice, but it is perfectly logical, because it is a protest against the gratification of a strong instinct while the duties attaching to it are avoided. Still our moral repugnance should not

[1] *Essay on Population*, p. 292.
[2] *The Coal Question*, p. 170.
[3] *Essay on Population*, pp. 266, 286, 512.

prevent our considering the question. Let us examine results. What evidence is there as to the effects of a system of artificial checks ? We know that at least one European nation, the French, has to some extent adopted them. Now we find that in the purely rural Department of the Eure, where the population, owing presumably to the widespread adoption of artificial checks, is on the decline, although the district is the best cultivated in France and enjoys considerable material prosperity, the general happiness promised is not found. This Department comes first in statistics of crime ; one-third of these crimes are indecent outrages ; another third are paltry thefts ; and infanticide also is rife.[1] Though this is very incomplete evidence, it shows at least that you may adopt these measures without obtaining the promised results. The idea that a stationary and materially prosperous population will necessarily be free from vice is unreasonable enough in itself, and there is the evidence of experience against it. Indeed, one strong objection to any such system is to be found in the fact that a stationary population is not a healthy condition of things in regard to national life ; it means the removal of a great stimulus to progress. One incentive to invention, in particular, is removed in France by attempts to adapt population to the existing means of subsistence ; for in this respect it is certainly true that the struggle for existence is essential to progress. Such practices, moreover, prove injurious to the children themselves. The French peasant toils ceaselessly to leave each of his children a comfortable maintenance. It would be better for them to be brought up decently, and then left to struggle for their own maintenance. Much of the genius and inventive power in English towns has come from the rural districts with men belonging to large families, who started in life impressed with the idea that they must win their own way. It is wrong to consider this question from the point of view of wealth alone ; we cannot overrate the importance of family life as the source of all that is best in national life. Often the necessity of supporting and educating a large family is a training and refining influence in the lives of the parents, and the one thing that makes the ordinary man conscious of his duties, and turns him into a good citizen. In the last resort we may say that such

---

[1] See M. Baudrillart's book on Normandy, where not only moral considerations but enlightened self-interest is invoked against the system.

practices are unnecessary in England at the present day. A man in the superior artisan or middle classes has only to consider *when* he will have sufficient means to rear an average number of children; that is, he need only regulate the time of his marriage. Postponement of marriage, and the willing emigration of some of his children when grown up, does, in his case, meet the difficulty. He need not consider whether there is room in the world for more, for there *is* room; and, in the interests of civilisation, it is not desirable that a nation with a great history and great qualities should not advance in numbers. For the labouring masses, on the other hand, with whom prudential motives have no weight, the only true remedy is to carry out such great measures of social reform as the improvement of their dwellings, better education and better amusements, and thus lift them into the position now held by the artisan, where moral restraints are operative. Above all, it must be remembered that this is not a purely economic problem, nor is it to be solved by mechanical contrivances. To reach the true solution we must tenaciously hold to a high ideal of spiritual life. What the mechanical contrivances might perchance give us is not what we desire for our country. The true remedies, on the other hand, imply a growth towards that purer and higher condition of society for which alone we care to strive.

XI.

THE WAGE-FUND THEORY.

Malthus originated the Wage-fund Theory—Mill's statement of it—Its bearing on Trades-Unions—Its application to wages at a given time—Its fallacies—Origin of the theory.—Difficulty of forming a complete theory of wages—Wages in a given country depend upon the total amount of produce, and the division of that produce—Why wages are higher in America than in England—Influence of Protection and of commercial "rings" on wages—Comparison of wages in England and on the Continent—High wages in England mainly due to efficiency of labour—Limits to a rise in wages in any particular trade—Possible effects of a general rise in wages—Explanation of the fall in wages between 1790 and 1820.

BESIDES originating the theory of population which bears his name, Malthus was the founder of that doctrine of wages which, under the name of the wage-fund theory, was accepted for fifty years in England. To ascertain what the theory is we may take Mill's statement of it, as given in his review of Thornton *On Labour* in 1869. " There is supposed to be," he says, " at any given instant, a sum of wealth which is unconditionally devoted to the payment of wages of labour. This sum is not regarded as unalterable, for it is augmented by saving, and increases with the progress of wealth; but it is reasoned upon as at any given moment a predetermined amount. More than that amount it is assumed that the wages-receiving class cannot possibly divide among them; that amount, and no less, they cannot possibly fail to obtain. So that the sum to be divided being fixed, the wages of each depend solely on the divisor, the number of participants."[1] This theory was implicitly believed from Malthus's time to about 1870; we see it accepted, for instance, in Miss Martineau's Tales. And from the theory several conclusions were deduced which, owing to their practical importance, it is well to put in the forefront of our inquiry as to its truth. It is these conclusions which have made the theory itself and the science to which it belongs an offence to the whole working class. It was said in the first place that, according to the wage-fund theory, Trades-Unions could not at any given time effect a general rise in wages. It was, indeed, sometimes admitted that in a particular trade the workmen could obtain a rise by combination, but this could only be, it was alleged, at the expense of workmen in other trades. If, for instance, the men in the building trade got higher wages through their Union, those in the iron foundries or in some other industry must suffer to an equivalent extent. In the next place it was argued that combinations of workmen could not in the long-run increase the fund out of which wages were paid. Capital might be increased by saving, and, if this saving was more rapid than the increase in the number of labourers, wages would rise, but it was denied that Unions could have any effect in forcing such an increase of saving. And hence it followed that the only real remedy for low wages was a limitation of the number of the labourers. The rate of wages, it was said, depended entirely on the efficacy of checks to population.

The error lay in the premisses. The old economists, it may be

---

[1] *Fortnightly Review,* May 1869: reprinted in *Dissertations and Discussions,* vol. iv. p. 43.

observed, very seldom examined their premisses. For this theory assumes—(1.) That either the capital of a particular individual available for the payment of wages is fixed, or, at any rate, the total capital of the community so available is fixed; and (2.) That wages are always paid out of capital. Now it is plainly not true that a particular employer makes up his mind to spend a fixed quantity of money on labour;[1] the amount spent varies with a number of circumstances affecting the prospect of profit on the part of the capitalist, such, for instance, as the price of labour. Take the instance of a strike of agricultural labourers in Ireland, given by Mr. Trench to Nassau Senior. He was employing one hundred men at 10d. a day, thus spending on wages £25 a week. The men struck for higher pay—a minimum of 1s. 2d., and the more capable men to have more. Trench offered to give the wages asked for, but greatly reduced his total expenditure, as it would not pay to employ so many men at the higher rate. Thus only seventeen were employed; the other eighty-three objected, and it ended in all going back to work at the old rate.[2] The fact is, that no individual has a fixed wage-fund, which it is not in his power either to diminish or increase. Just as he may reduce the total amount which he spends on labour, rather than pay a rate of wages which seems incompatible with an adequate profit, so he may increase that total amount, in order to augment the wages of his labourers, by diminishing the sum he spends upon himself or by employing capital which is lying idle, if he thinks that even with the higher rate of wages he can secure a sufficiently remunerative return upon his investment. Thus the workman may, according to circumstances, get higher or lower wages than the current rate, without any alteration in the quantity of employment given. When wages in Dorset and Wilts were 7s.,[3] the labourers, if they had had sufficient intelligence and power of combination, might have forced the farmers to pay them 8s. or 9s., for the latter were

---

[1] The employer does not say, "I will spend so much in wages," or "I will employ so many labourers," but "I will spend so much if labour is at, say 30s., and so much if it is at 20s." On the other hand, Mr. Heath's statement as to the farmers in 1872 shows that men may determine to spend a fixed sum; that they would not vary it, however, he attributes to the accidental cause of "characteristic obstinacy."—See Heath's *English Peasantry*, p. 121; *Peasant Life*, p. 348.

[2] Senior's *Journals, etc., relating to Ireland*, vol. ii. p. 15.

[3] Caird, *English Agriculture in* 1850, p. 519.

making very high profits. As a matter of fact, where the work-men have been strong, and the profits made by the employers large, the former have often forced the employers to give higher wages.

Neither is it true that there is in the hands of the community as a whole, at any given time, a fixed quantity of capital for supplying the wants of the labourers, so much food, boots, hats, clothes, etc., which neither employers nor workmen can increase. It used to be said that a rise in money wages would simply mean that the price of all the commodities purchased by the labourers would rise proportionately, owing to the increase of demand, and that their real wages, *i.e.* the number of things they could purchase with their money, would be no greater than before. But, as a matter of fact, the supply can be increased as fast as the demand. It is true that between two harvests the available quantity of corn is fixed, but that of most other commodities can be increased at a short notice. For commodities, are not stored up for consumption in great masses, but are being continually produced as the demand for them arises.

So far I have been speaking of the theory as applied to wages at a particular time. Now, what did it further imply of wages in the long-run? According to Ricardo's law, which has been adopted by Lassalle and the Socialists, wages depend on the ratio between population and capital. Capital may be *gradually* increased by saving, and population *may* be gradually diminished; but Ricardo thought that the condition of the labourer was surely on the decline, because population was advancing faster than capital. While admitting occasionally that there had been changes in the standard of comfort, he yet disregarded these in his general theory, and assumed that the standard was fixed; that an increase of wages would lead to an increase of population, and that wages would thus fall again to their old rate, or even lower. The amount of corn consumed by the labourer would not diminish, but that of all other commodities would decline.[1] Later economists have qualified this statement of the supposed law. Mill showed that the standard of comfort was not fixed, but might vary indefinitely. This being the case, the labourer might sink even lower than Ricardo supposed possible, for population might increase till the labourer had not only less of everything else, but was forced down to a

---

[1] Ricardo (M'Culloch's edition, 1881), pp. 54-5.

lower staple of life than corn, for instance, potatoes. And this has, as a matter of fact, taken place in some countries. But, on the other hand, the standard might rise, as it has risen in England; and Mill thought that it would rise yet more. At first this was his only hope for the working classes.[1] At a later period he trusted that the labourer, by means of co-operation, might become more and more self-employing, and so obtain both profits and wages.

It is interesting to inquire how this wage-fund theory grew up. Why was it held that employers could not give higher real wages? Its origin is easy to understand. When Malthus wrote his essay on population, there had been a series of bad harvests, and in those days but small supplies of corn could be obtained from abroad. Thus year after year there seemed to be a fixed quantity of food in the country and increasing numbers requiring food. Population was growing faster than subsistence, and increased money wages could not increase the quantity of food that was to be had. Thus in 1800, when corn was 127s. the quarter, it was clear that the rich could not help the poor by giving them higher wages, for this would simply have raised the price of the fixed quantity of corn. Malthus assumed that the amount of food was practically fixed; therefore, unless population diminished, as years went on, wages would fall, because worse soils would be cultivated and there would be increased difficulty in obtaining food.[2] But the period he had before his eyes was quite exceptional; after the peace, good harvests came and plenty of corn; food grew cheaper, though population advanced at the same rate. So that the theory in this shape was true only of the twenty years from 1795 to 1815. But, when it had once been said that wages depended on the proportion between population and food, it was easy to substitute capital for food and say that they depended on the proportion between population and capital, food and capital being wrongly identified.[3]

[1] See in the earlier editions the chapter on the Probable Future of the Labouring Classes in his *Political Economy*, Bk. iv. c. vii.

[2] *Essay on Population*, vol. ii. pp. 64, 71, 76 (6th ed.). In reality the agricultural produce of the country was increased by one-fourth between 1803 and 1813. See Porter, p. 149.

[3] See Malthus's letter to Godwin in Kegan Paul's *Life of Godwin*, vol. i. p. 322: *Essay on Population*, vol. ii. pp. 93, 94 ; James Mill's *Elements of Political Economy*, ch. ii. p. 29 (1821).

Then when the identification was forgotten, it was supposed that there is at any given moment a fixed quantity of wage-capital— food, boots, hats, furniture, clothes, etc.—destined for the payment of wages, which neither employers nor workmen can diminish or increase, and thus the rate of wages came to be regarded as regulated by a natural law, independent of the will of either party.[1]

We have already seen that this theory is false; we have now to substitute for it some truer theory, and explain thereby the actual phenomena of the labour market, such, for instance, as the fact that wages at Chicago or New York are twice as high as they are in England, while the prices of the necessaries of life are lower. Though modern economists have pointed out the fallacies of the old wage-fund theory, no economist has yet succeeded in giving us a complete theory of wages in its place. I believe indeed that so complicated a set of conditions as are involved cannot be explained by any one formula, and that the attempt to do so leads to fallacies. Yet I am also aware that the public seem to feel themselves aggrieved that economists will not now provide them with another convenient set phrase in place of the wage-fund theory, and are inclined to doubt the validity of their explanations in consequence. Now, wages in a given country depend on two things : the total amount of produce in the country, and the manner in which that produce is divided. To work out the former problem we must investigate all the causes which affect the whole amount of wealth produced, the natural resources of the country, its political institutions, the skill, intelligence, and inventive genius of its inhabitants. The division of the produce, on the other hand, is determined mainly by the proportion between the number of labourers seeking employment and the quantity of capital seeking investment ; or, to put the case in a somewhat different way, instead of saying that wages are paid out of stored-up capital, we now say that they are the labourer's share of the produce.[2] What the labourer's share will be depends first on the quantity of produce he can turn out, and secondly, on the nature

---

[1] Mill's *Political Economy* (1st edition), vol. i. p. 475.
[2] This solution was first given by Mr. Cliffe-Leslie in an Article on "Political Economy and Emigration" in *Fraser's Magazine*, May 1868; but its full bearing was first shown by Mr. Walker in his books on the *Wage Question*.

of the bargain which he is able to make with his employer. We
are now in a position to explain the question put above, why wages
in America are double what they are in England. An American
ironmaster, if asked to give a reason for the high wages he pays,
would say, that the land determines the rate of wages in America,
because under the Free Homestead Law, any man can get a piece
of land for a nominal sum, and no puddler will work for less than
he can get by working on this land.[1] Now, in the Western States
the soil is very fertile, and though the average yield is lower than
in Wiltshire, the return in proportion to the labour expended is
greater. Moreover, labour being scarce, the workman has to be
humoured; he is in a favourable position in making his bargain
with the employer, and obtains a large share of the produce. Thus
agricultural wages are very high, and this explains also the cause
of high wages in the American iron-trade and other American
industries. In consequence of these high wages the manufacturer
is obliged to make large use of machinery, and much of our English
machinery, *e.g.* that of the Leicester boot and shoe trade, has been
invented in America. Now, better machinery makes labour
more efficient and the produce per head of the labourers greater.
Further, according to the testimony of capitalists, the workmen
work harder in America than in England, because they work with
hope; they have before them the prospect of rising in the world
by their accumulations. Thus it is that the produce of American
manufactures is great, and allows of the labourer obtaining a large
share. High wages in America are therefore explained by the
quantity of produce the labourer turns out being great and by the
action of competition being in his favour.

There are, however, other causes influencing the rate of wages
in America which are less favourable to the workmen. Protection,
for instance, diminishes real wages by enhancing the cost of many
articles in common use, such as cutlery. It is owing to Protection
also that capitalists are able to obtain exceptionally high profits at
the expense of the workmen. By combining and forming rings
they can govern the market, and not only control prices but dictate

---

[1] *Trades-Union Commission* (1867), Qu. 3770 (Report II. p. 3). A. S. Hewitt,
ironmaster, said "the rate of wages is regulated substantially in our country (U. S.)
by the profits which a man can get out of the soil which has cost him little or
nothing except the labour which he himself and his family have put upon it."

the rate of wages. Six or seven years ago, the whole output of Pennsylvanian anthracite was in the hands of a few companies. Hence it was that, in the Labour War of 1877, the workmen declared that, while they did not mind wages being fixed by competition, they would not endure their being fixed by rings, and that such rings would produce a revolution. And the monopoly of these companies was only broken through by a great migration of workmen to the West. The experience of America in this instance is of interest in showing how, as industry advances, trade tends to get concentrated into fewer hands; hence the danger of monopolies. It has even been asserted that Free Trade must lead to great natural monopolies. This may be true of a country like America which has internal but not external free trade, but only of such a country; for foreign competition would prevent a knot of capitalists from ever obtaining full control of the market.

I have shown why wages are higher in America than in England. We may go on to inquire why they are higher in England than in any other part of Europe. The great reason is that the total amount of wealth produced in this country is larger, and that from a variety of causes, material and moral. The chief material cause are our unrivalled stores of coal and iron, and perhaps, above all, our geographical position. On the moral side, our political institutions, being favourable to liberty, have developed individual energy and industry in a degree unknown in any other country. On the other hand, it has been said that the exclusion of the labourer from the land in England must have tended to lower wages. And no doubt the adoption of a system of large farms has driven the labourers into the towns, and made the competition for employment there very keen. But, to set against this, the efficiency of English manufacturing labour is largely due to this very fact, that it is not able to shift on to the land. While in America the whole staff of a cotton factory may be changed in three years, in England the artisan "sticks to his trade," and brings up his children to it; and thus castes are formed with inherited aptitudes, which render labour more efficient, and its produce greater. I believe the higher wages obtained in England, in comparison with the Continent, are mainly due to greater efficiency of labour,—that this is the chief cause why the total produce is greater. But if we go further, and ask what determines the division of the produce, the answer must be: mainly competition. To return to the comparison with America, the reason why the English labourer gets lower wages than the American is the great competition for employment in the over-stocked labour-market of this country.

I must notice an objection to the theory of wages as stated above. Wages, I have explained, are the labourers' share of the produce, and are paid out of it. But, it may be said, while our new Law Courts, or an ironclad, are being built—operations which take a long time before there is any completed result—how can it be correctly held that the labourer is paid out of the produce? It is of course perfectly true that he is maintained during such labours only by the produce of others; and that unless some great capitalist had either accumulated capital, or borrowed it, the labourer could not be paid. But this has nothing to do with the rate of wages. That is determined by the amount of the produce and is independent of the method of payment. What the capitalist does is merely to pay in advance the labourer's share, as a matter of convenience.

We will next inquire what are the limits to a rise of wages in any particular trade? The answer depends on two things. First, Is the capitalist getting more than the ordinary rate of profits? If he is not, he will resist a rise on the ground that he "cannot afford" to pay more wages. This is what an arbitrator, for instance, might say if he examined the books, and he would mean by it that, if the employer had to raise his wages, he would have to be content with lower profits than he could make in other trades. As a matter of fact, however, capitalists often do make exceptionally high profits, and it is in such cases that Trades-Unions have been very successful in forcing them to share these exceptional profits with their men. Secondly, though the employer be getting only ordinary profits, his workmen may still be strong enough to force him to give higher wages, but he will only do so permanently if he can compensate himself by raising the price of his commodity. Thus the second limit to a rise in wages in a particular trade is the amount which the consumer can be forced to pay for its products. Workmen have often made mistakes by not taking this into account, and have checked the demand for the articles which they produced, and so brought about a loss both to their masters and themselves.[1] In a particular trade then the limit to a rise in wages is reached when any further rise will drive the employer out of the trade, or when the increased price of the commodity will check the demand. When dealing with the general trade of a country, however, we can neglect prices altogether, since there can be no such thing as a general rise in prices while the value of the precious metals is stationary. Could, then, the whole body of the workmen throughout the kingdom, by good organisation, compel employers to accept lower profits? If there was a general strike, would it be the interest of the employers to give way? It is impossible to answer such a question beforehand. It would be a sheer trial of strength between the two parties, the outcome of which cannot be predicted, for nothing of the kind has ever actually taken place. And though there is now a nearer approximation than ever before to the supposed conditions, there has as yet been nothing like a general organisation of workmen.

Assuming, however, that the workmen succeeded in such a strike, we can then ask what would be the effect of a general rise of wages in the long-run? One of several results might ensue. The remuneration of employers having declined, their numbers might diminish, and the demand for labour would then diminish also and wages fall. Or again the decline in the rate of interest might check the accumulation of capital, thus again diminishing the demand for labour. Or, on the other hand, the rise in wages might be permanent, the remuneration of employers still proving sufficient, and the accumulation of capital remaining unchecked. Or lastly, higher wages might lead to greater efficiency of labour, and in this case profits would not fall. It is impossible to decide on *à priori* grounds which of these results would actually take place.

Returning to our period, we may apply these principles to explain the fall in wages between 1790 and 1820. During this period, while rent was doubled, interest also was nearly doubled (this by the way disproves Mr. George's theory on that point),[2] and yet wages fell. We may take Mr. Porter's estimate. " In some few

---

[1] *E.g.*, in the horse-nail trade wages advanced 50 per cent. between 1850 and 1864, but since then " horse-nail workmen during some time have not had half-work, their wages also declining."—Timmins, p. 116.

[2] *Progress and Poverty*, book iii. ch. vii. p. 197.

cases there had been an advance of wages, but this occurred only to skilled artisans, and even with them the rise was wholly incommensurate with the increased cost of all the necessaries of life. The mere labourer . . . did not participate in this partial compensation for high prices, but was . . . at the same or nearly the same wages as had been given before the war." In 1790 the weekly wage of skilled artisans and farm labourers respectively would buy 82 and 169 pints of corn; in 1800 they would buy 53 and 83.[1] According to Mr. Barton, a contemporary writer, wages between 1760 and 1820, "estimated in money, had risen 100 per cent.; estimated in commodities, they had fallen 33 per cent." [2] What were the causes of this fall? Let us first take the case of the artisans and manufacturing labourers. One cause in their case was a series of bad harvests. To explain how this would affect wages in manufactures we must fall back on the deductive method, and assume certain conditions from which to draw our conclusions. Let us suppose two villages side by side, one agricultural, the other manufacturing, in the former of which the land is owned by landowners, and tilled by labour employed by farmers. Suppose the manufacturing village to be fed by its neighbours in exchange for cutlery. Then, if there is a bad harvest in the agricultural village, every labourer in the manufacturing village will have to spend more on corn. The owners of land will gain enormously; the farmers will be enriched in so far as they can retain the increased prices for themselves, which they will do, if holding on leases. But every one else will be poorer, for there has been a loss of wealth. In order to get his corn, the labourer will have to give more of his share of the produce; and hence the demand for all other goods, which are produced for the labourers' consumption, will diminish. Nothing affects the labourer so much as good or bad harvests, and it is because of its tendency to neutralise the consequences of deficient crops at home, that the labourer has gained so much by Free Trade. When we have a bad harvest here, we get plenty of corn from America, and the labourer pays nearly the

---

[1] *Progress of the Nation*, 1847, p. 478.
[2] *Inquiry into the Depreciation of Agricultural Labour*, by J. Barton (1820), p. 11. At Bury, in Suffolk, a labourer in 1801 remembered when wages were 5s.; in order to buy as much in 1801 as their 5s. would have bought at the earlier date, they should have been £1, 6s. 5d.; they actually were 9s. plus 6s. from the rates, or altogether 15s.

same price for his loaf, and has as much money as before left to spend on other commodities. Still, even at the present day, some depression of trade is generally associated with bad harvests. And though Free Trade lessens the force of their incidence on a particular locality, it widens the area affected by them—a bad harvest in Brazil may prejudice trade in England.

The next point to be taken into consideration is the huge taxation which fell upon the workmen at this time; even as late as 1834 half the labourers' wages went in taxes. There was also increase in the National Debt. During the war we had nominally borrowed £600,000,000, although owing to the way in which the loans were raised, the actual sum which came into the national exchequer was only £350,000,000. All this capital was withdrawn from productive industry, and the demand for labour was diminished to that extent. Lastly, the labourer was often actually paid in bad coin, quantities of which were bought by the manufacturers for the purpose; and he was robbed by the truck system, through which the employer became a retail trader, with power to over-price his goods to an indefinite extent.

Some of these causes affected the agricultural and manufacturing labourers alike; they suffered, of course, equally from bad harvests. But we have seen in former lectures that there were agrarian and social changes during this period, which told upon the agricultural labourer exclusively. The enclosures took away his common rights, and where the land, before enclosure, had been already in cultivation, they diminished the demand for his labour, besides depriving him of the hope of becoming himself a farmer, and, to mention a seemingly small but really serious loss, cutting off his supply of milk, which had been provided by the "little people" who kept cows on the commons. He was further affected by the enormous rise in cottage rents. Mr. Drummond, a Surrey magistrate, told the Commission on Labourers' Wages in 1824, that he remembered cottages with good gardens letting for 30s. before the war, while at the time when he was speaking the same were fetching £5, £7, or £10.

This rise was due to causes we have before had in review, to the growth of population, the expulsion of servants from the farmhouses, and the demolition of cottages in close villages. When the labourers, to meet the deficiency, built cottages for themselves on the wastes, the farmers pulled them down, and, if the labourers rebuilt them, refused to employ them, with the result that such labourers became thieves and poachers.[1] Again, during this period, it was not uncommon for the farmers absolutely to determine what wages should be paid, and the men in their ignorance were entirely dependent on them.   Here are two facts to prove their subservience. In one instance, two pauper families who had cost their parish no less than £20 a year each, were given instead an acre of land rent free, and the rates were relieved to that amount; but though successful, the experiment was discontinued, "lest the labourer should become independent of the farmer." [2]   And this is the statement of an Essex farmer in 1793: "I was the more desirous to give them an increase of pay, as it was unasked for by the men, who were content with less than they had a right to expect." The agricultural labourer at this time was in an entirely helpless condition in bargaining with his employer.   Nor were the farmers the only class who profited by his deterioration; for the high rents of the time were often paid out of the pocket of the labourer.   The period was one of costly wars, bad seasons, and industrial changes.   The misfortunes of the labouring classes were partly inevitable, but they were also largely the result of human injustice, of the selfish and grasping use made of a power which exceptional circumstances had placed in the hands of landowners, farmers, and capitalists.

XII.

RICARDO AND THE GROWTH OF RENT.

Influence of Ricardo on economic method—His public life—His relation to Bentham and James Mill—Ricardo supreme in English Economics from 1817 to 1848—His Law of Industrial Progress—His influence on finance and on general legislation—The effect of the idea of natural law in his treatise—The Socialists disciples of Ricardo—Assumptions on which he grounds his theory of the constant rise in rents—His correct analysis of the cause of Rent—Rent not the cause, but the result of price—Explanation of rise in rents between 1790 and 1830—Rise of rents in towns—Proposal to appropriate rent to the State.

In Political Economy, as in other sciences, a careful study of method is an absolute necessity.   And this subject of method will

---

[1] *Committee on Labourers' Wages* (1824), p. 47.   [2] *Ibid.* p. 48.

come into special prominence in the present lecture, because we have now to consider the writings of a man of extraordinary intellect and force, who, beyond any other thinker, has left the impress of his mind on economic method. Yet even he would have been saved from several fallacies, if he had paid more careful attention to the necessary limitations of the method which he employed. It may be truly said that David Ricardo has produced a greater effect even than Adam Smith on the actual practice of men as well as on the theoretical consideration of social problems. His book has been at once the great prop of the middle classes, and their most terrible menace; the latter, because from it have directly sprung two great text-books of Socialism, *Das Kapital* of Karl Marx, and the *Progress and Poverty* of Mr. Henry George. And yet for thirty or forty years Ricardo's writings did more than those of any other author to justify in the eyes of men the existing state of society.

Ricardo's life has little in it of external interest. He made his fortune on the Stock Exchange by means of his great financial abilities, and then retired and devoted himself to literature. During the few years that he sat in Parliament, he worked (we have it on Huskisson's testimony) a great change in the opinions of legislators, even in those of the country squires—a remarkable fact, since his speeches are highly abstract, and contain few allusions to current politics, reading in fact like chapters from his book. We may notice one direct effect of his speeches: they were the most powerful influence in determining the resumption of cash payments. In his private life he associated much with Bentham and James Mill.

James Mill, like Bentham and Austin, was a staunch adherent of the deductive method, and it was partly through Mill's influence that Ricardo adopted it. Mill was his greatest friend; it was he who persuaded him both to go into Parliament, and to publish his great book. Ricardo's political opinions in fact merely reflect those of James Mill, and the other philosophical Radicals of the time, though in Political Economy he was their teacher. Ricardo reigned without dispute in English Economics from 1817 to 1848, and though his supremacy has since then been often challenged, it is by no means entirely overthrown. His influence was such that his method became the accepted method of economists; and to understand how great the influence of method may be, you should turn from his writings and those of his followers to Adam Smith, or to Sir Henry Maine, where you come in contact with another cast of mind, and will find yourselves in a completely different mental atmosphere. Now what is this deductive method which Ricardo employed? It consists in reasoning from one or two extremely simple propositions down to a series of new laws. He always employed this method, taking as his great postulate that all men will on all matters follow their own interests. The defect of the assumption lies in its too great simplicity as a theory of human nature. Men do not always know their own interest. Bagehot points out that the £10 householders, who were enfranchised by the first Reform Bill, were after 1832 the most heavily taxed class in the community, though the remedy was in their own hands; because they were ignorant and apathetic. And even when men know their interests, they will not always follow them; other influences intervene, custom, prejudice, even fear. Cairnes frankly admits these defects in Ricardo's method;[1] but it took economists some thirty or forty years to learn the necessity of testing their conclusions by facts and observation.[2] Since 1848 their attitude has improved; it is now seen that we must insist upon the verification of our premises, and examine our deductions by the light of history.

Ricardo has deduced from very simple data a famous law of industrial progress. In an advancing community, he says, rent must rise, profits fall, and wages remain about the same.[3] We shall find from actual facts that this law has been often true, and is capable of legitimate application, though Mr. Cliffe Leslie would repudiate it altogether; but it cannot be accepted as a universal law. The historical method, on the other hand, is impotent of itself to give us a law of progress, because so many of the facts on which it relies are, in Economics, concealed from us. By the historical method we mean the actual observation of the course of economic history, and the deduction from it of laws of economic progress; and this method, while most useful in checking the

---

[1] *Logical Method of Political Economy*, p. 42, 2d ed. 1875.
[2] This was first pointed out in a review of Mill's *Principles* in *Fraser's Magazine* for 1848.
[3] *Works* (M'Culloch's edition, 1876), pp. 54, 55, 375.

results of deduction is, by itself, full of danger from its tendency to set up imperfect generalisations. Sir H. Maine and M. Laveleye for instance, have taken an historical survey of land-tenure, and drawn from it the conclusion that the movement of property in land is always from collective to individual ownership ; and Mr. Ingram,[1] again, alluding to this law, accepts it as true that there is a natural tendency towards private property in land. He can build his argument on the universal practice from Java to the Shetlands, and it would seem a legitimate conclusion that the tendency will be constant. Yet there is at the present day a distinct movement towards replacing private by collective owner-ship, due to the gradual change in the opinions of men as to the basis on which property in land should rest. Mill, in 1848, argued that where the cultivator was not also the owner, there was no justification for private ownership ; later in his life, he advocated the confiscation of the unearned increment in land.[2] If we ask, Was he right?—the answer must be : Every single institution of society is brought to the test of utility and general national well-being ; hence, private property in land, if it fails under this test, will not continue. So too with the rate of interest : older econo-mists have insisted on the necessity of a certain rate, in order to encourage the accumulation of capital ; but we may fairly ask whether the rate of remuneration for the use of capital is not too high—whether we could not obtain sufficient capital on easier terms ? These considerations show that, in predicting the actual course of industrial progress, we must not be content to say that because there has been a movement in a certain direction in the past—for example, one from status to contract—it will therefore continue in the future. We must always apply the test, Does it fit in with the urgent present requirements of human nature ?

Ricardo's influence on legislation, to which I have already alluded, was twofold ; it bore directly upon the special subject of currency and finance ; and, what is more remarkable, it affected legislation in general. As regards finance, his pamphlets are the real justification of our monetary system, and are still read by all who would master the principles of currency. With respect to

---

[1] *The Present Position and Prospects of Political Economy*, p. 22.

[2] See the papers of the Land Tenure Reform Association, in *Dissertations and Discussions*, vol. iv.

other legislation, he and his friends have the great credit of having helped to remove not merely restrictions on trade in general, but those in particular which bore hardest on the labourer. When Joseph Hume, in 1824, proposed the repeal of the Combination Laws, he said he had been moved thereto by Ricardo. But though Ricardo advocated the removal of restrictions which injured the labourer, he deprecated all restrictions in his favour; he ridiculed the Truck Acts, and supported the opposition of the manufacturers to the Factory Acts—an opposition which, be it remembered, though prompted by mere class interest, was also supported in the name and on the then accepted principles of economic science.

In this way Ricardo became the prop, as I have called him, of the middle classes. Throughout his treatise there ran the idea of natural law, which seemed to carry with it a sort of justification of the existing constitution of society as inevitable. Hence his doctrines have proved the readiest weapons wherewith to combat legislative interference or any proposals to modify existing institutions. Hence, too, his actual conclusions, although gloomy and depressing, were accepted without question by most of his contemporaries. Another school, however, has grown up, accepting his conclusions as true under existing social conditions, but seeing through the fallacy of his " natural law." These are the Socialists, through whom Ricardo has become a terror to the middle classes. The Socialists believe that, by altering the social conditions which he assumed to be unalterable, Ricardo's conclusions can be escaped. Karl Marx and Lassalle have adopted Ricardo's law of wages; but they have argued that, since by this law wages, under our present social institutions, can never be more than sufficient for the bare subsistence of the labourer, we are bound to reconsider the whole foundation of society. Marx also simply accepts Ricardo's theory of value. The value of products, said Ricardo, is determined by the quantity of the labour expended on them ; and Marx uses this statement to deduce the theorem that the whole value of the produce rightly belongs to labour, and that by having to share the produce with capital the labourer is robbed.

Mr. Henry George, again, the latest Socialist writer, is purely and entirely a disciple of Ricardo. The whole aim of his treatise, *Progress and Poverty*, is to prove that rent must rise as society advances and wealth increases.[1] It is not the labourer, Ricardo reasoned, who will be richer for this progress, nor the capitalist, but the owner of land. Mr. George's theory of progress is the same. Putting aside his attempt to show a connection between the laws of interest and wages, which he contends will rise and fall together, there is little difference between his conclusions and Ricardo's. Others before Mr. George had clearly enough seen this bearing of the law of rent. Roesler, the German economist, says : " Political Economy would only be a theory of human degradation and impoverishment, if the law of rent worked without modification."[2]

Now let us see what are the assumptions on which Ricardo grounded his law about the course of rent, wages, and profits in a progressive community. The pressure of population, he argued, makes men resort to inferior soils ; hence the cost of agricultural produce increases, and therefore rent rises. But why will profits fall ? Because they depend upon the cost of labour,[3] and the main element in determining this is the cost of the commodities consumed by the workmen. Ricardo assumes that the standard of comfort is fixed. If, therefore, the cost of a quartern loaf increases, and the labourer is to obtain the same number of them, his wages must rise, and profits therefore must fall. Lastly, why should wages remain stationary ? Because, assuming that the labourer's standard of comfort is fixed, a rise of wages or a fall in prices will only lead to a proportionate increase of population. The history of the theory of rent is very interesting, but it is out of our road, so I can only lightly touch upon it. Adam Smith had no clear or consistent theory at all on the subject, and no distinct views as to the relation between rent and price. The modern doctrine is first found in a pamphlet by a practical farmer named James Anderson, published in 1777, the year after the appearance of *The Wealth of Nations* ;[4] but it attracted little attention till it was simultaneously

---

[1] We find almost exactly the same theoretical conclusions drawn from Ricardo's premises by Professor Cairnes. See his *Leading Principles of Political Economy* (p. 333), published in 1864. Of course he does not also draw the same socialistic conclusions as Mr. George.

[2] Roesler, *Grundsätze*, p. 210, quoted in Roscher's *Grundlagen*, p. 352.

[3] That is, accepting Mill's correction of Ricardo's theory.—See his *Political Economy*, vol. i. p. 493 (1st ed. 1848).

[4] *Inquiry into the Nature of the Corn Laws* (Edinburgh, 1777).

re-stated by Sir Edward West, and by Malthus in his pamphlet on the Corn Laws.[1] Had the theory, however, been left in the shape in which they stated it, it would have had little influence. It was Ricardo, who, puzzled by the question of rent, snatched at the theory, and gave it currency by embodying it in his whole doctrine of value and of economic development.

Ricardo's two great positive conclusions are : first, that the main cause of rent is the necessity of cultivating inferior soil as civilisation advances ; and secondly, that rent is not the cause but the result of price.[2] The theory has been disputed and criticised, but nearly all the objections have come from persons who have not understood it. We may say conclusively that, as a theory of the causes of rent, apart from that general doctrine of industrial develop- ment of which in Ricardo it forms a part, the theory is true. The one formidable objection which can be urged against it is, that the rise in rents in modern times has been due not so much to the necessity of resorting to inferior soils, as to improvements in agriculture ; but when Professor Thorold Rogers [3] attacks the theory on this ground, he merely proves that Ricardo has overlooked some important causes which have led to an increase of rents since the Middle Ages.

What, then, are we justified in stating to be the ultimate causes of rent ? First, the fertility of the soil and the skill of the cultiva- tor, by which he is able to raise a larger produce than is necessary for his own subsistence ; this makes rent physically possible. Next, the fact that land is limited in quantity and quality ; that is, that the supply of the land most desirable from its situation and fertility is less than the demand : this allows of rent being exacted.[4] The early colonists in America paid no rent, because there was an abund-

---

[1] *Essay on the Application of Capital to Land,* by a Fellow of University College, Oxford (1815) ; *Observations on the Effect of Corn Laws* (1814), by Rev. T. R. Malthus.

[2] Notice the verbal ambiguity of the text-books. When they say that "rent is not an *element* of price," they mean that it is not a *cause* of price. For in- stance, the great rent paid for mills *is* an *element* in the price of yarn.

[3] *Contemporary Review,* April 1880.

[4] *E.g.,* "As a consequence both of their difference of situation and their fer- tility, in the Himalaya, the farmers low down on the sides pay 50 per cent. of the gross produce as farm rent, and higher up 20 per cent. less."—Roscher, *Political Economy* (English translation, Chicago, 1878), ii. 19. In Buenos Ayres, "only a short time since, an English acre, fifteen *leguas* from the capital, was worth from 3d. to 4d., and at a distance of fifty *leguas*, only 2d."—*Ibid.* ii. 28.

ance of land open to every one ; but twenty years later, rent was paid because population had grown. Let us see exactly what happens in such a case. A town is founded on the sea-coast ; as it grows, the people in that town have to get some of their food from a distance. Assume that the cost of raising that corn and bringing it to the town is 20s., and that the cost of raising it close to the town is 15s. for every five bushels (we will suppose that in the latter instance the cost of carriage is *nil*) ; then, as both quantities will be sold at the same price, the surplus 5s. in the latter case will go for rent. Thus we find that rent has arisen because corn is brought into the market at different costs. In twenty years more, rents will have risen still further, because soils still more inferior in fertility or situation will have been brought into cultivation. But the rise of rent is not directly due to the cultivation of inferior soils ; the direct cause is the increase of population which has made that cultivation necessary.

Going back to the question raised by Professor Rogers, as to the effect of agricultural improvements on rent, we may notice that the controversy on this question was first fought out between Ricardo and Malthus. Ricardo thought that improvements would lead to a fall in rents ; Malthus maintained the opposite, and he was right. Take an acre of land close to the town, such as we were considering above, with an original produce of five bushels of wheat, but which, under improved cultivation, yields forty bushels. If the price of wheat remains the same, and all the land under cultivation has been improved to an equivalent extent, the rent will now be 5s. multiplied by eight. Yet there are a few historical instances where agricultural improvements have been followed by a fall in rents. For instance, during the Thirty Years' War the Swiss supplied Western Germany with corn, and introduced improvements into their agriculture, in order to meet the pressure of the demand. After the peace of Westphalia the demand fell off ; the Swiss found they were producing more than they could sell ; prices fell, and, as a consequence, rents fell also.[1]

Professor Rogers has further objected to Ricardo's theory that it does not explain the historical origin of rent. The term "rent" is ambiguous ; it has been used for the payment of knight-service, for the performance of religious offices, for serfs' labour and

[1] Roscher, *op. cit.* ii. 32, note.

the sums of money for which it was commuted. In Ricardo's mouth it meant only the money rent paid by a capitalist farmer, expecting the usual rate of profits; but it is quite true that these modern competition rents did not arise till about the time of James I.[1]

The last point in the theory of rent is the relation between rent and price. Before Ricardo's time most practical men thought that rent was a cause of price. Ricardo answered, There is land cultivated in England which pays no rent, or at least there is capital employed in agriculture which pays none; therefore there is in the market corn which has paid no rent, and it is the cost of raising this corn, which is grown on the poorest land, that determines the price of all the corn in the same market.[2] Probably he was right in his statement that there is land in England which pays no rent; but even if all land and all farmers' capital paid rent, it would not affect the argument, which says that rent is not the cause but the result of price. We may conclude that at the present day rent is determined by two things: the demand of the population, and the quantity and quality of land available. These determine it by fixing the price of corn.

Now let us turn to facts, to see how our theories work. We will take the rise in rents between 1790 and 1830, and ask how it came about. The main causes were—(1.) Improvements in agriculture, the chief of which were the destruction of the common-field system, rendering possible the rotation of crops, the consolidation of farms with the farmhouse in the centre of the holding, and the introduction of machinery and manures; (2.) the great growth of population, stimulated by mechanical inventions; (3.) a series of bad harvests, which raised the price of corn to an unparalleled height; (4.) the limitation of supply, the population having to be fed with the produce of England itself, since, during the first part of the period all supplies from abroad were cut off by war, and later, higher and higher protective duties were imposed, culminating in the famous corn bill of 1815. After 1815, however, a fall in rents —not a very great one—took place, a process which greatly puzzled people at the time. It was the consequence of a sudden coincidence of agricultural improvements and good harvests; there was for a

[1] *Contemporary Review*, April 1880.
[2] *Works*, p. 40 (M'Culloch's ed. 1876).

time an over production of corn, and wheat fell in price from 90s. to 35s. This fact is the explanation of Ricardo's mistaken idea that agricultural improvements tend to reduce rents. Having no historical turn of mind, such as Malthus had, he did not recognise that this effect of agricultural improvements was quite accidental. This case, indeed, and the instance of Switzerland given above, with the similar events in Germany about 1820, are the only historical examples of such an effect. For a time there was great agricultural distress; the farmers could not get their rents reduced in proportion to the fall in prices, and many, in spite of the enormous profits they had before made under beneficial leases, were ruined; the farming class never wholly recovered till the repeal of the Corn Laws. But the fall was temporary and exceptional. Taking the period as a whole its striking feature is the rise of rents, and this rise was due to the causes stated: increased demand on the part of an increased population, and limitation of quantity, with improved quality, of the land available.

I have hitherto been considering the theory of agricultural rents; I now pass to a subject of perhaps greater present importance—ground-rents in towns. If the rise in the rent of agricultural lands has been great, the rise in that of urban properties has been still more striking. A house in Lombard Street, the property of the Drapers' Company, was in 1668 let for £25; in 1877 the site alone was let for £2600. How do we account for this? It is the effect of the growth of great towns and of the improvements which enable greater wealth to be produced in them, owing to the development of the arts, and to the extension of banking and credit. Are town rents then a cause of the rise in prices? Certainly not. Rent may be an element in price, but the actual amount of rent paid depends upon these two things: the demand of the population for commodities, which determines price, and the value of a particular site for purposes of business.

These considerations bring us to the question now sometimes raised: Is rent a thing which the State can abolish? Is it a human institution, or the result of physical causes beyond our control? If we abolished agricultural rent, the result would simply be, as Ricardo says, that the rent would go into the pockets of the farmers, and some of them would live like gentlemen. Rent itself is the result of physical causes, but it is within our power to say who shall receive the rent.   This seems a fact of immense importance, but the extent of its significance depends largely on the future course of rent in England; and so we are bound to inquire whether Ricardo was right in assuming that rents must necessarily rise in a progressing state.   Many think the contrary, and that we are now on the eve of a certain and permanent fall in agricultural rents; and if rents continue steadily to fall, the question will become one of increasing insignificance.   As means of communication improve, we add more and more to the supply of land available for satisfying the wants of a particular place; and as the supply increases, which it is likely to do to an increasing extent, the price of land must fall.   Social causes have also influenced rents in England, and social changes are probably imminent, which will at once reduce the value of land for other than agricultural purposes, and increase the amount of it devoted to agriculture. Such changes would likewise tend to diminish rent.   We may say therefore that, since there are these indications of a permanent fall in rents, so great a revolution as the transference of rent from the hands of private owners to the nation would not be justified by the amount which the nation would acquire.   The loss and damage of such a revolution would not be adequately repaid.

But will rent in towns fall ?   Here it is impossible to predict. For instance, we cannot say whether London will continue to grow as rapidly as it has done heretofore.   Now it is the monetary centre of the world; owing to the greater use of telegraphy, it is possible that it may not retain this pre-eminence.   The decay of the provincial towns was largely due to the growth of great estates, which enabled their proprietors to live and spend in London; but if changes come to break up these large properties, London will cease to be the centre of fashion, or at any rate to have such a large fashionable population.   Politics, moreover, are certainly tending to centre less in London.   And further inventions in the means of locomotion and the greater use of electricity may result in causing a greater diffusion of population.

XIII.

TWO THEORIES OF ECONOMIC PROGRESS.

Distribution of Wealth the problem of the present time—Ricardo's theory that
wages will remain stationary and interest fall—Facts disprove both propositions—Henry George's theory of economic progress likewise contradicted
by facts.

SINCE Mill, in 1848, wrote his chapter on the future of the
working classes, the question of the distribution of wealth has become of still greater importance. We cannot look round on the
political phenomena of to-day without seeing that this question is
at the root of them. We see the perplexity in which men stand,
and the divisions springing up in our great political parties, because
of the uncertainty of politicians how to grapple with it. Political
power is now widely diffused; and whatever may be the evils of
democracy, this good has come of it, that it has forced men to
open their eyes to the misery of the masses, and to inquire more
zealously as to the possibility of a better distribution of wealth.
Economists have to answer the question whether it is possible for
the mass of the working classes to raise themselves under the
present conditions of competition and private property. Ricardo
and Henry George have both answered, No; and the former has
formulated a law of economic development, according to which, as
we have seen, rent must rise, profits and interest fall, and wages
remain stationary, or perhaps fall. Now is there any relation
of cause and effect between this rise in rent and fall in wages?
Ricardo thought not. According to his theory, profits and wages
are fixed independently of rent; a rise in rent and a fall in wages
might be due to the same cause, but the one was not the result of
the other, and the rise in rent would not be at the expense of the
labourers. Yet practical opinion goes in the opposite direction.
From the evidence of farmers and land-agents we see that it is
widely believed that the high rents exacted from farmers have
been partly taken out of the pockets of the labourers. "If there
is a fall in the price of corn, agricultural wages will fall, unless
there is a corresponding fall in rent," was said before a Parliamen-

tary Commission in 1834.[1] Ten years ago the connection was admitted in Ireland; and the Land Act of 1870 was founded on the belief that rack-rents were not really the surplus left when capital and labour had received their fair returns, and that the only limit to the rise of rents was the bare necessities of the peasantry. In England it has been assumed that wages and profits have fixed lines of their own independent of rent, but this is not universally true; where the farmers have suffered from high rents, they in their turn have ground down the labourers. Thus even in England rent has been exacted from the labourer; and this is not an opinion but a fact, testified by the evidence of agents, clergy, and farmers themselves. What appears accurate to say about the matter is, that high rents have in some cases been one cause of low wages.

This direct effect of rent on wages under certain conditions is quite distinct from the " brazen law of wages " which Lassalle took from Ricardo. It is impossible, according to Ricardo, for labourers to improve their position under existing industrial conditions, for if wages rise, population will advance also, and wages return to their old level; there cannot therefore be any permanent rise in them. Ricardo, indeed, did not deny that the standard of comfort varied in different countries, and in the same country at different times; but these admissions he only made parenthetically, he did not seem to think they seriously touched the question of population, and they did not affect his main conclusions. For instance, he argues that a tax on corn will fall entirely on profits, since the labourer is already receiving the lowest possible wages. This statement may be true with regard to the very lowest class of labourers, but it certainly does not apply to artisans, nor to a large proportion of English working men at the present time. With them, at any rate, it is not true that they are already receiving the lowest possible wage, nor that there is an invincible bar to their progress. Let us turn to the test of facts and see if wages have

---

[1] See *Agricultural Commission*, 1882, vol. iii. pp. 37-38; on the other hand, Kebbel's *Agricultural Labourer*, p. 22, and Heath's *English Peasantry*, pp. 67, 348. Mr. Kebbel's statement really bears out the assertion in the text; he says, "The present writer could point to more than one large estate, where a very low rental has been paid for years, but where the wages of the labourer are perhaps at the lowest point, *though the attention of the tenants has been repeatedly directed to the anomaly.*"

risen since 1846. Henry George says that free trade has done nothing for the labourer;[1] Mill, in 1848, predicted the same. Professor Cairnes came to a very similar conclusion; writing in 1874 he said, that "the large addition to the wealth of the country has gone neither to profit nor to wages, nor yet to the public at large, but to swell . . . the rent-roll of the owner of the soil."[2] Yet it is a fact that though the cost of living has undoubtedly increased, wages have risen in a higher ratio. Take the instance of a carpenter as a fair average specimen of the artisan class. The necessaries of a carpenter's family in 1839 cost 24s. 10d. per week; in 1875 they cost 29s. But meanwhile the money wages of a carpenter had risen from 24s. to 35s. Thus there had been not only a nominal but a real rise in his wages. Turning to the labourer, his cost of living was about 15s. in 1839, it was a little under 15s. in 1875. The articles he consumes have decreased in cost, while in the case of the artisan they have increased, because the labourer spends a much larger proportion of his wages on bread. The labourer's wages meanwhile have risen from 8s. to 12s. or 14s.; in 1839 he could not properly support himself on his wages alone.[3] These facts seem conclusive, but certainty is difficult from the very varying estimates of consumption and money wages. For strong proof of a rise in agricultural wages we may take a par-

---

[1] *Progress and Poverty*, book iv. c. iii. p. 229, 4th ed. 1881.
[2] *Leading Principles*, p. 333.
[3] Weekly Expenses of a Carpenter with Wife and 3 Children—

	In 1839.		In 1875.	
	s.	d.	s.	d.
8 quartern loaves, .	5	8	4	4
8 lbs. meat,	4	4	6	0
1½ lbs. butter,	1	6	1	9
1 lb. cheese,	0	7	0	8
2 lbs. sugar,	1	2	0	8
¼ lb. tea, .	1	6	0	8
1 lb. soap, .	0	5	0	4
1 lb. candles,	0	6	0	6
1 lb. rice, .	0	4	0	2
2 quarts milk,	0	4	0	8
Vegetables,	0	6	1	0
Coals and firing, .	1	0	2	4
Rent, .	4	0	6	6
Clothes and sundries,	3	0	3	6
	24	10	29	1

ticular instance. On an estate in Forfar the yearly wages of a first ploughman were by the wages-book, in

1840, . .	£28 2 0	1870, . . £42 5 0
1850, . .	28 15 0	1880, . . 48 9 0
1860, . .	39 7 0	

According to his own admission the standard of comfort of the first ploughman employed on this estate in 1880 had risen, for he complained, in a letter describing his position, of his increased expenditure, increased not because things were dearer, but because he now needed more of them.

We may take as further evidence the statistics of the savings of the working classes; it is impossible to get more than an approximate estimate of them, but they probably amount to about £130,000,000.[1] To these we may add the savings actually invested in houses. In Birmingham there are 13,000 houses owned by artisans. All this is small compared with the whole capital of the country, which, in 1875, was estimated at £8,500,000,000 at least, with an annual increase of £235,000,000—this latter sum far exceeding the total savings of the working classes.[2] The comparison will make us take a sober view of their improvement; yet the facts make it clear that the working classes can raise their position, though not in the same ratio as the middle classes. Mr. Mulhall

Weekly Expenses of a Farm Labourer with Wife and 3 Children.

	In 1839.	In 1875.
	s. d.	s. d.
9 quartern loaves, ...	6 4½	4 10½
1½ lb. meat and bacon, . . .	0 9¾	1 0¾
1 lb. cheese, ...	0 7	0 8
½ lb. butter, ...	0 6	0 7
2 oz. tea, ...	0 9	0 4
1 lb. sugar, ...	0 7	0 4
½ lb. soap, ...	0 3	0 2
½ lb. candles, . . .	0 3	0 3
Coals and firing, . . .	1 0	1 6
Rent, ...	1 0	1 6
Clothes and Sundries, . .	3 0	3 6
	15 1¼	14 9¼

[1] This sum has been carefully calculated from the statistics of Building Societies, Savings Banks, Co-operative Societies, Trades-Unions, Friendly Societies, and Industrial and Provident Societies.

[2] Giffen's *Essays on Finance*, p. 173-5. See also Mulhall, in *Contemporary Review*, December 1881.

also estimates that there is less inequality between the two classes now than 40 years ago. He calculates that the average wealth of a rich family has decreased from £28,820 to £25,803, or 11 per cent.; that of a middle-class family has decreased from £1439 to £1005, or 30 per cent.; while that of a working-class family has *increased* from £44 to £86, or nearly 100 per cent.[1] But without pinning our faith to any particular estimate, we can see clearly enough that the facts disprove Ricardo's proposition that no improvement is possible; and there are not wanting some who think that the whole tendency of modern society is towards an increasing equality of condition.

Was Ricardo any more correct in saying that interest and profits (between which he never clearly distinguished) must fall? As a matter of fact, for the last century and a half, interest in England has been almost stationary, except during the great war. In Walpole's time it was three per cent.; during the war it doubled, but after the peace it dropped to four per cent., and has remained pretty steady at that rate ever since. Ricardo thought that the cost of the labourer's subsistence would necessarily increase, owing to the necessity of cultivating more land, and as he would thus require a greater share of the gross produce, less wealth would be left for the capitalist. He overlooked the fact that the rate of interest depends not merely on the cost of labour, but on the field of employment as well. As civilisation advances, new inventions and new enterprises create a fresh demand for capital: some £700,000,000 have been invested in English railways alone. No doubt, if the field for English capital were confined to England, the rate of interest might fall; but Ricardo forgot the possibility of capital emigrating on a large scale. Thus Ricardo's teaching on this point is deficient both in abstract theory and as tested by facts. What we really find to have taken place is, that though rent has risen, there is good reason to suppose that in the future it may fall; that interest has not fallen much; and that the standard of comfort and the rate of wages, both of artisans and labourers—of the former most decidedly, and to a certain extent also of the latter, has risen.

[1] *Contemporary Review*, February 1882. He defines a rich family as one spending over £5000; a middle-class family as one spending between £5000 and £100; a working-class family, as one spending under £100.

I wish next to examine Mr. George's theory of economic progress.[1] Mr. George is a disciple of Ricardo, both in his method and his conclusions ; he has as great a contempt for facts and verification as Ricardo himself.[2] By this method he succeeds in formulating a law, according to which, in the progress of civilisation, interest and wages will fall together, and rents will rise. Not only is the labourer in a hopeless condition, but the capitalist is equally doomed to a stationary or declining fortune. "Rent," he says, "depends upon the margin of cultivation, rising as it falls, and falling as it rises. Interest and wages depend on the margin of cultivation, falling as it falls, and rising as it rises."[3] The returns which the capitalist obtains for his capital and the labourer for his work, depend on the returns from the worst land cultivated ; that is, on the quality of land accessible to capital and labour without payment of rent.

Now Mr. George's observations are derived from America, and what he has done is to generalise a theory, which is true of some parts of America, but not of old countries. His book seems conclusive enough at first sight. There is little flaw in the reasoning, if we grant the premisses ; but there are great flaws in the results when tested by facts. Do interest and wages always rise and fall together? As an historical fact they do not. Between 1715 and 1760, while rents (according to Professor Rogers) rose but slowly (Arthur Young denies that they rose at all), interest fell, and wages rose. Between 1790 and 1815 rent doubled, interest doubled, wages fell. Between 1846 and 1882 rents have risen, interest has been stationary, wages have risen. Thus in all these three periods the facts contradict Mr. George's theory. Rent indeed has generally risen, but neither profits nor wages have steadily fallen, nor have their variations borne any constant relation to one another. Coming to Mr. George's main position, that rent constantly tends to absorb the whole increase of national wealth, how does this look in the light of fact? Does all the increase of wealth, for instance, in the Lancashire cotton manufactures, go simply to raise rents? Evidently not. Wages have

[1] The arguments here used against Henry George are expanded in the two published lectures on *Progress and Poverty*, which were delivered in January 1883.—Ed.
[2] *Progress and Poverty*, book iii. ch. vi. (4th ed. p.184).   [3] *Ibid.* p.197.

risen owing to improvements in machinery; and in most cases profits have also risen. We can prove by statistics that in England the capitalists' wealth has increased faster than that of the landowners'; for in the assessments to the income-tax there has been a greater increase under Schedule D, which comprises the profits of capitalists and the earnings of professional men, than under Schedule A, which comprises revenues from land. At the same time, Mr. George has made out a strong case against private property in land in great towns; but here he has only restated more forcibly what Adam Smith and Mill advocated, when they recommended taxes on ground rents as the least objectionable of all taxes. Under existing conditions the working people in great towns may be said to be taxed in the worst of ways by the bad condition of their houses. An individual or a corporation lets a block of buildings for a term of years; the lessee sublets it, and the sub-lessee again for the third time. Each class is here oppressing the one beneath it, and the lowest units suffer most. This is why the problem of the distribution of wealth is sure, in the near future, to take the form of the question, how to house the labourers of our towns.

XIV.

THE FUTURE OF THE WORKING CLASSES.

Causes of improvement in the condition of the working classes since 1846—
Free trade—Steady price of bread and of manufactured produce—Steadiness
of wages and regularity of employment—Factory legislation—Trades-
Unions—Co-operation—Will the same causes continue to act in the future?
—Moral improvement among the working classes—Better relations between
workmen and employers—Evil as well as good in the close personal relation-
ships of former times—Trades-Unions have improved the relations of the
two classes—Can the workmen really secure material independence?—
Various solutions of the problem—Industrial partnership—Communism—
Modified Socialism.

I HAVE thus far tried to show that the material condition of the workman is capable of improvement under present social conditions.

I wish now to explain the causes which have contributed to its actual improvement since 1846. The most prominent of these causes has been Free Trade. In the first place, Free Trade has enormously increased the aggregate wealth of the country, and therefore increased the demand for labour; this is an indisputable fact. Secondly, it has created greater steadiness in trade,—a point which is often overlooked in discussions of the subject. Since 1846 workmen have been more regularly employed than in the preceding half-century. Free trade in wheat has, moreover, given us a more steady price of bread, a point of paramount importance to the labouring man; and this steadiness is continually becoming greater. From 1850 to 1860 the variation between the highest and lowest prices of wheat was 36s., between 1860 and 1870 it was 24s., and in the last decade it has been only 15s. And since the sum which the workman has spent on bread has become more and more constant, the amount which he has had left to spend on manufactured produce has also varied less, and its price in consequence has been steadier. But why then, it may be asked, the late great depression of trade since 1877? I believe the answer is, because other countries, to which we sell our goods, have been suffering from bad harvests, and have had less capacity for buying. The weavers in Lancashire have had to work less time and at lower wages because far-off nations have not been able to purchase cotton goods, and the depression in one industry has spread to other branches of trade.

The greater steadiness of wages which has been caused by Free Trade is seen even in trades where there has been no great rise. But besides the amount of the workman's wages per day we must take into consideration the number of days in the year and hours in the day, during which he works. He now finds employment on many more days (before 1846 artisans often worked only one or two days in the week), but each working day has fewer hours; so that his pay is at once steadier and more easily earned. And hence even where his daily wages have remained nearly the same, with more constant employment and with bread both cheap and fixed in price, his general position has improved.

What other agencies besides Free Trade have been at work to bring about this improvement? Factory legislation has raised the condition of women and children by imposing a limit on the hours of work, and especially the sanitary environment of the labourer; the factory laws seek to regulate the whole life of the workshop. Trades-Unions, again, have done much to avert social and industrial disorder, and have taught workmen, by organisation and self-help, to rely upon themselves. Herein lies the difference between the English and the Continental workman; the former, because he has been free to form voluntary associations, does not look to the State or to revolutionary measures to better his position. For proof of this, it is enough to compare the parliamentary programme of the last Trades-Unions Congress with the proceedings of the International at Geneva. English Trades-Unions resort to a constitutional agitation which involves no danger to the State; indeed, as I have said, their action averts violent industrial dislocations. And beyond this, Trades-Unions have achieved some positive successes for the cause of labour. By means of their accumulated funds workmen have been able to hold out for better prices for their labour, and the Unions have further acted as provident societies by means of which their members can lay up sums against sickness or old age. The mischief and wastefulness of strikes is generally enough insisted on, but it is not as often remembered that the largest Unions have sanctioned the fewest strikes; the Amalgamated Engineers, who have 46,000 members, and branches in Canada and India, expended only six per cent. of their income on strikes from 1867 to 1877. The leaders of such a great Union are skilful, well-informed men, who know it to be in their interest to avoid strikes.[1]

Lastly, we must not forget to mention the great Co-operative Societies, which in their modern shape date from the Rochdale Pioneers' Store, founded in 1844, under the inspiration of Robert Owen's teaching, though the details of his plan were therein abandoned. These, like Trades-Unions, have taught the power and merit of voluntary association and self-help. At present, however, they are only big shops for the sale of retail goods, through which the workman gets rid of the retail dealer, and shares himself in the profits of the business, by receiving at the end of each quarter a dividend on his purchases. Such stores, however useful in cheapening goods, and at the same time encour-

---

[1] See Howells' *Conflict of Capital and Labour.*

aging thrift, do not represent the ultimate object of co-operation. That object is to make the workman his own employer. Hitherto the movement has not been successful in establishing productive societies; the two great difficulties in the way being apparently the inability of a committee of workmen to manage a business well, and their unwillingness to pay sufficiently high wages for superintendence. The chief obstacles are thus moral, and to be found in the character of the workmen, and their want of education; but as their character and education improve, there is no reason why these difficulties should not vanish.

Such are the chief agencies to which we trace the improvement in the position of the labourer during the last forty years. At the beginning of this period Mill insisted on one thing as of paramount importance, namely restriction upon the increase of population, and without this he believed all improvement to be impossible. Yet we find that during this period the rate of increase has not slackened. It is nearly as great now as between 1831 and 1841. It was greater during the last decade than it had been since 1841. On the other hand, there has undoubtedly been an enormous emigration which has lightened the supply of labour. Three millions and a half of people have emigrated from Great Britain since 1846.

The question which now most deeply concerns us is, Will the same causes operate in the future? Will Free Trade continue to be beneficial? Will our wealth continue to increase and our trade to expand? On this point a decided prediction is of course impossible. Competition in neutral markets is becoming keener and keener, and we may be driven out of some of them, and thus the national aggregate of wealth be lessened. But, on the other hand, we have reason to believe that increased supplies of corn from America and Australia will give an enormous impetus to trade. As in the past so in the future corn is the commodity of most importance to the labourer; and if the supply of corn becomes more constant, trade will be steadier and wages will probably rise. Besides, cheap corn means that all over the world the purchasing power of consumers is increased, and this again will stimulate trade. So that in this respect the labourers' outlook is a hopeful one. As to emigration also, there is no reason to suppose that there will be any check on this relief to the labourer for the next fifty years at least. Again, there is every prospect of co-operation and even productive co-operation making great progress in the future, though I do not think that the latter is likely for some time to be an important factor in improving the status of the workmen. The moral obstacles to co-operative production which I mentioned will disappear but slowly. In certain directions, however, it is likely to develop; I mean in the direction of manufacturing for the great Wholesale Co-operative Societies, because here the market is secured. Trades-Unions too are likely to expand.

Turning to the moral condition of the workpeople, we find an improvement greater even than their material progress. When we see or read of what goes on in the streets of our great towns, we think badly enough of their morality; but those who have had most experience in manufacturing districts are of opinion that the moral advance, as manifested, for example, in temperance, in orderly behaviour, in personal appearance, in dress, has been very great. For the improvement in the inner life of workshops as early as 1834, take the evidence of Francis Place, a friend of James Mill, before a Committee of the House of Commons in that year. He told the Committee that, when he was a boy, he used to hear songs, such as he could not repeat, sung in respectable shops by respectable people; it was so no longer, and he was at a loss how to account for the change.[1] Similar statements are made by workmen at the present day. Conversation, they say, is bad at times, but opinion is setting more and more against immoral talk. The number of subjects which interest workpeople is much greater than before, and the discussion of the newspaper is supplanting the old foul language of the workshop. We have here an indirect effect of the extension of the suffrage. Add to this the statistics of drunkenness. In 1855 there were nearly 20,000 persons convicted for drunkenness, in 1880 there were not many more than 11,000.

Again, the relations between workmen and employers are certainly much better. The old life, as described by Owen and Cobbett, of an apprentice in the workshop, or a boarded labourer in the farm-house, is at first sight most attractive; and the facts told to the Commission of 1806 seem to realise the ideal life of industry. The relations between masters and workmen were

[1] Porter, pp. 683-685.

then extremely close, but this close relationship had its bad side. There was often great brutality and gross vice. The workman was at his employer's mercy: in Norfolk the farmer used to horse-whip his labouring men, and his wife the women.[1] There existed a state of feudal dependence, which, like all feudalism, had its dark and light sides. The close relationship was distinctly the result of the small system of industry, and hence it was shattered by the power-loom and the steam-engine. When huge factories were established there could no longer be a close tie between the master and his men; the workman hated his employer, and the employer looked on his workmen simply as hands. From 1800 to 1843 their mutual relations, as was admitted by both parties, were as bad as they could be. There could be no union, said employ-ers, between classes whose interests were different, and farmers, contrary to ancient usage, ruthlessly turned off their men when work was slack. The "cash-nexus" had come in, to protest against which Carlyle wrote his *Past and Present ;* but Carlyle was wrong in supposing that the old conditions of labour could be re-established. Feudalism, though it lingers in a few country places, has virtually disappeared alike in agriculture and in trade. The employer cannot offer and the workman cannot accept the old relations of protection and dependence : for, owing to the modern necessity of the constant movement of labour from place to place and from one employment to another, it has become impossible to form lasting relations, and the essence of the old system lay in the permanency of the workmen's engagements. Trades-Unions too have done much to sever what was left of the old ties. Workmen are now obliged, in self-defence, to act in bodies. In every workshop there are men who are attached to their masters, and who on occasion of a strike do not care to come out, but are yet compelled to do so in the common interest. Before this obli-gation was recognised by public opinion, the effect of Unions was, no doubt, to embitter the relations between masters and men. This was especially the case between 1840 and 1860.

Since the latter date, however, Trades-Unions have distinctly improved the relations between the two classes. Employers are beginning to recognise the necessity of them, and the advantages

---

[1] See Dr. Jessop, in the *Nineteenth Century,* May 1882.

of being able to treat with a whole body of workmen through their most intelligent members. Boards of Conciliation, in which workmen and employers sit side by side, would be impossible without Unions to enforce obedience to their decisions. In the north of England, at the present moment, it is the non-unionists who are rejecting arbitration. And the reason why such Boards have succeeded is, because the employers have of their own accord abandoned all ideas of the feudal relation. They used to say that it would degrade them to sit at the same board with their workmen; but it is noticeable that directly the political independence of the latter was recognised, as soon as he possessed the franchise, these objections began to disappear. The new union of employers and workmen which is springing up in this way, is based on the independence of both as citizens of a free state. The employers meet their workmen also in political committees, on School Boards and similar bodies, and the two classes are learning to respect one another. Thus this new union bids fair to be stronger than the old one.

Still the question remains, Can this political independence of the workman be combined with secure material independence? Until this is done he will be always at the mercy of his employer, who may practically stultify his political power by influencing his vote, as Mr. George asserts is done in New England.[1] Among the many solutions of this problem proposed in our own country two deserve especial prominence. The first is that of the English Positivists. Comte, although he had but a glimpse of the English Trades-Unions, understood the meaning of them far better than Mill. Inspired by him, Mr. Frederick Harrison and his friends deny the possibility of solving the labour question by co-operative production or any such schemes. They rely on a gradual change in the moral nature of capitalists; not that they expect the old system of feudal protection to return, but they hope that the " captains of industry " of the future will rise to another conception of their position, will recognise the independence of the workman, and at the same time be willing to hand over to him an increased share of their joint produce. This belief may seem ridiculous, and we must expect for a long time yet to see capitalists still striving

[1] *Progress and Poverty,* Book x. c. iv. p. 480.

to obtain the highest possible profits. But observe, that the passion for wealth is certainly in some senses new. It grew up very rapidly at the beginning of the present century; it was not so strong in the last century, when men were much more content to lead a quiet easy life of leisure. The change has really influenced the relations between men; but in the future it is quite possible that the scramble for wealth may grow less intense, and a change in the opposite direction take place. The Comtists are right when they say that men's moral ideas are not fixed. The attitude of public opinion towards slavery was completely changed in twenty or thirty years. Still I am obliged to believe that such a moral revolution as the Comtists hope for is not possible within a reasonable space of time.

I should have more hope of Industrial Partnership as elaborately described by Mr. Sedley Taylor.[1] This also implies a certain change in the moral nature of the employers, but one not so great as the alternative system would require. It has been adopted in over a hundred Continental workshops, though the experiment of Messrs. Briggs in England ended in failure. There is hope of its being more successful in the future, because by promoting the energy of the workmen and diminishing waste, it coincides with the interest of the employer. I think that in some industries it will extend, but that it will not be generally adopted.

There remains the ordinary Communist solution. This has taken various forms; the simplest being a voluntary association of individuals based on the principle of common property, and in which every person works for the community according to fixed rules. There are many successful instances of this, on a small scale, in the United States,[2] but we cannot suppose such a solution to be possible for society as a whole. It has only been tried with picked materials, whereas our object is rather to improve the great mass of the population. The Communism of recent European theorists, of whom the best known is Lassalle, presents a somewhat different aspect.[3] It aims at the appropriation of all instruments of production by the State, which is to take charge of the whole national

---

[1] *The Participation of Labour* (London: 1881), and *Profit-sharing between Capital and Labour* (Cambridge: 1882).

[2] See Nordhoff's *Communistic Societies.*

[3] See the account of his system in M. de Laveleye's *Le Socialisme Contemporain.*

industry and direct it. But the practical difficulty of such a scheme is obviously overwhelming.

The objections to a Communistic solution do not apply to Socialism in a more modified shape. Historically speaking, Socialism has already shown itself in England in the extension of State interference. It has produced the Factory Laws, and it is now beginning to advance further and interfere directly in the division of produce between the workmen and their employers. The Employers' Liability Act recognises that workmen, even when associated in Trades-Unions, cannot without other aid secure full justice, and in the name of justice it has distinctly handed over to the workmen a certain portion of the employers' wealth. The extension of regulative interference however, though it is to be expected in one or two directions, is not likely to be of much further importance. With regard to taxation, on the other hand, Socialist principles will probably attain a wide-reaching application, and here we shall see great changes.

The readjustment of taxation would enable the State to supply for the people many things which they cannot supply for themselves. Without assuming the charge of every kind of production, the State might take into its hands such businesses of vital importance as railways, or the supply of gas and water. And should not the State attempt in the future to grapple with such questions as the housing of the labourers? Municipalities might be empowered to buy ground and let it for building purposes below the full competition market value. I think that such a scheme is practicable without demoralising the people, and it would attack a problem which has hitherto baffled every form of private enterprise; for all the Societies put together, which have been formed in London with this object since 1842, have succeeded in housing only 60,000 persons. And this brings up the whole question of public expenditure for the people. A new form of association, which has become common of late years, is that of a certain number of private individuals combining to provide for some want of the public, such as Coffee Taverns, or Artisans' Dwellings, or cheap music. Such Societies are founded primarily with philanthropic objects, but they also aim at a fair interest on their capital. Might not municipalities seek in a similar way to provide for the poor? In discussing all such schemes, however, we must remember that the real problem is not how to produce some improvement in the condition of the working man—for that has to a certain extent been attained already—but how to secure his complete material independence.[1]

---

[1] The subject of this lecture is also treated of in the Address *Are Radicals Socialists?*—ED.

POPULAR ADDRESSES.

1. WAGES AND NATURAL LAW.
2. INDUSTRY AND DEMOCRACY.
3. ARE RADICALS SOCIALISTS?

———————

THE EDUCATION OF CO-OPERATORS.

———————

THE IDEAL RELATION OF CHURCH AND STATE.

I.

WAGES AND NATURAL LAW.[1]

When I was invited to deliver this lecture, anticipating that my audience would be largely composed of working men, I thought I could not do better than try to dispel some of those prejudices which working men in the past have entertained, and still to some extent entertain, towards Economic Science. I do not mean to say these prejudices are unjust. On the contrary, many of them are most just, and many of the statements made by economists have been not only false in the abstract, but most mischievous from the point of view of workpeople. Perhaps the most striking example of the false statements made by economists has been their assertions with regard to the causes which determine the rate of wages —I mean those assertions which throw ridicule on the efforts of working men, by means of Trades-Unions and other organisations, to improve their condition. Economists have said that Trades-Unions were a foolish, and perhaps a wicked, resistance to the inevitable laws of nature. Political economists have had, on this point, to make a great recantation; and my desire to-night is, to state the nature of that recantation, and to explain what I mean by natural law in Political Economy, and what the causes are which really determine the condition of workpeople.

Perhaps the most prominent idea of the present age is this idea of natural law. If you look back into the beginnings of civilisation you will find that the idea of natural law is entirely absent, and that men then attributed all things to will, arbitrary chance, or caprice. But after Newton's great discovery of the law of gravitation, two or three thinkers began to trace law and order in human society also. All our vast fabric of civilisation, all our arts, and sciences, and literature, which seem the creation of the wilful mind of man, appeared to them to be the product of law. The first to

[1] A Lecture given at the Mechanics' Institute, Bradford, in January 1880, and repeated in part at Firth College, Sheffield, in February 1882.

lay hold of this idea clearly were the economists; Adam Smith it was who first insisted, in a way understood by every one, on the presence of law in human society; and, dealing only with a part of society, he established the laws which determine the production of wealth. This idea of law in human society was a great discovery. We have not come to the end of it yet; and I do not know what revolution it may not yet be destined to effect in our habits of thought and in our daily action. But I am not now going to deal with this very wide subject; I intend to confine myself to one narrow point—Are the laws regarding the distribution of wealth as laid down by economists, by Malthus, Ricardo, and John Stuart Mill, really laws of nature in the same sense as the law of gravity is a law of nature?

Now, the idea of law as applied to some social and economic facts, such as the increase in the number of marriages when corn is cheap, and the rise that takes place in the price of cotton when there is a short supply in the market, is intelligible, because these events do take place with a sequence almost as invariable as that of a law of nature; but, as you will see presently, the idea of law is also applied in an altogether indefensible way to the influences which determine the distribution of wealth among the various classes of the community. I do not hesitate to say that this question of the distribution of wealth is the greatest question of our time. But in considering to-night how a portion of the wealth of the nation *is* distributed, remember that we are not considering how the wealth of the nation *ought* to be distributed. We are only going to investigate the so-called laws of wages, profits, and interest; indeed, it is obvious that the way in which wealth is now distributed must be studied before we can apply with any effect our notions of how it ought to be distributed. We have to explain how wealth is distributed under a system of private property and of division of employments, how it is distributed, in fact, in England at the present time. Having done this we can then go on, if we choose, to frame practical precepts for the guidance of workmen and employers under existing circumstances, or to enable them to modify these circumstances, if they think fit, and establish a new method of distribution for the future.

Political economy has a twofold character: it is a theoretical science and a practical science. In explaining how wages are

determined under the existing system of society, I shall have to
exhibit political economy as a theoretical science. I shall say
nothing as to whether this system of society is or is not right;
I shall simply endeavour to explain how wealth is distributed
under existing conditions among men as they are at present constituted. The distinction between theoretical and practical economics, which is a very important one, has been constantly neglected,
not only by journalists, but by employers and working men.
Because the laws of Political Economy express the action of self-
interest, men have said that Political Economy enjoins men to
value their self-interest to the disregard of their humanity, their
morality, and their religion. That is not true. Political Economy
as a practical science bids men follow their own self-interest only
when it promotes the good of the community. Political Economy
never said that there was no room for humanity or morality or
religion in the world.

I will show you by three illustrations the truth of what I
have said as to the mistake made by journalists, working men,
and employers, as to the nature of Political Economy. In the
first place, I will take a case which occurred in America. In
the great labour war of 1877, which was followed by a long
controversy in the American magazines and newspapers, Colonel
Scott, the manager of the Pennsylvanian Railway, wrote an
elaborate defence of the policy of his company in the reduction
of wages. He said: "We have kept in our employment more
men than we wanted, and this I know is contrary to the hard
rules of Political Economy"—as if, as I have observed before,
Political Economy bade men discard humanity. Again, in a recent arbitration question the representative of the men, in arguing
his case before the arbitrators, said : "If in 1872 we had followed
our own interest on the true principles of Political Economy, then
our wages would be double what they are at the present time."
There again that man thought that because the laws of Political
Economy expressed the action of self-interest, therefore the political
economist enjoined men always to act from self-interest and not
from any other motive. Lastly, let me give a quotation from the
Times. In a leading article on a great strike the *Times* said, con-
demning the action of the workmen : " It is true that the sternest
economist, when he thinks of the sufferings of some classes of

labour, gives an involuntary shudder.   He involuntarily wishes the laws of economy might be relaxed in favour of this class of workmen." Did that writer suppose that the laws of Political Economy were of the same character as the laws of gravity, that they expressed facts which were unalterable by human endeavour ? He did, and he was entirely wrong.   In 1848, many years before that leading article was written, John Mill had shown the great distinction between those laws of Political Economy which are true laws of nature—true as the law of gravity to which the laws of Political Economy have been compared with wearisome iteration— and those laws of Political Economy which are true only under certain assumptions—that is, under a certain existing social system which is alterable by human endeavour; under existing human passions which can be modified in the progress of civilisation by higher passions and higher ideals.   This is what I wish to enforce upon you before proceeding to the immediate subject of my lecture —that a large portion of the laws of Political Economy simply ex- press the action of human beings as they are at present constituted under the existing system of law and social institutions, and that though we cannot expect rapidly or completely to change the nature of man, the nature of man is being slowly but surely changed by the progress of civilisation, of morality, and of religion, and therefore if a man alleges in his behalf, when he has done an inhuman thing, the laws of Political Economy, he is discarded alto- gether by all the economists of the most recent school.

It is true that certain economists of the old school, misled by the influence of physical science, believed that the law of the dis- tribution of wealth, the law of wages, was an inevitable and eternal law, and this conception gave rise to the wage-fund theory. Though John Mill distinctly said the laws of distribution of wealth were true only under existing social conditions which might be altered, he yet maintained that granting these conditions the law of wages was inevitable and unalterable by human endeavour, and in saying this he undid the chief benefit of his treatise.   It was not until a late period of his life that he gave up this theory; in 1869, he publicly, in an article in the *Fortnightly Review*, confessed that he had been wrong.   What economists for a long time had been saying to working men who were trying by com- bination to raise their wages, was : " You are doing a very foolish thing. You might as well try to make iron swim as to alter the rate of wages by your individual will. The rate of wages, like the succession of night and day, is independent of the will of either employer or employed. Neither workmen nor employers can change the rate determined by competition at any particular time." Such an assertion as this was not only made in text-books and by abstract theorists, but it was made by journals and by members of Parliament. Mr. Roebuck is an example. Mr. Roebuck was in his own way a great friend of the working man, but he was a very strict political economist of the old school, and opposed to Trades-Unions. Some of you may remember that Mr. Roebuck was a member of the Trades-Union Commission in 1867, and examined the leaders of the Trades-Unions adversely. In 1847, in the course of the great debate on the Ten Hours' Bill, when the country gentlemen eagerly tried to avenge themselves on the manufacturers for the repeal of the Corn Laws, Mr. Roebuck took the side of the manufacturers, and urged that landowners ought to look at home. " Think," he said, " of the low wages you are paying your labourers ; don't be always insisting upon the miserable condition of the operatives of the north." And notice how he went on : " I am not going to retort upon you because the wages which you pay your workmen are low. You cannot, I know, afford to pay more wages to them." In other words, Mr. Roebuck meant to say that the 6s. a week which the Wiltshire peasant was getting at that time was the result of an inevitable law which neither landowner, nor farmer, nor labourer could change. But though the wage-fund theory has been given up by economists, it is extremely difficult to frame another theory in its place which shall explain the facts. The facts of our present industrial system are of so complicated a nature that they have not only defied the attention of economists for the last fifty years, but they have deceived practical men who have given to them not only the time economists have given, but their whole lives. This is the peculiar difficulty under which the economist lies. The geologist or the physicist has the facts of the physical world before him ; he can quietly observe them, he can make experiments ; but the economist has to deal with facts which are far more complicated, which are obscured by human passions and interests, and, what is still more to the point, which are perpetually in motion.

I believe the wage-fund theory was the great cause of the un-popularity of Political Economy among working men; first because the theory contradicted obvious facts known to the working classes, such as a rise of wages caused by the action of Trades-Unions ; secondly, because it strengthened the hands of the employer in bargaining with the workman by bringing public opinion to bear on his side, for the workmen were represented as kicking against an in-evitable law of nature ; and thirdly, because it affected to place an immoveable barrier to the improvement of the working classes, tell-ing them that there was only one escape for them, limitation of their numbers—a hard saying. But before going on to an explanation of the law of wages as it exists at the present time, I wish to state, as shortly as I can, what the wage-fund theory really was. In the first place, it said that at any given moment the rate of wages was determined by causes entirely beyond the control of the em-ployer and the working man. It said, " Wages are paid from past accumulations of capital. A certain portion of that capital is put aside by the employer for the payment of wages. That portion and no more the working man can get. The wages question is a question of saving and not of bargaining." Therefore, the political economist condemned Trades-Unions, which are an organised attempt to bargain for the rate of wages ; therefore, the English political economist said that wages were a question of population. He said, " The only way for the working man to improve his con-dition is to limit his numbers." He looked upon the working man as a divisor, and not as a multiplier. He said, " The working man cannot increase the dividend, therefore let him diminish the divisor." That was the only hope which English economists for fifty years held out to the working classes. All the endeavours of the working classes to improve their condition were condemned by this theory, and therefore it was that the working man said, " If Political Economy is against the working man, it behoves the working man to be against Political Economy."

And the working man was right. The economists had made a vast mistake, but there were certain deceptive appearances which misled them. It must not be supposed that because they made a mistake about the most important question of their time, these men were either blindly prejudiced or thoroughly incapable. They were deceived by certain facts which are very difficult to interpret. The first fact is, that though wages are not paid out of capital, they are always *advanced* out of capital. The next fact is that, though the rate of wages is not determined by the proportion of food capital to the population that exists at a given moment, yet the existence of that food capital is a necessary condition of the employment of the working man; and therefore the economist said, that it formed also the limit to his wages, because according to the theory of population, wages are always at the level of bare subsistence. During the past ten years economists in Germany, in America, and in England have been busy pointing out the mistakes committed by the old school, but no economist has yet succeeded in constructing another complete theory of wages. The fact is, that no simple formula or phrase can cover so complicated a set of facts, and the most I can do this evening is to explain certain leading conditions which determine the rate of wages. I shall not pretend to exhaust the subject, but I think I can put in a clear way the most prominent and important causes affecting wages in England at the present time.

In order to render my statement clear, I must make certain divisions. These divisions will be necessarily artificial, and therefore to a certain extent misleading, but they are absolutely essential to a clear exposition of my subject. We must first ask, Why are wages paid at all? and secondly, What determines the real wages received by the working man—that is, what determines, in Adam Smith's language, " the amount of the necessaries, conveniences, and luxuries of life received by the working man?" Now, in answering the first question, we must remember that three things are necessary to the employment of the labourer. (1.) There must be an unsatisfied want—that is, there must be a demand for the commodities produced by his labour. (2.) There must be what we may call " food capital;" somebody must have saved, or abstained from the consumption of so much food and clothing as is absolutely indispensable to the labourer until the product of his labour is realized. (3.) The labourer must find an employer, some one who will provide the capital, manage the industry, and undertake to satisfy the want of the consumer. The function of the employer in the modern industrial system seems to have been very little understood. It is a function at the present time of enormous importance. The employer scrutinises the natural resources of the country; he detects new possibilities; he creates a new industry out of the waste of old industries; he gathers together men in factories; he takes the whole risk of the business; he guarantees the wages of the workmen, and he studies the wants of the consumer. He must know where to buy his raw material; he must know how to buy it in the cheapest market, when to sell his goods, and when not to sell them. He must undertake operations which involve relations with all sorts of men, not only in his own country but in distant countries. Without him it is absolutely impossible, as long as the present industrial system lasts, for the workman to live. These three things, then, are necessary :—First of all, demand for the commodities; secondly, capital; and, thirdly, the employer. If there is demand for a certain commodity, and if there is an employer who will advance the capital and take the risk of satisfying that demand, then the labourer gets employment. Observe that if the capital, the labour, and the business knowledge and enterprise 'all belonged to the same man there would be no question of distribution. But as a fact the three things often belong to three sets of people, and the question therefore arises, how are we to divide the price of the produce? for wages are paid out of the price of the produce. This brings us to the second division of our subject.

When the labourer is employed, what determines the amount of his wages? We will first of all consider the wages question as a question of production. As wages are primarily determined by the amount of the produce, our first business is to inquire what determines this amount. Now, the amount of the produce depends to a large extent upon the efficiency of labour. It is this which chiefly determines the quantity of wealth the labourer can create. If we look at different countries—at America, at France, at Germany, at Russia, and at England, we shall see that there are different rates of wages in these countries. What is the main cause of this difference in the rate of wages? It is the difference in the efficiency of labour, as well as in the natural resources of the country. Here is the first great hope which the latest analysis of the wages question opens out to the labourer. It shows him that there is another mode of raising his wages besides limiting his numbers. He can increase the dividend by increasing the amount of the produce.

Let us consider for a moment on what the efficiency of labour depends. First of all it depends on the physical strength and the technical skill of the labourer. Next, it depends upon the state of the mechanical arts, on the kind of machinery with which the labourer has to work. Next, it may be said to depend upon climate. A climate may or may not be like that of England, which permits continuous labour and stimulates a hardy and vigorous existence. Next, it depends upon the foresight and skill of the employer in the distribution of labour, and in the management of the economy of the factory. The amount of the produce is affected by all these things. Recently many statistics have been collected in order to show the different efficiency of labour in different countries.

I shall give one or two instances to illustrate my position. One reason why wages in England are high compared with wages on the Continent, is that the machinery used in England is more efficient than that used on the Continent, and that the physical strength and skill of the working man here enables him to superintend more machinery than the working man on the Continent is able to superintend. You may say that machinery is an injury to the working man. Well, machinery, like many other things in the progress of mankind, has been an injury to certain classes of working men. If a man has got a special aptitude for a special occupation, and a machine is invented which displaces him, he may become a pauper. That raises the question, how to promote industrial progress without unnecessary suffering to the individual—a question which is too wide to be dealt with in my present lecture. But remember that machinery has also had a great effect in raising wages; first because it has made labour more efficient, and the labourer thus produces more; and secondly because it has cheapened commodities, and therefore the labourer can buy more. You have probably heard of the bitter complaints of American manufacturers, of the high wages they have to pay, of their desperate competition with the " pauper labour" of Europe. Now, why do men get high wages in America? Partly for the very reason we are considering, because workmen produce more in America than in other countries, for labour-saving machinery has been more rapidly invented there than in any other country. At the very time when American manufacturers were complaining of the competition of "pauper labour" in Europe, it was shown that in the American hardware industries, in which wages were double as high as they were in England, America was underselling other countries in their own markets. Again, take the coal industry. The output of a single collier in England has been calculated at 272 tons per annum. In Belgium it is 185 tons. This is due to a difference of physical strength, and to improved mechanical appliances. Sir Thomas Brassey considers that though French wages are twenty per cent. cheaper than English, yet the cost of making iron in France is greater; this is due to the "want of appliances for the saving of labour."

Thus far we have seen that the labourer receives wages according to the amount of the produce of his labour. We have next to consider the price for which that produce will sell. Wages, in the second place, depend upon the price of the produce. What determines the price of a manufactured commodity is a very complicated question, and one which has very much exercised the minds of economists. I think it is possible to put the facts pretty simply for our purpose. Commodities may be divided into two classes; those produced under free competition, and those produced under monopoly. The price of commodities produced under free competition is the lowest which the producers will work for; the consumer in these cases has his wants satisfied at the minimum cost. The price of such commodities is determined by the actual cost of production; and the product is sold at the lowest price at which any man can afford to make it. If it fell lower, the producer would throw up the business. The lock-trade, for instance, is not carried on like most trades by large employers of labour with immense capital, but by small masters employing six or eight apprentices. The competition among them is so keen that the price of locks is reduced to the lowest point. Here the individual master can do very little indeed to determine the price, and the individual workman can do very little to determine the price; it is decided by causes beyond the control of the producer, whether he is an employer or a workman. But with regard to commodities produced under a monopoly, their price is not determined by cost of production, but by the demand of the consumer. The consumer may have to pay three times as much for a monopolised commodity as he would have had to pay had it been produced under free competition, and the end of the satisfaction of all wants at the minimum cost is thus defeated. It is important to deal thoroughly with this question, because one of the most favourite proposals at the present time, of employers in America and working men in England, is a limitation of production in order to secure a rise in price, and therefore a rise in wages and profits ; to create, in fact, a monopoly price. But in considering this question we must keep in mind what is our fundamental aim—the satisfaction of wants at the minimum cost of life, and with the minimum antagonism of interests.

How far then can a working man increase his wages—not merely by increasing the efficiency of his labour, and thereby increasing the amount of his produce, but by getting a higher price for his produce ? We have to ask, in the first place, Can he do it ? and, in the next place, if he can do it, Is it a policy which a political economist, not as a scientific man analysing facts, but as a teacher framing precepts to guide men's actions, would recommend ? Now there is no doubt that under certain circumstances the thing can be done. It can be done by limitation in production, and by combination to raise wages—two things closely connected. To take a particular industry : supposing that the colliers, or the cotton-spinners and weavers of Lancashire, determined to limit production in order to raise their wages, it would be perfectly possible of course for the colliers to insist on limiting the output of coal, the spinners the manufacture of cottons ; but remember, unless the combination among them is universal it will not be successful. Unless they can get, not merely the colliery owners of any particular district but of the whole country, not merely the cotton-spinners of any particular district but of the whole country, to consent to that limitation, they will not gain their point. Supposing the manufacturers of Lancashire limited the output, and other manufacturers refused to do so, these latter would get the hold on the markets which the Lancashire manufacturers had abandoned, and consequently, when these again increased their production they would find others in the possession of the market. So you see it is not an easy matter to raise prices by limiting production. I do not, however, condemn such a policy, when it can be successfully attempted, if followed by men who wish for a time to adapt production to consumption. A temporary limitation of production, when there is a real glut of goods in the market, is a perfectly legitimate attempt to remedy a defect in our industrial system. But this is quite a distinct thing from a restriction of production to obtain a monopoly price; and what we have to consider at the present time is the policy of attempting to limit permanently the output of a particular industry, in order to draw into the hands of the producers of that industry a larger amount of the general wealth.

Now this object can, under certain circumstances, be effected by a combination among capitalist employers—a common enough policy in America, and a real danger of the modern industrial system—or by a combination among the men. Supposing what has been attempted by the employers in America had really succeeded, that what are called "rings" had been formed, and that such rings had determined to tax the whole body of consumers for their own benefit, the result of course would have been a small gain to themselves at the expense of a great loss to the whole people. That word "consumer" is a very misleading one. The body of the *mere* consumers in England is a small one. Most consumers are producers, and half the things produced are consumed by working men. If a particular group of working men and employers combine to raise the price of their own products, what they do is simply this: they just draw into their hands a larger quantity of commodities produced by other producers, and tax the whole people for their own benefit. I do not deny that such a policy is feasible, but as a practical political economist I condemn it. There is already one great antagonism of interest—that between employer and labourer—and here you would be creating a second antagonism of interests between one group of producers and the producers of the whole community, and the result would be an industrial war within the community. This would be, not a question of a struggle between two classes of the community for the division of legitimate gains, but a combination of two classes to obtain illegitimate gains at the expense of the whole people.

The same reasoning applies to combinations, not of employers and workmen, but of workmen alone to raise the price of their produce. The workmen of a given district, being all powerful owing to their Trades-Union, may insist upon a rise in wages, and the employer may grant such a rise, and try to throw the increased cost on the consumer. But will the consumer pay the higher price? That is the question. He will certainly pay it if the article be one which he *cannot do without;* but what is then the result? He has less to spend on other commodities; so that again one group of working men gain at the expense of all other groups of working men. You must remember it is the consumer who pays wages though the employer advances them. But it may be that the article in question is one which the consumer can do without, or of which he can, at any rate, diminish his consumption. In that case it is probable that the rise in prices will lead to a reduction in the demand for the article, and thus, though the rate of wages among the labourers producing the article has risen, they may be none the better off, because the amount of the article required, and consequently the amount of their employment, will be less. The only effect of the rise of price would thus be to diminish the production of some necessary or convenient article.

We have now come to the third circumstance which determines the rate of wages. I have spoken of the amount of the produce, and the price of the produce: we have lastly to consider the division of the price of the produce. The price of the produce has to be divided into three parts; first, the interest on capital; second, what is called by Mill " the wages of superintendence," or, to use the language of a more recent economist, " the earnings of management;" and third, the wages of labour. Over the first we need not linger. Whether capital is borrowed or belongs to the employer himself, the current rate of interest has to be paid on it. The hard point to ascertain is, how the rest of the price is divided between the employer and the workman. The rate of interest is ascertainable enough, but the rate of profits and the rate of wages is a matter of continual dispute. You are all familiar with the old formula of supply and demand, but I shall be obliged again to make use of it. As a fact, the rate of profit—the wages of management—and the rate of wages—the reward of labour— are determined by the famous law of supply and demand, that dubious, hateful, convenient phrase. Primarily the remuneration of the employer is determined by the number of employers compared with the demand for them, the remuneration of the labourer is determined by the number of labourers compared with the demand for them. In other words, the rate of wages and the rate of what I will call profits, as distinguished from interest, are determined by the comparative supply of employers and labourers. You all remember the famous saying of Cobden's: "Wages rise when two masters run after one workman; wages fall when two men run after one master."

If I were going into a complete investigation of the subject, I should have to inquire into all the causes which determine the supply of employers, and all the causes which determine the supply of labourers, but that is far too intricate a question for me to enter on to-night. What I wish to deal with is this: What determines the actual bargains made between employers and workmen, assuming a certain state of supply and demand? In the first place let us ask whether there is a minimum rate of profit; that is, a rate of profit on less than which the employer refuses to carry on his business. In all the discussions which you meet with in the newspapers, and in books written by impartial, fair-minded men like Mr. Brassey, you will find it constantly said that the employer must have his fair rate of profit. What is really meant by the word "fair"? If you will look into it closely you will see that it means this: that the fair rate of profit which the employer must have, is that rate which, if he does not obtain in his own particular industry, he can obtain either by moving to some other locality, or by moving to some other occupation. There are actual instances of employers doing this. You know that certain trades have been driven from certain districts by the action of Trades-Unions, which have refused to recognise that there is this minimum rate of profit. I am saying nothing whatever as to whether the employer is right or not in insisting on this rate of profit; all I say is, that so long as human nature is what it is, so long as employers are what they are, so long will they insist upon this rate of profit while they can get it. But this fair rate of profit is not a fixed quantity. The employer, rather than throw up his business, may give higher wages, and the workmen get their rise in wages at the expense of the employer. The rate is not a fixed rate. Some employers will be content with less than others, but remember that there *is* a minimum rate of profit, there *is* a limit to the rise of wages at the expense of the employer.

Now let us turn to the workman's side of the case. Is there a minimum rate of wages ? We hear almost more about fair wages than we hear about fair profits. Let us try to see what meaning can be given to the term "fair," as applied to wages. It means that there is a certain rate of wages in a given occupation on less than which the workman refuses to carry on his business. He says, "If you won't give me this rate of wages, I can move to another occupation or to another locality." The workman's power of moving to another occupation depends very much upon his brains, and his power of moving to another locality depends upon the knowledge he has of the opportunities in other places. He may either migrate from one part of England to another, or he may leave the country altogether; there is thus a limit to a rise in profits. So far we have seen the limits to wages and profits, now we have to ascertain what determines the division of that part of the price which lies between these two limits.

You all know that it has been said, I suppose a hundred thousand times in the last fifty years, that the wages of labour are determined by the demand for and supply of labour, just as the price of other commodities is determined by the demand for and the supply of those commodities. This is what the newspapers have said and many economists also ; but there is an assumption in that statement which is not true. The writers who make that statement assume that the market for labour is identical in character with the market for commodities. Is that the case ? The most eminent recent economists of more than one school have denied it. They have shown that there is a radical difference between the market for commodities and the market for labour, and that in the bargain of the labourer with the employer the labourer is, as an isolated individual, under a natural disadvantage. Remember that in the market for commodities buyer and seller meet on equal terms. They have equal knowledge, and probably—though not necessarily—equal capital. They can hold out for their reserve price ; and if the merchant or the manufacturer cannot sell his commodities in one market, he has not the slightest difficulty in sending them to another. Further, a bargain about a bale of cotton goods does not convulse the industrial system, but the bargain about the price of labour involves the social condition of a whole class. In order to place the labourer on an equality with the employer in his bargain he must have equal knowledge with the employer of the market demand for employers and for labourers. But it is perfectly obvious that the employer has the advantage of the labourer in point of knowledge. He knows better when to strike a bargain and when to hold out. It is a fact that a few years ago labourers in the south and south-west of England had never heard of Lancashire and the demand for labour which existed there.

In the next place, in order that employer and labourer may bargain on equal terms they must both have a reserve price,—that is, equal power of using their knowledge of the market. The isolated labourer is very much in the position of a merchant who has to sell without being able to hold out for his price. To enable the labourer to hold out he must have capital. He must be able to say to the employer, " Very well: if you won't give me my price, I will wait;" and he must be able to live during the time he is waiting.   Trades-Unions have supplied capital to the labourer and enabled him (as far as regards this point) to approach the employer on a more equal footing.   The employer has a large capital; so has the Trades-Union, and the two are now a very much more equal match than in the old times before the repeal of the Combination Laws in 1824, when it was illegal for the labourers to combine to hold out for their " reserve price."   But again, in making the bargain the employer is one man united ; the labourers are many disunited. If the labourers unite in a Trades-Union then they can bargain as one man and maintain their price.   This is a second function of real importance which Trades-Unions perform in the bargain between employers and labourers ; they enable the men to bargain as a whole.   Again, if the employer and the labourer are to be on equal terms they must have equal mobility—that is, an equal power of moving from the place in which they are not wanted, to a place where they are wanted.   Has the labourer an equal mobility with the capitalist employer ?   No.   The labourer has to contend with ignorance of other localities, and with local attachment and domestic ties.   A bale of cotton goods has no domestic ties, has no local attachment. And not only can an employer ship his goods to another place, but he can transport his business power and his capital elsewhere, much more easily than the labourer can his labour.   In 1870 a large cotton-spinner in Glasgow took his capital and established a factory in New York. Trades-Unions, however, also occasionally send workmen from place to place.

There is another fact which I wish to insist upon. If two people are to be on an equal footing in making a bargain, they must have an equal indifference to each other. Is the labourer more in need of the employer, or the employer of the labourer? If the labourers are obstinate the employers can in many cases introduce fresh machinery. Some of the most famous machines of modern times have been introduced owing to strikes. Nasmyth, the inventor of the steam-hammer, introduced machinery in 1857 to the extent of reducing his hands one-half, thereby much increasing his profits. I believe the contractors for the Tubular Bridge in 1848 procured the invention of a machine for punching holes in iron plates, and thus got rid of men who had been troublesome. Have labourers yet discovered a machine which they can substitute for employers? And, again, employers have another resource—the introduction of foreign workmen. You have never heard of a labourer importing an employer; it is not the labourer who imports the employer, but the employer who imports the labourer. Thus the employer is, in many ways, more necessary to the labourer than the labourer to the employer. The employer, again, may even refuse to use the commodity which the labourer produces. He may, for instance, substitute concrete for stone, and so get rid of a troublesome bargainer.

All these cases show that there is a real, essential difference between the market for labour and the market for commodities. I am not stating this in any other than a perfectly scientific spirit. It represents the careful analysis of the labour market by impartial men, and is accepted by economists of different schools. To put it shortly, we have in the market for commodities organised competition on equal terms and no social question involved; in the labour market we have unorganised competition and a great social question involved; and the statement of the conditions necessary to assimilate the labour market to the goods market is seen to be a statement of the *labourers' disadvantage*. When we have the labourer as an isolated individual bargaining with the employer, this is unorganised competition on unequal terms; but if labourers, instead of bargaining singly, combine, accumulate capital, and bargain with the employer as one man, as they can do through their Trades-Unions, then there is organised competition on much more equal terms.

Before I leave the subject of Trades-Unions let us just consider the result of the action of a Union supposing it to gain a direct rise in wages. A rise in wages may be a benefit to the workman without being any real loss to the employer; the workman may be more efficient owing to the rise in his wages, and by turning out a larger produce may increase both wages and profits. This may happen, but you must also remember that if Trades-Unions not only endeavour to organise competition but attempt likewise to limit competition, that is, if they do not merely combine all the labourers in a given industry in one Union, but combine a certain number of labourers and exclude others, then they may get into difficulties, because if the combined labourers succeed in getting a higher rate of wages, that higher rate will attract other labourers from other districts. Now this happened as a fact in Glasgow about the year 1834. The wages of the cotton-spinners being kept up by their Union, the high rate attracted outsiders, and the Unionists were obliged to support these out of their own wages in order to prevent their competition!

I am not now about to discuss the question of how far Trades-Unions can solve the struggle for existence, by limiting competition to a select few. But I should like to point out that if by limiting competition the Trade-Unionist diminishes the produce of labour, in the end he defeats his own purpose, for one of the primary causes of higher wages is efficient labour. On the other hand the action of Trades-Unions in organising competition has been perfectly legitimate. They have organised supply where supply was unorganised, they have got rid of the influences of custom, and have forced employers to yield them a higher rate of wages where employers have succeeded in getting higher profits. But they cannot get a higher rate of wages than that determined by organised competition; if they do, employers will withdraw their capital, or new hands will be attracted by the high wages into the trade. Yet we see that it is not pure and simple competition in the market of workmen on one side and employers on the other which determines the rate of wages. Given the same number of workmen and the same number of employers under different conditions, and a different rate of wages would ensue.

But I wish particularly to draw your attention to one fact, that owing to the increased organisation of employers on the one hand and labourers on the other, arbitration and conciliation are becoming increasingly necessary. The struggle is becoming very definite. Vast groups of labourers are standing face to face with groups of employers. Both parties are beginning to see the true nature of the problem which they have been working out for the last one hundred years, and the result is that they see that neither can win any permanent advantage by protracted struggles. They find that it is far better to meet in council and discuss the facts of their business; they find it is far better to treat each other, not as natural opponents, but as merchants treat each other on the exchange, not looking upon each other as determined foes, but as men bargaining with a definite point at issue, a point which can be ascertained by increased knowledge on the part of the labourer, and increased willingness to take the labourer into his counsels on the part of the employer.

But I have not exhausted the analysis of the causes which determine the rate of wages. They are still influenced by custom, by Poor-Laws—a bad Poor-Law, like the old one in England before 1834, may distinctly keep wages down—by all kinds of institutions which seem but remotely connected with the labourer; and by the past history of the nation. Public opinion also is an influence of great importance. The London daily press in times past has unhappily been nearly always against the workmen. During the builders' strike in 1861 the *Daily Telegraph* wrote, " It has been settled by the expression of public opinion that ten hours is not an oppressive day's work for a mason or labourer;" the *Standard* wrote, " We know that if the masters attempted anything harsh or unusual the men would have public opinion with them, and the employers would have to yield;" the *Times* wrote, " They will not enlist the public on their side, and without the public they will not succeed against their masters." The power of public opinion in America has been more than once directly shown; a Shoemakers' Union was beaten in an attempt to obtain exorbitant wages by the spirit evinced by the people generally who supported the employers in the introduction of Chinese labour; and a printers' strike in Boston was defeated by the assistance lent to the publishers by the public, even a judge, it is said, helping to set type !

Happily public opinion exercises a considerable influence upon masters as well as upon workmen. I am not now referring to honourable employers, but to men who unfortunately exist in every trade, whose only desire is to make money and who are only too anxious to get it out of the weakness of their men. The action of this class of employer, is controlled, not only by the public opinion of the newspapers, but by the public opinion of their own class. Let me give an example of this. Mr. Mundella, who, singularly enough, was examined by Mr. Roebuck before the Trades-Union Commission, in the course of his evidence before that Commission on the truck system at Nottingham, said that some masters in his trade were as bad as they could be, that in fact their conduct almost justified the violence of the men. "But," Mr. Mundella added (he was then speaking of the Board of Arbitration), "since we have got our Board, we have put a stop to their exactions." In other words, the public opinion of the workmen and the employers, expressed through the Board of Arbitration, had coerced these masters, and had raised the wages of their men, hitherto robbed by payment in truck instead of in the coin of the realm.

I have said enough to show that it is not competition *alone* that determines the rate of wages, that Trades-Unions, that custom, that law, that public opinion, that the character of employers, all influence wages; that their rate is not governed by an inexorable law, nor determined alone by what a great writer once called "the brute natural accident of supply and demand." As a matter of fact, wages are influenced by a great many causes which are only too apt to escape our notice. That competition in England and still more in America is the main influence no one denies. In America the condition of the workmen is extremely good, and this is distinctly the result of competition joined to the accident of the existence in the western states of America of a vast extent of still unoccupied land. Unless manufacturers in the eastern states paid their men the same wages as they can earn with the farmers in the west, who are competing for their labour, or which they can obtain by themselves taking up unoccupied land and cultivating it, they would find that they were without hands. But why are wages in England only one-half of what they are in America? Curiously enough the land has a great deal to do with it, even in England, though in the opposite direction to its influence in America. From causes into which I cannot go now labourers have in this country been driven off the land, out of agricultural districts into the towns, where they compete with the manufacturing labourer, and thus depress wages. The main reason why wages are lower here than in America is because there are more labourers competing in the labour market. I admit, and for the second time, that competition is the main cause of low wages; also that unless we can modify competition by other things, the condition of the workmen in England is not likely to improve at any very great pace; but it is more important to recognise that competition is not the *sole* cause than to recognise that it is the main cause.

Wages on the whole have risen since the repeal of the corn-laws, bread has been cheaper and steadier in price, and some of the other necessaries of life more plentiful; an enormous emigration has also relieved the labour market. Socialists say all this is nothing, and that the only way permanently to improve the condition of working men is to abolish private property and get rid of competition entirely, substituting in their place collective property under the control of the State. We in England laugh at such conceptions, but if we are able to laugh at them, it is because we have here institutions like Trades-Unions, which have enabled working men to hold their own against employers, and to effect a considerable improvement in their condition.

But taking into account all that Trades-Unions have done and can do, we have to recognise that if human nature is to continue to be as it is; that if employers go on seeking to obtain the highest rate of profit possible, and exert their power to the full, workmen will find it extremely difficult to obtain any great improvement in their condition. But human nature is not always the same. It slowly changes, and is modified by higher ideals and wider and deeper conceptions of justice. Men have forgotten that although it is impossible to change the nature of a stone or a rock, human nature is pliable, and pliable above all to nobler ideas and to a truer sense of justice. We have no reason to suppose that human nature as it is now will always remain the same. We have reason, on the other hand, to suppose that employers under the influence of the wider and deeper conceptions of which I have spoken, may be willing to forego in the struggle for the division of wealth, some part of that share which would come to them if they chose to exert their force without restraint. It may be said: "This is chimerical; human nature will be the same, and always has been the same." This I deny, and I instance that great change of opinion which took place in England with regard to slavery. If such a rapid change could take place in our moral ideas within the last hundred years, do not you think it possible that in the course of another hundred years English employers and English workmen may act upon higher notions of duty and higher conceptions of citizenship than they do now? I am not speaking to employers alone. The matter is as much in the hands of the workman as it is in the hands of the employer. It is not merely a question of the distribution of wealth; it is a question of the right use of wealth. You know only too well that many working men do not know how to use the wages which they have at the present time. You know, too, that an increase of wages often means an increase of crime. If working men are to expect their employers to act with larger notions of equity in their dealings in the labour market, it is at least rational that employers should expect that workmen shall set about reforming their own domestic life. It is at least reasonable that they should demand that working men shall combine to put down drunkenness and brutal sports. High wages are not an end in themselves. No one wants high wages in order that working men may indulge in mere sensual gratification. We want higher wages in order that an improved material condition, with less of anxiety and less uncertainty as to the future, may enable the working man to enter on a purer and more worthy life. So far from high wages being an end in themselves, we desire them for the workman just in order that he may be delivered from that engrossing care for every shilling and every penny which engenders a base materialism. Therefore in dealing with the subject of wages, I do not hesitate to insist that you cannot separate it from the whole question of life.

I shall be content if I have succeeded in showing that the question is within the power of human will to determine; that man need not crouch and shiver, as he did in the past, under the shadow of an inexorable law; but that human will may largely modify human fate for good or ill. If also I have achieved a still more humble purpose; if I have shown working men that they should study economic science if they would understand within what limits they can raise wages under present social conditions, and taking human beings as they are—if I have succeeded in doing this, then also I shall be content.

In conclusion, I would entreat working men to believe that Political Economy is no longer an instrument for the aggrandisement of the rich and the impoverishment of the poor; that in as far as it is a science at all, it endeavours to explain the laws by which wealth is produced and distributed by men, as they are at present constituted under the existing institutions of society; that, as a theoretical science, it pronounces no judgment on these laws, nor on the conduct of labourers and employers; but that as a practical science, it does frame precepts, not in the interests of the employers alone, not in the interests of the workmen alone, but in the interests of the whole people.

II.

INDUSTRY AND DEMOCRACY.[1]

I FEEL that some explanation is due from me to those who are assembled here to-night, of my claim to deal with the subject I have chosen. It is a difficult subject, and seems to belong to the politician and the practical man. I am neither; I am simply a student,—a student who has stepped outside his usual sphere to handle a question which seems to raise issues beyond the power of a student to appreciate. And yet I am content to rest my claim to address you to-night, on the fact that I am a student, because in that capacity I have, I believe, certain qualifications not possessed in an equal degree by the politician and man of business. The student will not—at any rate at first—be suspected of class prejudice or political prejudice. This, I think, is a strong point, when we consider the delicacy of the question and its social importance. But there is a stronger point still in favour of the student: he is not only free from prejudice, he is able to take those wide, connected views of things which are often to the politician and practical man impossible. They live in the world, are immersed in its cares, distracted by its cries—are in the arena carrying on the struggle. The student lives retired, watches the world from afar, and discerns many things unnoticed by those who

[1] This Address was delivered in the earlier part of 1881, to audiences of working men at Newcastle, Chelsea, Bradford (where employers also were present), and Bolton. It is the only one of the addresses printed in this volume which was prepared for publication by Toynbee himself. A note in his own hand, which he wrote as a preface to the Address, says:—"With the exception of one or two passages, this Address was not written out till after it was spoken, but it is, I believe, here printed substantially as it was delivered. It has not been thought necessary to give authorities for the facts mentioned ; but it may be as well to state that the line of argument pursued is to be found, with variations, in Mr. Crompton's book on *Industrial Conciliation* (to which I would refer all who are interested in that subject) ; in Brentano's Essay, *Das Arbeitsverhältniss gemäss dem heutigen Recht ;* and in Mr. Lushington's essay published in the volume entitled *Questions for a Reformed Parliament.* The treatment of the subject is necessarily incomplete, and it is intended to deal with some of the points omitted in a second address, 'Socialism and Democracy.'" This second address was never written.—ED.

are too often borne along in the tumult they seek to guide. From his watch-tower he looks before and after, pursues with diligent eye the receding past, and with anxious expectation forecasts the future.

You must not, however, suppose that I am describing the student as a person of finer powers than the statesman; I am describing not his powers but his position, and on the advantages of that position I insist, because I believe it to be one of peculiar value at the present time. Owing to causes obvious to all, politicians have become less and less the leaders and teachers, and more and more the instruments of the people. I pass no judgment on the fact; I state it simply to show the necessity for the intervention in political and social affairs of a new order of men, who may indeed be enrolled as members of this party or that, but who shall not suffer party connections or personal aims to hamper them in the elucidation of the questions which it is the function of politicians to settle. Is it quite impossible to conceive of such men?—of men who shall be as students impartial, as citizens passionate?

I propose to-night to apply a familiar philosophical conception to the interpretation of a particular industrial problem. The conception I mean is that of a law of progress—of a certain definite order in human development which cannot be ignored or pushed aside. I shall try to show what light is thrown by our knowledge of this law on the relations between employers and workmen; and when you have listened to me, I venture to hope you will have received some little help towards an understanding of the problems which perplex the present and make the future dark with menace.

I have called my subject "Industry and Democracy." By "industry" I mean "the life and affairs of employers and workmen;" by democracy, "government of the people by the people." The relations between industry and democracy are innumerable; I shall deal with only one of them. I intend to trace shortly the industrial history of the last century and a quarter, and to show how democracy has contributed to the solution of the problems presented by industrial change. I shall also incidentally show how the growth of industry has stimulated the growth of democracy; for in human affairs no event is single.

I must ask you to transport yourselves in imagination to England as it was a century and a quarter ago. We are accustomed to think that, however the life of man may alter, the earth on which he moves must remain the same. But here the revolutions in man's life have stamped themselves upon the face of nature. The great landmarks, the mountain ranges, the river channels, the inlets and estuaries, are for the most part unaltered; nothing else remains the same. For desolate moors and fens, for vast tracts of unenclosed pasturage and masses of woodland, we have now corn-fields and orchards, and crowded cities with their canopies of smoke. Only a few years before the time of which I speak, men complained that half the country was waste. To-day we have a struggle to preserve any open land at all.

It is to a revolution in three industries, agriculture, cotton, and iron, that this transformation is principally due. The stupendous advances in manufactures towards the close of the last century, with which we are all familiar, have a little overshadowed the simultaneous and parallel changes in agriculture. Yet these were of equal importance. In the middle of the last century farms were small and the method of cultivation primitive. The old system of common cultivation was still to be seen at work in a large number of parishes in the Midland counties. Rotation of crops was only imperfectly understood; the practice of growing winter roots and artificial grasses was only slowly spreading. "As for the sheep," said an old Norfolk shepherd, speaking of a still more recent period, "they hadn't such food provided for them as they have now. In winter there was little to eat except what God Almighty sent for them, and when the snow was deep on the ground they ate the ling or died off." I am tempted to give many more details in illustration of the state of agriculture, but I cannot spare the time. Let us turn to the condition of manufactures. The cotton industry, which now supports more than half a million of persons, was then oppressed by Parliament as a possible rival to older industries, and was too insignificant to be mentioned more than once, and then incidentally, by Adam Smith in the great book which contains so full and accurate a description of the England of his time. The iron industry, with which the material greatness of England has during the present century been so conspicuously associated, was gradually dying out. Much of the ore was still smelted by charcoal in small furnaces blown by leather bellows worked by oxen. And it was not a trade upon which the nation looked with complacency or pride. On the contrary, it had long been denounced by patriots as the voracious ravager of the woods which furnished timber for our warships, and pamphleteers demanded that we should import all our iron from America, where vast forests still remained to be cleared in the interests of agriculture. Not cotton and iron, but wool was considered, in those days, the great pillar of national prosperity. There were few people who doubted but that the ruin of England would follow the decay of this cherished industry, and it was only philosophers like Bishop Berkeley who, going very deep into matters, ventured to ask whether other countries had not flourished without the woollen trade.

To show you the external conditions of industrial life in the middle of the last century, I cannot, I think, do better than give a short description of the way in which wool was manufactured in the neighbourhood of Leeds—a description drawn from a singularly full and interesting account contained in the evidence taken before a Parliamentary committee. The business was in the hands of small master-manufacturers who lived not in the town but in homesteads in the fields, and rented little pasture-farms—we are especially told that clothiers who took arable farms rarely prospered—of from 3 to 15 acres in size. Most of them kept horses to carry their cloth to the Hall in Leeds where it was sold. Every master worked with his own hands, and nearly all the processes through which the wool was put—the spinning, the weaving, and the dyeing—were carried on in his own house. Few owned more than three or four looms, or employed more than eight or ten people—men, women, and children. This method of carrying on the trade was called the domestic system. " What I mean," said a witness, " by the domestic system is the little clothiers living in villages or detached places, with all their comforts, carrying on business with their own capital: every one must have some capital, more or less, to carry on his trade, and they are in some degree little merchants as well as manufacturers, in Yorkshire." There are many other facts of extreme interest, but what I have told you may be taken as a fair description of an industrial system which was not by any means peculiar to one place or to one trade.

To make my description complete I ought, perhaps, to remind

you that the manufacture of wool was not confined to one or two special districts like the neighbourhood of Leeds or the valleys of Gloucestershire and Somersetshire. A spinning-wheel was to be found in every cottage and farm-house in the kingdom, a loom in every village. And the mention of this fact brings me to another point in the economic history of this period—the extremely narrow circle in which trade moved. In many districts the farmers and labourers used few things which were not the work of their own hands, or which had not been manufactured a few miles from their homes. The poet Wordsworth's account of the farmers' families in Westmoreland, who grew on their own land the corn with which they were fed, spun in their own homes the wool with which they were clothed, and supplied the rest of their wants by the sale of yarn in the neighbouring market town, was not so inapplicable to other parts of England as we might at first imagine. If the inland trade was thus circumscribed, we shall not be surprised to find that our foreign trade was, compared with its present dimensions, on a tiny scale. There is no doubt that it was in a far smaller proportion to the home trade than at the present time. I have mentioned these facts about the area of trade, because, taken in connection with the contemporary industrial conditions, they explain to a large extent why, in those days, though there were periods of keen distress, there was no such thing as long-continued wide-spread depression of trade. Over-production —of which we hear so much as the cause of trade depressions— over-production was impossible when the producer lived next door to the consumer, and knew his wants as well as the country shoemaker of to-day knows the number of pairs of boots that are wanted in his village. And when foreign trade was so insignificant, wars and rumours of wars could exercise but little influence over the general circle of commerce. So that not only was the whole state of industry then very different, but the most complicated of all the difficulties which beset us now had not made their appearance.

I have still to give some explanation of the extreme simplicity of our productive system, and of the limited character of the inland trade. The main cause was undoubtedly the badness of communications and the high cost of carriage. Brindley had only just cut the first canal; the great bulk of goods were borne in coasting vessels. The expense of carriage was enormous—it cost forty shillings to send a ton of coals from Manchester to Liverpool—and it was as slow as it was expensive. Adam Smith tells us that it took a broad-wheeled wagon, drawn by eight horses, and attended by two men, three weeks to carry four tons of goods from London to Edinburgh. The roads—even the main roads—were often impassable. A famous traveller describes how the high road between Preston and Wigan had, even in summer, ruts four feet deep, floating with mud : and in many parts of the country the principal means of communication were tracks used by pack-horses. The hosiery manufacturers of Leicester, in the very middle of England, employed this last mode of conveyance. Was it not natural that, shut up within such narrow confines, unstimulated by wide markets and varied intercourse, manufactures advanced but slowly and inventions were rare ? During the last century there has been a series of inventions, the greatest the world has seen ; but Adam Smith expressly declares that during the three centuries preceding the time in which he wrote, only three inventions of any importance had been made in the clothing trade, the staple industry of the English people. Man's life moved on from generation to generation in a quiet course which would seem to us a dull, unvarying routine.

Such then, briefly and imperfectly described, were the external forms or conditions of industry in the middle of the last century. If now we turn to its inner life—to the relations between employers and workmen—we shall find the revolution which has taken place equally startling. The majority of employers were small masters—manufacturers like those already described, who, in ideas and habits of life, were little removed from the workmen, out of whose ranks they had risen, and to whose ranks they might return once more. There were, of course, even then capitalist employers, but on a small scale ; nor was their attitude to their workmen very different from that of the little masters in the same trade. That they were not numerous is proved by the extreme rarity of the term "capitalist" in the writings of the period ; whilst the term "manufacturer" which now denotes the employer then described the workman—a change of meaning curiously significant of the transformation in the conditions of industrial life. Few of the small masters of whom I have spoken

did not work with their own hands; and it was the common thing
for them to teach their apprentices the trade. Both the apprentices,
for whose moral education he was responsible, and the journeymen were lodged and boarded in the master's house. Between
men living in such close and continuous relations (the journeyman was hired by the year, and seldom changed his master if
he was a good one) the bonds were naturally very intimate. Nor
were these bonds loosened when the journeyman married and
lived in his own house. The master knew all his affairs, his
particular wants, his peculiarities, his resources, the number of
his children, as well as he did before. If the weaver was sick,
the master lent him money; if trade was slack he kept him on
at a loss. This state of things had its dark side, no doubt,
but that it existed there is a mass of evidence to prove. "We
consider it a duty to keep our men," said one employer.
"Masters and men," said another, "were in general so joined
together in sentiment, and, if I may be permitted to use the term,
in love to each other, that they did not wish to be separated if
they could help it." And the workmen corroborated the assertions
of the masters. "It seldom happens," said a weaver, "that the
small clothiers change their men except in case of sickness and
death." It was not uncommon for a workman to be employed
by the same master for forty years; and the migration of labourers
in search of work was small compared with what goes on in the
present day. A workman would live and die on the spot where
he was born, and the same family would remain for generations
working for the same employers in the same village. It would be
difficult to find examples of this life in England now: but were
we to cross the sea and travel to the ancient town of Nuremberg
in Bavaria, in whose quaint, narrow streets the old industrial
system still survives, we should light upon many an example.
There we should discover, for instance, a certain family of Schmidts
employed by a certain firm named Sachs, whose ancestors three
hundred years ago entered the service of that same house; the
two families are united by an indissoluble tie. Under such conditions the master busies himself with the welfare of the workman,
and the education of his children; the workman eagerly promotes
the interests of the master, and watches over the fortunes of the
house. They are not two families but one.

And this warmth of personal attachment, this close dependence of the workman on the employer, existed at the time of which I am speaking not only in manufactures, but also in agriculture. The labourer, hired by the year, and boarded and lodged in the farm-house, was a member of the farmer's household. William Cobbett, the most graphic painter of English rural life we have ever had, describes life in the farm-house as he knew it when a boy, and as it had existed many years before his time. "The farmer," he says, "used to sit at the head of the oak table along with his men, say grace to them, and cut up the meat and the pudding. He might take a cup of strong beer to himself, when they had none; but that was pretty nearly all the difference in the manner of living." If we turn to a less prejudiced observer than Cobbett, to the old Norfolk shepherd, whom I have already quoted, we shall find that he tells us the same tale. "The farmer then worked like his men, and all messed together. He hadn't much more book-learning than we shepherds, who could neither read nor write." The farmer, in fact, like the master manufacturer, hardly belonged to a different class from his labourers.

There is yet one other characteristic of industry in those days which remains for us to scrutinise. This is the network of restrictions and regulations in which it was entangled, and which exercised an important influence over both its inner and its outer life. These laws and regulations were of two kinds—first, those which expressed ideas common to both workmen and employers; secondly, those which expressed the ideas of the employers alone. To the first kind I need only just allude. The most famous of them were the regulation of trade by corporations with exclusive privileges, the law of apprenticeship, and (perhaps) the settlement of wages by Justices of the Peace. Of the second kind I must speak a little in detail, for they throw a strong light on the status of the workman at that time. Most conspicuous were the combination laws,—laws which made it illegal for labourers to combine to raise wages, or to strike. "We have no Acts of Parliament," says Adam Smith, "against combining to lower the price of work, but many against combining to raise it." And in another passage he describes a strike as generally ending "in nothing but the punishment or ruin of the ringleaders." Cobbett has said the same thing in more vehement language. "There was a turn-out last winter," he writes, after a visit to the clothiers of the west of England some half century after the period in which Adam Smith wrote, " but it was put an end to in the usual way : the constable's staff, the bayonet, the gaol." And not only was combination to raise wages illegal, but emigration from parish to parish in search of work was rendered almost impossible by the law of settlement —part of the cumbrous machinery of the old Poor Law. The web of restrictions upon the labourer's movements was completed by laws which forbade him to emigrate. These laws, which cruelly hindered the workman in his efforts to secure a livelihood, were bad ; but there were other laws directly affecting the position of the workman as a citizen which were worse. I select one example. The law of Master and Servant made breach of contract on the part of an employer a civil offence, on the part of the labourer a crime.

Now, how was it that the English statute-book was disfigured by laws which robbed the labourer as a wage-earner, and degraded him as a citizen ? The explanation, I think, is simple. Except as a member of a mob, the labourer had not a shred of political influence. The power of making laws was concentrated in the hands of the landowners, the great merchant princes, and a small knot of capitalist-manufacturers who wielded that power—was it not natural ?—in the interests of their class, rather than for the good of the people. And different as the small master-workmen were from the classes who were supreme in Parliament, they had this in common with them—they were masters ; and when disputes with their workmen arose, they did not hesitate to appeal to the legislature for a support which it was only too ready to give. Nor is the famous assertion of the great economist that, whenever Parliament attempted to regulate differences between masters and their workmen, its counsellors were always the masters, unsupported by facts. It receives lively illustration from the pen of a pamphleteer of the period, who remarks with an air of great naturalness and simplicity that "the gentlemen and magistrates ought to aid and encourage the clothier in the reduction of the price of labour, as far as is consistent with the laws of humanity, and necessary for the preservation of foreign trade."

You must not suppose, however, that the ruling classes were utterly incapable of sympathy with the people, or of playing the part of protectors. When their interests were not imperilled, or their class prejudices involved, they frequently did interpose to shield the workmen from injustice. Parliament, even in its worst days, was never entirely on the side of the masters; there were always certain kinds of oppression against which it steadily set its face. Its attitude was a mixed one. For example, if we turn to a statute of the reign of George I. which forbids combinations of workmen under penalty of three months' imprisonment with hard labour, we shall find in the very same Act clauses making it illegal for employers to pay their workmen in truck under penalty of a ten pound fine. The country gentlemen, though they regarded combinations as insurrections against the established order of society, were quite capable of seeing that payment in kind was an instrument of fraud; and the benevolence of their intentions is not affected by the fact that in the first case the penalty is a heavy, in the second a light one. It is so important to understand this double attitude of the ruling classes towards the labourers that I cannot resist illustrating it by another example, designedly selected from a later period when the "Lords of the Loom" had taken their places in the legislature by the side of the "Merchant Princes" and the country squires, but when the workmen had not yet obtained the franchise. Sir Robert Peel, father of the famous statesman, was the author of the first Factory Act of 1802, and a man of honesty and benevolence. But when asked by a Committee of the House of Commons whether he would follow up his suggestion to repeal the law of apprenticeship by a proposal to repeal the law forbidding the emigration of artisans, he answered that there was a great want of workmen at home, and that on this point legislation would be premature. Now it is well known that the law of apprenticeship was repealed on the demand of the masters against the wishes of the great mass of workmen; and it is obvious that the "true principles of commerce" urged in favour of the first, applied with equal force in favour of the second. But whilst the repeal of the first was in the interest of the masters, the repeal of the second would have been in the interest of the workpeople. We see, therefore, that the disposition of the great manufacturers towards the labourers resembled that of the country gentlemen; but it was not, on the whole, so favourable. Though in mentioning this incident I have anticipated my narrative, I have yet obtained an

excellent illustration of the point I have been striving to prove—
namely, that the position of the workman was a transitional one.
He halted half-way between the position of the serf and the position of the citizen; he was treated with kindness by those who
injured him; he was protected, oppressed, dependent.

The England I have described was the England Adam Smith
saw when he was collecting materials for his great book.[1] But in
the facts contained in the book itself are traces of the industrial
revolution which had already begun when its publication took
place. Out of many instances I will choose one. Adam Smith
remarks that wages had recently risen in the neighbourhood of
Carron; and it was at Carron that Roebuck had, in 1760, set up
the first ironworks ever established in Scotland, and succeeded in
smelting iron by pit coal—an invention which revolutionised the
iron trade. It was, however, in Glasgow itself where Adam
Smith was teaching the new science of Political Economy, that
the signs of new movement in industry were most conspicuous.
The city is described by a contemporary writer as a " perfect bee-
hive of industry," and "filled with a noble spirit of enterprise."
And it was in Glasgow that Adam Smith saw a most startling
proof of the obstacles thrown in the way of industrial originality
by the old regulations of industry. Whilst he was Professor at
the University, there came to Glasgow James Watt, the inventor
of the condensing steam-engine, anxious to set up as a mathe-
matical instrument-maker; but the Corporation of Hammermen
refused him permission, on the ground that he was neither a
burgess of the town nor had served an apprenticeship to the
trade. Fortunately, however, for Watt, he had a friend among the
Professors, by whose influence he was allowed to establish his
workshop within the University buildings, where the power of the
corporation could not penetrate. No wonder that every page of
the *Wealth of Nations* is illumined with an illimitable passion for
freedom of industry and trade. In the spirit of that book still
more than in the facts contained in it, the dawn of a new epoch is
visible. The *Wealth of Nations* is the great proclamation of the
rights of industry and trade.

Let us pause and inquire what the proclamation really meant.

[1] Compare with this and the following paragraphs a similar passage in
" Ricardo and the Old Political Economy " above, pp. 13-15.—ED.

We shall find, if we consider it closely, that it contained two assertions; first, an assertion of the right of the workman to legal equality and independence ; secondly, an assertion that industrial freedom is essential to the material prosperity of the people. The first assertion—rather implied than insisted on—reflected the political ideas of the age. It is significant that the same year which witnessed the enunciation of the industrial rights of man in the publication of the *Wealth of Nations* witnessed the enunciation of the political rights of man in the Declaration of American Independence. All around, indeed, men pointed out signs of the dissolution of the old social and political system. "Subordination," said Dr. Johnson, who could compress keen observation into pregnant sentences—"subordination is sadly broken down in this age. No man, now, has the same authority which his father had —except a gaoler." The second assertion contained in this proclamation expressed the inarticulate desire for the removal of ancient restrictions once approved by both masters and men, a desire created by the rapid growth of material prosperity. Just now I said that in the middle of the last century there was comparatively little movement of workmen from place to place; but Adam Smith's fierce attack on the law of settlement shows that migration was on the increase. The world was, in fact, on the eve of an industrial revolution; and it is interesting to remember that the two men who did most to bring it about, Adam Smith and James Watt, met, as I have mentioned, in Glasgow, when one was dreaming of the book, and the other of the invention, which were to introduce a new industrial age.

For the *Wealth of Nations* and the steam-engine (with the great inventions, like the spinning-jenny and the power-loom, which accompanied or followed it) destroyed the old world and built a new one. The spinning-wheel and the hand-loom were silenced, and manufactures were transferred from scattered villages and quiet homesteads to factories and cities filled with noise. Villages became towns, towns became cities, and factories started up on barren heath and deserted waste. I cannot stop to describe this vast revolution in detail; I must try to carry you quickly over a period of seventy years, marking as strongly as I can the principal features of the change. Rapid as the revolution was it did not come at once. In the cotton trade, for instance, first the hand-wheel was thrown away, and mills with water-frames and spinning-jennies were built on the sides of streams; then the mule was invented, which supplied the weaver with unlimited quantities of yarn, and raised his wages and increased the demand for loom-shops, causing even old barns and cart-houses hastily pierced with windows to be adapted to that purpose; finally there came the intro-duction of the power-loom, the general application of steam to drive machinery, and the erection of the gigantic factories that we see around us at the present time. By these last changes the final blow was struck at the little master, half-manufacturer half-farmer, and in his place sprang up the great capitalist employer, the owner of hundreds of looms, the employer of hundreds of men, buying and selling in every market on the globe.

The revolution, however, was not entirely due to the substitu-tion of steam for hand power in production; it was partly the result of an enormous expansion of internal and external trade. The expansion of internal trade was the effect of unparalleled improvements in the means of communication, the establishment of the canal system, the construction of new roads by Telford, and the introduction of railways. The expansion of external trade was caused by the great war of 1793, which, closing the workshops of the Continent, opened every port in Europe to English iron and cotton. We should naturally expect such radical changes to give rise to new industrial and commercial problems, and this was the case. In the literature of this period we find, for the first time, discussions of those intricate questions of over-production and depression of trade with which we are now only too familiar—questions, remember, which never embarrassed an earlier age. On these points, however, I do not intend to speak to-night. I must proceed instead to a brief examination of a subject which is perhaps the most vital of those that I have considered; I mean the effects of the revolution in the external forms of industry upon its inner life.

These effects were terrible. In the new cities—denounced as dens where men came together not for the purposes of social life, but to make calicoes or hardware, or broad cloths—in the new cities, the old warm attachments, born of ancient, local contiguity and personal intercourse, vanished in the fierce contest for wealth among thousands who had never seen each other's faces before.

Between the individual workman and the capitalist who employed hundreds of "hands" a wide gulf opened: the workman ceased to be the cherished dependant, he became the living tool of whom the employer knew less than he did of his steam-engine. The breach was admitted by the employer, who declared it to be impassable. "It is as impossible," said one, "to effect a union between the high and low classes of society as to mix oil and water; there is no reciprocity of feeling between them." The absence of any mutual affection was openly attributed to an irreconcilable antagonism of interest. "There can be no union," said the same employer, "between employer and employed, because it is the interest of the employer to get as much work as he can, done for the smallest sum possible." We know that, in the old time, in spite of the intimate relations in which masters and workmen lived, there were disputes between them; we know that there were combinations on the one side and oppression on the other; but we may be sure it would have been difficult to find a master who openly used words like these. Contrast them with the statement I quoted before: "Masters and men were in general so joined together in sentiment, and if I may be permitted to use the term, in love to each other, that they did not wish to be separated if they could help it!" Masters in the domestic system were often brutal and ignorant enough, but the quotation I have just repeated was not, let me remind you, an exaggerated description of the relations which, in many cases, actually existed between them and their workpeople.

To return to my narrative. The destruction of the old bonds between employers and workmen was not peculiar to manufactures; it came to pass in agriculture also. An agrarian as well as an industrial revolution had taken place. Scientific methods of cultivation had been substituted for unscientific; vast enclosures had been made; traces of the old three-field system of apportioning the land were fast disappearing; small farms were giving way to large. A new race of farmers, corresponding to the new race of manufacturers, had sprung into existence, who, enriched by the high prices which prevailed during the great war, changed their habits of life. The labourer ceased to be a member of the farmer's household, and, to use Cobbett's words, was thrust out of the farm-house into a hovel. Exceeding bitter was the labourer's cry. "The farmers," said one, "take no more notice of us than if we were dumb beasts; they let us eat our crust by the ditch-side."

On the part of both the artisans in the cities and the labourers in the villages lamentation at the changed attitude of their employers was intensified by the physical distress into which great masses of them had fallen. Though many of the old restrictions attacked by Adam Smith had been abolished, or had become obsolete—though the law of apprenticeship had been abolished (not, as I before said, at the demand of the labourers)—though, owing to the growth of new cities and the extension of internal trade, corporations had lost their power—though the material wealth of the country had increased with enormous rapidity (the cotton trade had trebled in fifteen years)—yet the people seemed to have little share in the wealth they produced, and large numbers of them sank deeper and deeper into destitution and misery and vice. Why was this ? There were several causes: first the old Poor Law, which stimulated increase among a degraded population, and the Corn Laws, which made bread dear and difficult to get ; secondly, the exhausting conditions of the new industrial methods ; thirdly, the fact that this was a period of transition from one mode of industry to another—all transition is painful—and that many workmen were fighting with machinery for a miserable subsistence. It would serve no good purpose to enlarge on the sufferings of the people at this time. I shall content myself with showing by the example of one industry in one place the wretchedness of those who were striving still to maintain themselves under the old system, which was being fast trodden out by the new. In Leicester and its neighbourhood, about the middle of the last century, an eye-witness describes the stocking-makers as remarkably prosperous. They had each a cottage and a garden, rights of common for pig and poultry, and sometimes for a cow, a barrel of home-brewed ale, a work-day suit of clothes and another for Sundays, and plenty of leisure. It is stated that they seldom worked more than three days a week ; but the general average in the trade was probably five. The working day was about ten hours. Nearly a hundred years later Thomas Cooper, the Chartist, returning late at night from a Chartist meeting in Leicester, and hearing as he passed along the streets, the creak of the stocking frame, and seeing lights in the upper windows, turned to his companion and said,

"What do these people earn?" ",About four and sixpence," was the reply. "You mean four and sixpence a day?" said Cooper. "No," said his friend, "four and sixpence a week." Cooper, though a workman himself, was incredulous that men who were at their frames for sixteen hours a day could receive such a wretched pittance.[1]

The misery, of which this is only one instance, was spread far and wide; and about the time Cooper was in Leicester, that is about the year 1840, things had reached a crisis. It is true that the old Poor Law had been reformed, and the great Factory Act of 1833 passed, but many thought these and all other remedies were ineffectual or too late. "All schemes of reform," said an old reformer, "are far too late to prevent the tremendous evils which I have long seen gathering around us, and for which I see no remedy." That a social revolution was inevitable was an opinion generally held. "We are engulfed, I believe, and must inevitably go down the cataract," said Dr. Arnold. Nor was this belief confined to the upper and middle classes. Even Ebenezer Elliott, the Corn-law Rhymer, declared that had he known French he would have fled to France to avoid the coming revolution for the sake of his children. Whilst many were paralysed by the conviction that a revolution was at hand, hundreds of a more sanguine temperament raised their voices to offer remedies of their own, or to denounce the remedies of others. Not a few turned round and attacked the gospel of Adam Smith and James Watt. "Liberty," said Carlyle, "liberty, I am told, is a divine thing. Liberty, when it becomes the 'Liberty to die by starvation,' is not so divine."

Of all those who assailed the new industrial world created by the *Wealth of Nations* and the steam-engine, Carlyle was the greatest; and *Past and Present*, the book in which he flung out his denunciations, is the most tender and pathetic picture of the Past, the most unsparing indictment of the Present that exists in modern English literature. "England," wrote Carlyle, "is full of wealth, of multifarious produce, supply for human wants in every kind; yet England is dying of inanition." Throwing impatiently aside such explanations of this contradiction as those at which I

[1] The account I have given of this dialogue is condensed and not quite literal; but the original is too long for quotation, though well worth reading at length in Cooper's Autobiography.

hinted a few minutes ago, Carlyle fixed his eyes on two facts which he asserted to be at the root of the nation's suffering. The first was *want of permanence.* Gazing on the ever-shifting scene of the Present; the perpetual moving to and fro of men in search of wealth; workmen breaking away from masters, and masters discarding workmen; and contrasting this with the quiet, restful Past, when men lived together in contentment whole lifetimes, and formed unbroken habits of affection; Carlyle passionately declared that, unless we could bring back permanence, those habits of affection on which our whole life rests could never more be formed, and society must fall in pieces and dissolve. " I am for permanence," he cried, " in all things, at the earliest possible moment and to the latest possible. Blessed is he that continueth where he is." And only in the restoration of the old system of employment, in the substitution of the principle of permanent contract for temporary (then every day gaining ground), did he see some faint hope for the future. " The Principle of Permanence year by year better seen into and elaborated, may enlarge itself, expand gradually on every side into a system. This once secured, the basis of all good results were laid." The second fact which Carlyle singled out as closely connected with the first was what he called the *cash-nexus*—" man's duty to man resolving itself into handing him certain metal pieces, and then shoving him out of doors "—and the contemplation of it filled him with that same immeasurable indignation and rage which he poured out upon want of permanence. " We call it a society," he writes, " and go about proposing openly the totalest separation and isolation. Our life is not a mutual helpfulness; but rather, cloaked under due laws-of-war, named fair competition and so forth, it is a mutual hostility. We have profoundly forgotten everywhere that *cash-payment* is not the sole relation of human beings; we think, nothing doubting, that *it* absolves and liquidates all engagements of man. ' My starving workers ?' answers the rich mill-owner. ' Did I not hire them fairly in the market ? Did I not pay them to the last sixpence the sum covenanted for ? What have I to do with them more ?' " Do with them more ? Carlyle would have had him do infinitely more—would have had him cherish them as human beings and not forget them as hands ; would have had him guide and protect them, help them in sickness and misfortune, and not dismiss them even when trade was bad, and profits were gone. In one word, Carlyle would have had the rich govern and protect the poor as they did in the past.

But what said the poor themselves whose cause Carlyle so eagerly pleaded? Did they accept his view? No! The poor believed that the time for government by the rich had passed; that the time had come for government by the whole people. " Give us," cried the Chartists, who represented the aspirations of the people, " give us, not government by the rich, but government by the people, not protection, but political rights—give us, in one word, our Charter, and then will this dread interval of darkness and of anguish pass away; then will that dawn come for which we have watched so long, and justice, love, and plenty inhabit this land, and there abide."

Who was right, Carlyle or the people? The people! Yes! the people were right—the people who, sick with hunger and deformed with toil, dreamed that Democracy would bring deliverance. The people were right; Democracy, so giantlike and threatening, which, with rude strength severs sacred ties and stamps out ancient landmarks, Democracy, though in ways undreamt of, did bring deliverance. For Democracy is sudden like the sea, and grows dark with storms and sweeps away many precious things; but, like the sea, it reflects the light of the wide heavens and cleanses the shores of human life.

Democracy saved industry: let us see in what way. I have already drawn your attention to the fact that on the eve of the industrial revolution there were on every side signs of political change. But the French Revolution frightened statesmen, and political reform in England was delayed for nearly half a century. Nevertheless there were in Parliament disciples of Adam Smith who strove to obtain for the workman civil equality and independence, apart from the franchise. Owing to their endeavours, the Combination Laws were repealed in 1824; but the following year proved how insecure was the position of the workman when without a vote. In 1825 the fears of the employers were powerful enough to induce Parliament, while legalising the common deliberations of workmen, to make illegal any action in which such deliberations might result, and the workmen lost nearly all they had gained the year before. But though in Parliament their cause might fluctuate, in the country their power was rapidly increasing, owing to their concentration in large cities; and the Reform Bill of 1832 was largely due to their influence. Bitter disappointment, however, followed; for the working classes found that they had only thrown additional power into the hands of their masters and the middle classes, whilst they themselves remained oppressed and fettered as before. The disappointment bore fruit in the agitation for the Charter, which assumed formidable proportions during that time of misery of which I have spoken, but died away when the repeal of the Corn-Laws restored prosperity to the nation. In the lull that followed, the workmen ceased to agitate, but they were not idle; they were quietly organising themselves; and in 1867, after a sharp struggle, the triumph came. The workmen had gained the key of the position when they obtained the suffrage. You have only to mark the results. In 1871 Trades-Unions were legalised—this is not merely a fact in the history of Trades-Unions, but in the history of English citizenship; in 1875 the law of conspiracy was abolished, and the old law of master and servant was replaced by a law putting master and servant on exactly the same footing. The workman had at last reached the summit of the long ascent from the position of a serf, and stood by the side of his master as the full citizen of a free state.

Meanwhile, during this whole period of struggle the gulf between workman and employer was becoming every day more wide. The causes of this growing estrangement were manifold; I can only mention one or two of them. First, the introduction of machine-tools, in many cases, enabled the master to dispense with a body of highly skilled mechanics; he was no longer reluctant, as in the old days, to dismiss a man whom it would be difficult, perhaps impossible, to replace. Next, Trades-Unions sprang up: and though it is essential to remember that, without these associations, giving as they did both material power and organisation to the workmen, Democracy would have been impotent to effect a solution of the labour question; yet it is equally important to recognise that by forcing the workmen to act in masses through delegates, they tore away the last remnants of personal ties between individual workmen and employers, and seemed to make their separation complete. The change was deeply regretted by the best members of both classes. " In the strike of 1859," said a master builder before the Trades-Union Commission, " men came to us who had worked at the place for thirty or forty years, and said to us—' This is the saddest day that ever happened to us in our lives, but we must go, we are bound to go.'" And as the men had, as we have seen, upbraided the masters with their changed conduct, so now the masters in their turn justly complained of the men. " There is a difference in the very behaviour of the men; some hardly address you with ordinary civility," remarked the same employer, dwelling on the altered bearing of his men after they had joined a Union. Again, though Carlyle had pleaded passionately for permanent instead of temporary engagements, short contracts became more and more the rule. Yearly hirings ceased in every industry except agriculture, where they are also beginning to disappear; and in many trades, for instance in the building and iron trades, what is called the minute system was established—a system by which men can leave and be discharged at a moment's notice. For this change also the Trades-Unions are, in the main, responsible. Yearly hirings were condemned by them as a kind of slavery, since they put the workmen in the power of the employer, and only allowed the Union to step in and defend his interests once a year, instead of every minute. And apart from the system of short contracts, which does not necessarily mean transient ties, there was a cause for separation between employer and workmen in the very constitution of modern industrial life— with its rapid migration of men from occupation to occupation, and from place to place. This is most conspicuous in a new country like America, where the whole staff of a cotton factory is sometimes changed in three years, and where the western farmer, hiring labourers for the season, seldom sees the same faces a second time. How could personal bonds exist under such conditions as these ? Not only, moreover, did the workman become more and more divided from his employer; he had, as De Tocqueville long ago pointed out, become more and more unlike him. The modern capitalist understands nothing of the details of his business. He leaves the management of his factory and the engagement and discharge of his men to a subordinate, lives in a mansion far away from the works, and knows nothing of, cares nothing for, the condition of his workpeople. Frequently the employer is not an individual but a company ; and towards a company at any rate warm personal attachment is impossible.

As the result of all these changes, the workman, divided from his employer and receiving from him no benefits, regarded him from a distance with hatred and suspicion, as the member of a dominant class. The employer divided from his workman and conferring upon him no benefit, looked upon him uneasily as the member of a subject class claiming a dangerous independence. The gulf between the two classes seemed, and to many still seems, impassable.

It is not impassable—it is bridged by Democracy, which, by making workmen and employers equal, makes union possible.

You will ask at once—Where is this union visible ? I answer, that the conditions of union—the altered disposition of both classes towards each other, the changed tone of the public press on industrial questions,—are visible everywhere; and if I cannot point to many actual unions of workmen and employers, there is one plain and palpable instance which is of extreme significance. I mean the Boards of Conciliation established at Nottingham and other towns which are not, like many other schemes, artificial expedients of the hour, but the outgrowth of a long history based upon a great principle—the full, ungrudging recognition by the employer of the workman's equality and independence.

It is not difficult to show how completely Boards of Conciliation rest upon this principle. An equal number of workmen and employers, elected by their respective classes, sit intermixed at the same table, and discuss questions of wages, and everything connected with the interests of the trade. The expenses are borne equally by both sides. What is the principle involved may be most clearly seen if we turn to Mr. Mundella's description of the opposition he encountered in establishing such boards at Nottingham and elsewhere. " My obstacle, my difficulty whenever I go to get a board formed," he complained, " is that masters have that old feudal notion, they will deal with their men one at a time : they expect the men to give up the advantages of association ; and until the masters acknowledge that the men are right in associating there is no chance, I think, of peace." Then some employers, he found, thought it would degrade them to sit at the same table with their men. Next there was suspicion on both sides. " It is impossible to describe to you," said Mr. Mundella to the Trade-

Union Commissioners, " how suspiciously we looked at each other." Finally the principle flashes full upon us in Mr. Mundella's statement of his own attitude. " We consider in buying labour we should treat the seller of labour just as courteously as the seller of coal or cotton." That is the point; that is the solution. Democracy transforms disputes about wages from social feuds into business bargains. It sweeps away the estranging class elements of suspicion, arrogance, and jealousy, and freeing the pent-up economic elements whose natural tendency is not towards division, it enables workmen and employers to take the first step to unite.

But how hard to admit that this is the solution! How reluctant we are to confess that questions of wages—questions which affect the comfort, nay the whole life-status, the health, the happiness of thousands of families—that these questions should be treated like questions about coal and cotton. How tempting to bend over the faded past with its kindly protection and willing dependence! Even Mr. Mundella himself, the originator of Boards of Conciliation, cannot help giving a pathetic, backward glance at the old industrial conditions—" we employ thousands ; we do not know their faces, they are hands to us, they are not men." For the moment he forgot that what the employer buys *is* the workman's hands and not his life; that his life is now his own, to be cherished in a noble independence.

The old system is gone never to return. The separation lamented by Carlyle was inevitable : but we can now see that it was not wholly evil. A terrible interval of suffering there was indeed when the workman, flung off by his master, had not yet found his feet : but that is passing away, and the separation is recognised as a necessary moment in that industrial progress which enabled the workman to take a new step in advance. The detested cash-nexus was a sign, not of dissolution but of growth ; not of the workman's isolation, but of his independence. If, however, Carlyle was mistaken in denouncing the revolution, he was right in proclaiming that isolation is not the permanent condition of human life. If history teaches us that separation is necessary, it also teaches us that permanent separation is impossible. The law of progress is that men separate—but they separate in order to unite. The old union vanishes, but a new union springs up in its place.

The old union founded on the dependence of the workman disappears—a new union arises based on the workman's independence. And the new union is deeper and wider than the old. For workman and employer parted as protector and dependant to unite as equal citizens of a free state.

Democracy makes union possible—creates its initial conditions —but a profounder and more delicate power can alone make it an enduring fact of social life. Though it is a mistake to attempt to bring back the old moral relations which were the product of past social conditions, it is equally a mistake to assert that questions of wages can be treated as business bargains and nothing more. In spite of a fundamental identity of interest between employers and workmen revealed by the subsidence of social strife, there always will be, there always must be, antagonisms of interest; and these can only be met by moral ideas appropriate not to the feudal, but to the citizen, stage. Men's rights will clash, and the reconciliation must come through a higher gospel than the gospel of rights—the gospel of duty; that gospel which Mazzini lived to proclaim; for not Adam Smith, not Carlyle, great as he was, but Mazzini is the true teacher of our age. He, like Carlyle, wrote a great book, *The Duties of Man*, which is the most simple and passionate statement published in this century of man's duties to God and his fellows. Mazzini was a democrat who spent his life in struggling to free his country; but he believed in liberty not as an end but as a means—a means to a purer and nobler life for the whole people. The time has come to preach this gospel : not because it is not always true, but because there are social conditions in which it is little better than a mockery to preach it. How could you preach duty to men who were conscious that they had not their rights ? " Who made it ?" said workmen speaking of the old law of master and servant. " Not we ; we had no hand in making it ; it was made by those who employ us, and by those who govern us." But now that law has been repealed ; and the bitter sense of injustice is gone. Democracy, to be praised for many things, is most to be praised for this : that it has made it possible, without shame or reluctance, to preach the gospel of duty to the whole people.

I have not come to preach that gospel to-night; but before I sit down, I would venture, from this long historical review, to draw a single practical conclusion. It is this; that we should do all that in us lies to establish Boards of Conciliation in every trade when the circumstances—economic or moral—are not entirely un-favourable. I know it is not easy to form them; and that it is difficult to maintain them may be learned in Nottingham at the present time. But, notwithstanding failures and obstacles, I believe these Boards will last: and more than that, I believe that they have in them the possibilities of a great future. If I might trust myself on the unsure ground of prediction I would point out that Boards of Conciliation may grow into permanent councils of employers and workmen, which,—thrusting into the background, but not superseding Trades-Unions and Masters' Associations—for these must long remain as weapons in case of a last appeal to force,—should, in the light of the principles of social and industrial science, deal with those great problems of the fluctuations of wages, of over-production and the regulation of trade, which workmen and employers together alone can settle. However remote such a consummation may appear—and to many it must seem remote indeed—of this I am convinced, that it is no dream, but a reasonable hope, born of patient historical survey and sober faith in man's higher nature. And it is reasonable above all in England, where, owing to a con-tinuous, unbroken history, some sentiment of mutual obligation between classes survives the dissolution of the ancient social system.

It is true indeed that, as we move in the chill and tedious round of daily work, this hope will sometimes seem to us a dream. History will grow dim, faith will die, and we shall see before us, not the fellow-citizen, but the obstinate, suspicious workman, the hard, grasping employer. Yet let us remember, even in these moments of depression, that there never has been a time when such union between classes has been so possible as it is to-day or soon will become. For not only has the law given to workman and employer equality of rights, but education bids fair to give them equality of culture. We are all now, workmen as well as employers, inhabitants of a larger world; no longer members of a single class, but fellow-citizens of one great people: no longer the poor recipients of a class tradition, but heirs of a nation's history. Nay more, we are no longer citizens of a single nation, we are participators in the life of mankind, and joint-heirs of the world's inheritance. Strengthened by this wider communion and ennobled by this vaster heritage, shall we not trample under foot the passions that divide, and pass united through the invisible portals of a new age to inaugurate a new life ?

III.

ARE RADICALS SOCIALISTS ?[1]

WHEN I had the honour of speaking at Newcastle last year, I ventured to explain that I was not a politician, but a student; and though the subject with which I have undertaken to deal is a political one, it is still as a student that I wish to address you to-night. It may be asked what business a student has to meddle with political questions in a town like Newcastle, which is so great a centre of political activity and intelligence. I acknowledge the weight of the objection, and confess that it was not without hesitation, and even fear, that I resolved to approach so formidable a subject before so formidable an audience; for I had to consider not only the character of my audience, but that of my subject—a subject full of snares and pitfalls for a person without political experience. I felt also that I lacked that minute acquaintance with the actual course of political affairs which is necessary to give reality and appropriateness to political utterance. Nevertheless I determined to face my difficulties; for I am convinced that, however deficient in many respects he may be, a student who is not devoid of the interest and passion of a citizen, ought to be able to contribute something towards the solution of such a question as I propose.

The times are troubled, old political faiths are shaken, and the overwhelming exigencies of the moment leave but small breathing-space for statesmen to examine the principles on which they found their practice. The result has been that startling legislative measures, dictated by necessity—with which no compact is to be made—have been defended by arguments in sharp contradiction to the ancient principles of those who have pressed these arguments into their service. I think this contradiction is undeniable. It is asserted in connection with the support given by Radicals to recent Acts of Parliament, not only by enraged

[1] This address was delivered in the earlier part of 1882 to audiences of workmen and employers at Newcastle, Bradford, Bolton, and Leicester.

political opponents, but by adherents of the Radical and Liberal party who have refused to abandon their allegiance to their former principles. The gravest of the charges brought against Radicals is the charge of Socialism, a system which in the past they strained every nerve to oppose. Accusations of Socialism are common enough; the *Times* once accused Mr. Cobden of inciting the peasants to seize the land and divide it in small pieces among themselves, because he advocated the abolition of entail and primogeniture; but on the present occasion the accusation has been made with a definiteness and elaboration that render it worthy of patient examination. It is not a wholesome state of things that a great party should be in doubt—as I think I am justified in saying certain sections of the Radical party are—as to the principles by which it is guided. A great party which is uncertain as to its principles ceases to be a party, and becomes an aggregate of factions without vigour or coherence.

I propose in this address first of all to show what the old Radical creed was which we are accused of silently deserting; next, to state the opinions to which it was opposed; and finally, to explain what changes this creed has undergone by the adoption of some of its opponents' principles under the pressure of external circumstances.

I shall carry you back forty years to a time of great national calamity, and seek to ascertain what Radical principles were at that time. I go back thus far for two reasons; first, because at that distance we shall be able to find Radical principles in their original purity ; and, secondly, because a period of national distress is a period in which opinions get sharply and clearly stated, and men are forced to ascend to the fountain-head, in order to see if their principles are adequate to the necessities of the time. The old Radical creed may be summed up in three words—justice, liberty, and self-help. To obtain justice and liberty they believed all classes should be admitted to the suffrage; to promote self-reliance they believed that every restriction on trade should be abolished, that labour and commerce should be as free as the winds. Two things are observable in this creed, the intense dislike of the old Radicals to State interference, and their complete faith in the people. Others might fear, they trusted the people; and nothing shook this faith,—not the wild cries of starving multitudes, not ignorant tumults, not violence. Nor was their stanch belief in the power of the people to help themselves ever weakened; nothing changed it, not even revelations of hideous suffering and degradation amongst the poorest and weakest of the labouring classes.

There was much to upset their confidence in both liberty and self-help in the circumstances of that dreadful time before the repeal of the Corn-Laws, a time which can no more be compared to the period of distress through which we are just now passing, than the sleet and hail of a winter hurricane can be compared to a summer shower. A full description of its misery is impossible in the time I have at my command; but I can tell you enough to make you understand the need that all political parties felt to do something to save the people.

This was the state of the great towns: in Manchester 12,000 families were supported by charity; 2000 families were without a bed; 5492 houses were shut up, and 116 mills and workshops idle; and it was calculated that there were 8666 persons whose weekly income was not 14½d. each. In Stockport, so many houses were untenanted, that a wag chalked up on a shutter, " Stockport to let!" There may be persons still living in Bolton who can remember a letter written by Colonel Thompson, to a paper now defunct, *The Sun*, in which he described what he called the siege of Bolton. In the year 1842 he said: " Have you ever seen a pennyworth of mutton? Come to Bolton and see how rations are dealt out under the landlord's siege" (he was alluding to the Corn Laws). " A pennyworth of mutton might bait a rat trap; but a well-fed rat would not risk his personality for such a pittance." Pennyworths of mutton and half-pennyworths of bread, that was the way in which the shopkeepers sold their goods to the inhabitants in the time of Colonel Thompson, who went about Bolton visiting the houses of the poor in company with Mr. Ashworth. One of the lecturers of the Anti-Corn-Law League reported at the time that out of fifty mills in Bolton thirty were idle, or only working four days a week, and there were 7000 people in Bolton whose average income per head was not much more than 1s. a week. There were 1500 houses empty at this time. In Leicester one-third of the workmen in the hosiery trade are said to have been out of employment. At the same time the population was huddled together in these towns in filthy dens like wild animals, and women worked like beasts of burden in the mines. The country labourers were almost worse off than the weavers of the towns ; they famished in their dark hovels ; no wonder that the skies were reddened by the flames of burning ricks. Not only was there distress, but there was tumult and anger amongst the people, the like of which we have not seen since. On the Lancashire and Yorkshire moors torch-light meetings were held and addressed by angry and vehement orators, who uttered deep threats, and incited the people to take up arms for vengeance. And not only were the poor excited, but men who by their position were secure against want were driven to despair ; to them also everything seemed too late and revolution at hand, so terrible was the distress, the suffering, and the bewilderment of that period.

What were the remedies proposed by the different parties of the day ? What did the Radicals, men like Joseph Hume, Sir William Molesworth, Cobden, Bright, Fox, and Villiers propose ? They said, " Repeal the Corn-Laws, and then all the rest will come—you will then have cheap bread and steady prices." The Corn-Laws, which sent the quartern loaf up to 1s. 10d., they declared to be at the root of the evil. But the working men, curiously enough, were not eager in their support of the Anti-Corn-Law League. They did not deny that the Corn-Laws were bad ; but they said the Corn Laws were only a bad part of a bad system. What they wanted was to get rid of the bad system ; and in order to do this the working man must have the suffrage. The working-class Radicals, such men as William Lovett, Henry Heatherington, and James Watson, set their hearts on a political measure, and demanded the passing of their Charter, including the ballot, electoral districts, annual parliaments, manhood suffrage, payment of members, and the abolition of the property qualification. There were those who said that the cry for cheap bread only meant low wages, and those who held this view went to the meetings of the Anti-Corn-Law League and tried to break them up. Ultimately the League triumphed ; but Cobden himself admitted that the workmen never heartily joined in the agitation. On the other hand, many of the middle-class Radicals supported the Charter, only they were convinced that the first thing to do was to repeal the Corn-Laws. This the Chartists denied. Lovett said, " The Corn-Laws, though highly mischievous, are only one of the effects of the great curse we are seeking to remove, and in justice we think the question of their repeal ought to be argued by the representatives of all the people." Others denounced the Anti-Corn-Law movement as a middle-class manœuvre; Thomas Cooper spoke thus : " If you give up your agitation for the Charter to help the Free-traders, they will not help you to get the Charter. Don't be deceived by the middle-classes again. You helped them to get their votes. You swelled their cry of ' the Bill, the whole Bill, and nothing but the Bill,' but where are the fine promises they made you ? Gone to the winds !—and now they want to get the Corn-Laws repealed, not for your benefit, but for their own. Cheap bread they cry, but they mean low wages. Do not listen to their cant and humbug. Stick to your Charter, you are veritable slaves without your votes." It is a mistake, however, to suppose that the genuine Chartists, men like Lovett, Heatherington, and Watson, had a mere blind belief in the suffrage ; nothing is more striking than the intelligence of their manifestoes; they argued on the true ground, " We cannot get justice until every class is represented in the State." Neither were these men advocates of violence, for though they were willing to frighten the middle-class they were not prepared to hurt them. Their real position was vividly put by a Scotch Chartist—" We must shake our oppressors well over hell's mouth, but not let them drop in ! "

But though the genuine Chartists repudiated violence, they were displaced by Feargus O'Connor and his physical force Chartists, who openly advocated it. The opinions of these men are of little interest, but associated with them were men whose opinions are of great importance; I mean, Joseph Raynor Stephens and Richard Oastler, the " Factory King," whose opinions were again closely allied to those of a distinguished man who had died a few years before, M. T. Sadler, one of the most benevolent and self-devoted of citizens. The number of these men was small, but their popular influence was immense. Stephens and Oastler, though acting with the Chartists, denied that they themselves belonged to that body. Both were orators of great power. They insisted that the ancient constitution of the realm, and the laws as they were, were sufficient to meet the difficulties of the time; they exalted the throne, and declared the powers that be to be ordained of God.

But whilst denying and attacking the Radical doctrine that political power should be confided to the people, they insisted that the Queen and her Parliament should protect and succour the people. They believed that the poor must be dependent for much of the comforts and necessaries of life upon the rich and the powerful, and were unsparing in their invective against those who neglected the people. Because the poor were weak and helpless they asserted that not only was it the duty of the rich to help them, but that the poor had a right to help, had a claim on the national wealth independent of individual merit or virtue. These men made assertions which were really as dangerous as any ever made in England. In one of Stephens' speeches he said, "The man who is without a home has a quarrel with society. A man who has no home, or a home which is not what God intended it to be, that man is robbed." Oastler also said, "If you take away the industrious poor man's right to relief" (he was speaking of the old poor-law) "all other advantages crumble into dust and become worthless." Now, if you examine these statements closely, you will find they amount to this: an assertion of an unconditional claim on the part of the people to an indefinite share in the national wealth, which is, to say the least, a most pernicious doctrine. It is to maintain that every individual has a right to a share in other men's wealth, that is, that your property and mine is not ours absolutely, but the beggar and the pauper have a right to a part of it. These men were sometimes called Tory Chartists, but they ought to have been called Tory Socialists, for their doctrine was Socialism in the most unmistakable form. The occasion of these wild assertions was the agitation against the new Poor Law of 1834, which was, although now forgotten, certainly a more popular agitation than that carried on by the Anti-Corn-Law League. The new Poor Law, while not denying the right to relief, had attached stringent conditions to the receipt of it, had, in fact, made the relief conditional in many cases on entering the workhouse—on imprisonment in a Bastille, as Stephens and Oastler called it. The old Poor Law had given relief without conditions, and had completely demoralised the people. Any one who asked for relief could get it, in any form he liked, with the result that the burden on the land had become so terrible that we read of one parish in Buckinghamshire where nearly the whole of the land had gone out of cultivation; and with a still worse effect upon the people. Family affection was stamped out, mothers threatened to leave their children out of doors if they were not paid for keeping them, children deserted their bed-ridden parents. Under this régime the idle were confounded with the honest poor, and the Poor Law was well described at the time as a national institution for the encouragement of vice and idleness and the discouragement of honesty and thrift.

Although unsuccessful in their fierce attacks upon the new Poor Law, Oastler and Stephens carried on successfully the agitation for the Ten Hours' Bill. And they conducted this agitation on the same principle as the first one—that there were certain members of society who, being unable to protect themselves, had a right to the protection of the State. It is a remarkable thing that these opinions were held also by rich men, by landowners and capitalists; they were held by one man who afterwards became Prime Minister of England. We are not accustomed to call Lord Beaconsfield a Socialist, but I think we may apply the title to his lordship without injustice. Let me show you what I mean. Lord Beaconsfield was in the habit of expressing his political opinions not in pamphlets but in novels; and about this time he published his *Sybil*, in which is contained a description of the Chartist movement, and in which an opinion exactly on all-fours with those of Oastler and Stephens is expressed. He writes, " The people are not strong; the people never can be strong. Their attempts at self-vindication will end only in their suffering and confusion," and then he goes on to show how people must rely on an aristocracy who " are the natural leaders of the people." Some think Lord Beaconsfield was not sincere, but I think he was, and his opinion as to the condition of the people and as to the state of political opinion in 1845 is of great importance. Lord Beaconsfield's practical proposals were, however, very curious, if all he could suggest was that the land-owners should set up the Maypole once more on the village greens; that they should revive the old English sports; and that they should join with the peasantry in these sports.

I have called Stephens and Oastler Socialists, and have hinted at the connection between their views and those of Disraeli—and indeed those of a far deeper thinker than Disraeli, Thomas Carlyle, were in substance the same—but there was another body of men who deliberately adopted the title of Socialists—Robert Owen and his followers. These men did not agree with either the Chartists or the Anti-Corn-Law League. They scoffed at political remedies for bettering the condition of the people, declaring that what was required were social changes. "The Chartists," wrote Owen in his *Rational System of Society*, "have been and now are beating the air, or, like Don Quixote, fighting with windmills;" political changes are useless "that do not at the same time effect social changes." The evil, according to Owen, was competition and the struggle for existence; his plan was to substitute association and brotherhood for competition. His practical scheme was to found what he called Home Colonies, associations of about 2000 or 2500, who should have property in common, who should work in common, and amongst whom the produce should be divided equally. Owen neither wished to use force nor to confiscate property; he hoped gradually to transform society by the silent force of example. Socialism with him meant not that the poor had a claim on the wealth of the rich, but voluntary associated life with common property and equal division of wealth. Some of his colonies were actually founded, but ended in failure. Owen, nevertheless, should be remembered as the first great English Socialist, and as a man who has exercised immense influence on English institutions.

I have described thus briefly the Radical creed and the opinions to which it was opposed. Now, what was the answer which the middle-class Radicals, Joseph Hume, Mill, Bright, and Cobden, gave to the various parties who opposed them? Robert Owen they ignored. To the Tory Socialists they declared: "Your system of patronage and of patriarchal government is now physically impossible. Newspapers, railways, great cities, have made the workman independent. The old system may linger on a while in country districts, but its extinction is only a question of time. You are trying to revive the habits and relations of a bygone age; but the workmen having once tasted the sweets of independence, will never go back into dependence." A still more trenchant reply to the Tory Socialists was given when the Radicals turned on the land-owners and those who supported them, and said, "Who are you who are coming forward as the protectors of the people? Why, you are the very men who have robbed and injured the people by the Corn-Laws. If you wish to prove your sincerity, repeal the

Corn and Game laws. What a suffering people requires is not benevolence, but justice." To the Chartists their answer was, "We agree with you, we think you ought to have the suffrage; but you know very well that you cannot get the suffrage except by violence. You know that the great bulk of the middle-class are not sufficiently intelligent to grant you the suffrage; and the only thing for you to do is to join us in getting the repeal of the Corn Laws, and when we have done that, we will unite, and ultimately obtain the suffrage for you." Bright added, "The principles of the charter will one day be established, but years may pass over, months must pass over, before that day arrives."

We all know that the League won. In 1846 the Corn-Laws were repealed, and much of what the League had prophesied came true. Cheap bread did not mean low wages, as many of the Chartists had supposed, and bread from that time was not only cheaper but steadier. The Chartists seemed baffled and beaten, yet as time went on certain portions of the Charter were realised. The result of the repeal of the Corn-Laws and of Free-Trade was to restore material prosperity to the people, while the repeal of other duties, such as the stamp-duty on newspapers, and the paper duties, for which Watson and Heatherington struggled, brought knowledge within the reach of the masses. The working men obtained the suffrage in 1867, and it is noticeable that as soon as they exercised it, many of those laws which pressed most heavily on their class, and which were most iniquitous, were repealed. The law which made Trade-Unions illegal was repealed in 1871, and the cruel law of conspiracy in 1875. And mark the effect on the relations between workmen and employers. The workmen, ceasing to look upon the employers as the authors of unjust laws, are prepared to treat with them, and the employers, forced by granting the workmen the suffrage to recognise their independence, are in their turn prepared to meet them as equal citizens of a free State, and the consequence is that, with varying success, Boards of Conciliation and Arbitration have taken the place of the brute method of settling trade disputes by lockouts and strikes. The further points of the Charter which have been obtained are the ballot and the abolition of property qualification; some points still remain to be carried out. We have yet to assimilate the borough and county franchise, and to obtain free-trade in land. We have yet to consider the reform of the House of Lords, or, some prefer to say, its abolition, and not far off looms the possibility of universal suffrage.

But while such measures as free-trade and the extension of the franchise are generally esteemed great and solid gains to the community, while the improvement and prosperity to which I have alluded is generally acknowledged, there are men who watch the course of events and draw different conclusions from them. These are not fanatics nor Socialists. They are thinking men, and men learned in the economic history of England; and they see in the history of the country for the last forty years nothing but a preparation for revolution. They confront us with the declaration that the very things of which I speak, Free-Trade and Democracy, are bringing society to the verge of it. They point out that Free-Trade, whilst it has made some things cheaper, has also led to a concentration of wealth into fewer and fewer hands, and they say, "While you have been doing this you have had the extraordinary audacity to diffuse political power." Wealth is in the hands of the few rich, the suffrage in the hands of the many poor; in the concentration of wealth and the diffusion of political power lies the great danger of modern society. The danger becomes every day greater, and democracy, which seemed to save society, is really destined to overturn it.

Men like Karl Marx and Lassalle, the German Socialists, contend that it is impossible for working men under the present conditions of private property and competition, to raise themselves above the level of bare subsistence, and they say that Mr. Gladstone, the present Prime Minister, has expressed the same opinion. Mr. Gladstone, in his Budget speech of 1864, after having dwelt on the enormous growth of wealth in the country, said, speaking of the distress of the working classes in the large towns, "What is human life, in the great majority of instances, but a mere struggle for existence?" There are some who point to this contradiction with grim satisfaction, who, whilst ridiculing what they call political democracy, yet see in the diffusion of political power a means by which a social revolution can be achieved. Without this, they say, the workman can never better his condition, he is a slave to "the brazen law of wages." They describe vividly the gradual rolling together of huge masses of capital, whilst at its feet lie masses of workmen living in penury though in nominal independence. In the end, they say, the people will arise, and the present social system with its slavery be swept away. Some declare that the ground beneath us is already undermined. Nay, some go further, and whisper that the catastrophe, if we did but know it, is at hand. I am reminded of an incident in the siege of Sebastopol. One calm moonlight night the sentinels of the allied armies suddenly saw a vast column of smoke shoot high into the air from the Mamelon Tower, spread over the heavens, and cast acres of black shadow over the sleeping camps. Another minute, and those slumbering hosts were aroused by the roar and thunder of a great explosion. So some keen-eyed watchers believe that they can see the shadow of a great convulsion stealing over the sleeping nations, soon to be awakened by a crash that will shake all Europe.

Is the conclusion of the German Socialists a correct one? We in England smile at all this as a mere dream, so remote does revolution seem from our slow course of even progress. But if it is remote, it is because we in England have taken steps to modify the conditions which make revolutions imminent. If we can rightly smile at such pictures it is because we have developed among artisans and labourers vast voluntary societies wielding masses of capital, and have partially realised the Socialist programme. There are two great agencies which have been at work in England to produce that result: First, those voluntary agencies, the result of the self-help in which Radicals believe; and secondly, the action of the State in which Socialists believe.

Let us see how far the efforts of the people themselves have been sufficient to mitigate that inequality of conditions and of material wealth of which the Socialists speak. Let us see what the working classes, oppressed as they are described to be, have been able to save. In the savings banks last year there was £78,000,000, not wholly, but for the most part deposited by the working classes; in friendly societies, exclusively working class savings, £12,000,000; building society investments amounted to £31,000,000; and in co-operative societies there was £6,500,000. Allowing for other savings of which I can obtain no estimate this makes a total of about £128,000,000,—a very large sum to have been saved by men " struggling for existence." I contend that if the workmen were only able to obtain a bare subsistence they would not have been able to save. Again, there are the Trades-Unions formed for the purpose of confronting the power of these ever-increasing accumulations of capital, and these too are possessed of great funds. All this has been done by self-help; and when we come to consider what has been done by the State, we find curiously enough that some of the things the Socialists of Germany and France are now working for, we have had since 1834. The new Poor Law was based upon a recognition of the principle that the poor had a right to relief from the State, a doctrine attacked by the Radicals, but which others say has saved England from revolution; and our Factory Acts are also Socialism. They interfere to protect the weak, and not only women and children but also men, regulating not only the sanitary conditions of factories but also the working hours.

Now, who really initiated these movements, and who opposed them? Robert Owen was the founder of co-operation, and let us be candid and confess that the Radicals of that time derided it. The same was the fact as regards Trades-Unions. The Radicals had an exclusive belief in individual enterprise, and these movements they considered as infringements upon individual right. As an instance, Richard Cobden spoke very strongly against Trades-Unions as likely to become tyrannous. These are his words: "Depend upon it, nothing can be got by fraternising with Trades-Unions. They are founded upon principles of brutal tyranny and monopoly. I would rather live under a Dey of Algiers than a Trades Committee!" Dr. Arnold called them "gangs of conspirators;" but while some at home have thus condemned them as agents of revolution, foreign writers, like Lange and Brentano, have hailed them as averters of revolution.

Again, who passed the factory legislation? Not the Radicals; it was due to Owen, Oastler, Sadler, Fielden, and Lord Shaftesbury, to Tory-Socialists and to landowners. And let us recognise the fact plainly, that it is because there has been a ruling aristocracy in England that we have had a great Socialist programme carried out. This may seem a paradox, but it is not. The explanation is simple. The landowners always have—when their own interests were not concerned—attempted, in a rough and blind sort of way, to do justice to the people; and factory legislation harmonised more with their notions of the people's dependence than with the Radical manufacturers' idea of the people's independence. Next, from their position, they had a stronger feeling about protecting the people than these manufacturers ever had ; they had an idea of duty connected with their position. The claim made once by Lord John Manners to this effect is not altogether false. The landowners, like all men possessed of power for a long period, have had noble traditions as to its exercise, and where their own interests were not touched, they tried to use their power for the good of the people. They believed not only that the poor were, but ought to be, in a state of dependence ; but they recognised at the same time their consequent duties towards the poor. Cobden was right : the supremacy of the landowners, which has been the cause of so much injustice and suffering, has also been the means of averting revolution. If they robbed the peasant of his land, they gave him the right to relief from the land ; if they passed the Corn-Laws, they also secured the passing of the Factory Acts. I tremble to think what this country would have been without the Factory Acts. Let us do justice to the landowners of England even if there mingled in their action an unworthy motive—that of taking their revenge upon the capitalists and millowners of Lancashire for their repeal of the Corn-Laws. And abroad, these Acts, passed by Tory country gentlemen, are looked upon as Socialistic.

Let us now come to the last and most startling piece of Socialistic legislation—the Irish Land Bill of 1881. When we examine the debates on this bill we find that the Radicals and Tories have completely changed places. The reason for it is this : the Tories felt that the whole basis of their power was being touched when the land was meddled with ; before it was only a question of capital, now it was a question of land. It is a striking fact that many of the arguments used in the House of Commons by members of the Government in support of the Land Bill are almost exactly parallel to the arguments formerly used by men like Mr. Sadler in favour of the Factory Laws. They even used some of the illustrations employed in discussing the Poor Laws, dwelling upon the fundamental principle that there is no freedom of contract between men who are unequal. "The boasted freedom of our labourers in many pursuits," said Mr. Sadler in 1832, "will, in a just view of their condition, be found little more than nominal." " People forget the condition of society, the unequal division of property, or rather its total monopoly by the few; leaving the many nothing whatever but what they can obtain by their daily labour; which very labour cannot become available for the purpose of daily subsistence without the consent of those who own the property of this community, all the materials, elements, call them what you please, on which labour is bestowed, being in their possession." The Radicals now use arguments like Sadler's, and they are right. Let me insist that the principle of the Irish Land Act is not retrograde but progressive. That Act marks not only an epoch in the history of Ireland, but also in the history of democracy. It means—I say it advisedly—that the Radical party has committed itself to a Socialist programme. I do not mean the Socialism of the Tory Socialists; I do not mean the Socialism of Robert Owen; but I mean that the Radicals have finally accepted and recognised the fact, which has far-reaching applications, a fact which is the fundamental principle of Socialism, that between men who are unequal in material wealth there can be no freedom of contract.

The material inequality of men under the present social conditions is a fact. The Poor Law, factory legislation, Trades-Unions, may lessen the pressure of the strong upon the weak; savings banks, building societies, co-operation, may lessen the inequality of wealth; the power of the stronger may never be fully exercised, but be modified by custom, by public opinion, by benevolence—it is well not to forget the noble generosity of English landowners, and Irish, in the times of the Famine; economic causes, such as the fall of interest and of rent, may be at work to mitigate the inequality of condition; yet, notwithstanding all, this fact remains, and the maxims which Radical Socialists have founded on this fact are these: First, that where individual rights conflict with the interests of the community, there the State ought to interfere; and second, that where the people are unable to provide a thing for themselves, and that thing is of *primary social importance*, then again the State should interfere and provide it for them.

Having definitely accepted this principle, we may now ask what further application of it is necessary? I have no intention to sketch a new Radical programme, but in order to bring the principle to a definite issue, I will apply it to one matter of urgent importance—the dwellings of the people, a subject upon which it is difficult to understand why so little is said.[1] The importance of the *home* it is impossible to exaggerate. What is liberty without it ? What is education in schools without it ? The greatness of no nation can be secure that is not based upon a pure home life. But is a pure home life possible under present conditions for the bulk of the labouring class ? I answer, No. I do not deny that artisans have good dwellings in many towns, but I assert that the dwellings of the great mass of the people are a danger to our civilisation. It is not necessary to describe what has been so often described before; the dark dens into which the sun can never penetrate, the noisome air, the rotten floors, the broken roof through which the rain beats and the wind,—we know them all too well. Why do we sit still and quietly behold degradation worse than that from which we have rescued women and children in mines and factories ? Why are we content to see the sources of national life poisoned ? I believe it is because we think this condition of things inevitable. But if only we had the courage to stamp it out, I believe it is not so. People have no idea of the universality of the evil. It is recognised perhaps in such great cities as London or Liverpool, but take a quiet cathedral town in the south of England, and listen to some of the facts about dwellings there. Perhaps the description of one house will suffice : it has four rooms, the largest 11 ft. by 9 ft., and 8 ft. by 5 ft. 10 in. At the time to which my report refers, the drain underground was stopped up ; there was a perceptibly offensive smell; the upper rooms let in the rain; the staircase was rotten; one child had died recently, and the woman had been ill ever since she was in the house. The landlord had been complained to, and had made improvements,—that is, had pasted paper over the holes in the door. The medical officer had ordered drainage, but of this nothing had been done. Rent, 3s. 6d. a week. The gentleman from whom my information is derived purchased the house, and found that the former owner had made nearly fifty per cent. per annum on his purchase-money. No wonder that a Fair Rent Society has been founded among householders.

What means have we of grappling with the problem ? First,

---

[1] This was spoken more than a year before the discussion of the question in the public press, and the consequent action taken.—ED.

we might reform our local government. We have now inequality of local taxation, and sanitary laws and Building Acts are not enforced, because sanitary officers are not independent, and because local authorities would have to bear the expense. Further, the representation of workmen upon all Boards and Town-Councils should be insisted on. Next, we know what can be done by private enterprise. Building societies are stated to have investments to the amount of £31,000,000. Mr. T. M. Sadler, the Registrar, tells me that, in 1881, 237 were registered. The Artisan's Dwellings' Company in Newcastle had, in 1879, 108 tenements. In London, after forty years' efforts, improved industrial dwellings have been provided for 60,000 people. But, notwithstanding all such voluntary agencies, the evidence is clear that it is scarcely possible to furnish decent dwellings for the very poor at a remunerative price. The average weekly wage of the occupants of the Peabody buildings is £1, 3s. 10d.; that of the occupants of the houses of the Improved Industrial Dwellings' Company, 28s., of a whole family, 35s. to 40s. The circumstances of different localities differ, and I am perfectly aware that, in some manufacturing towns, artisans have often been able to buy houses and provide for themselves, but it was distinctly admitted by the Home Secretary that nothing could be done for the poorest class without State assistance; and the witnesses examined before the Committee on the Artisans' Dwellings Act of 1875 nearly all declared that the great mass of labourers cannot be provided with decent houses at a remunerative price.

Well, what are we to do? I do not hesitate to say the community must step in and give the necessary aid. These labourers cannot obtain dwellings for themselves; municipalities, or the State in some form, should have power to buy up land and let it below the market value for the erection of decent dwellings. It will be objected, "Why, this is rank Socialism!" Yes, it is. Mr. Waddy was denounced as a Communist for making such a suggestion once in the House. But the principle is only the principle of the Poor Law, and, if we look closely into the matter, we shall find that, as usual in England—where practice always precedes theory—the thing is already done. In London, the Peabody Trustees keep their interest at three per cent. gross, thirty or forty per cent. below that of other companies, and house 10,000 people. Land-

owners in the country building cottages, will tell you that no
cottage pays more than two per cent. Here are examples of
houses let below market value, and without the demoralisation of
their occupants. I believe we could make no better investment
of national capital. A higher standard of comfort would be
reached, and improved habits of living established among the
people; a great diminution in pauperism, drunkenness, and crime,
would inevitably follow.

But would not this be class legislation which Radicals have
always opposed? No, because it would be in the interest of the
whole community. We cannot call ourselves safe until all citizens
have the chance of living decent lives; the poorest class need to
be raised in the interest of all classes. But would it not diminish
self-reliance? No, I conceive of it as a help towards doing without help. It is doing for the people what they cannot do for
themselves, that they may thus gain a position in which they shall
not need assistance. Radicals are as keenly alive as ever to the
necessity for self-reliance; I would say, abolish outdoor relief
under the Poor Law, because outdoor relief lowers wages, degrades
the recipient, and diminishes self-reliance; I would have this
done with workmen themselves sitting as Poor-Law guardians.

In conclusion, I would ask what is the difference between
the Socialism of which I have spoken, Tory Socialism, and the
Socialism of the Continent? The Radical creed, as I understand
it, is this: We have not abandoned our old belief in liberty,
justice, and self-help, but we say that under certain conditions the
people cannot help themselves, and that then they should be
helped by the State representing directly the whole people. In
giving this State help, we make three conditions: first, the matter
must be one of primary social importance; next, it must be proved
to be practicable; thirdly, the State interference must not diminish
self-reliance. Even if the chance should arise of removing a great
social evil, nothing must be done to weaken those habits of individual self-reliance and voluntary association which have built up
the greatness of the English people. But—to take an example of
the State doing for a section of the people what they could not do
for themselves—I am not aware that the Merchant Shipping Act
has diminished the self-reliance of the British sailor. We differ from
Tory Socialism in so far as we are in favour, not of paternal, but

of fraternal government, and we differ from Continental Socialism because we accept the principle of private property, and repudiate confiscation and violence. With Mazzini, we say the worst feature in Continental Socialism is its materialism. It is this indeed which utterly separates English Radical Socialists from Continental Socialists—our abhorrence and detestation of their materialistic ideal. To a reluctant admission of the necessity for State action, we join a burning belief in duty, and a deep spiritual ideal of life. And we have more than an abstract belief in duty, we do not hesitate to unite the advocacy of social reform with an appeal to the various classes who compose society to perform those duties without which all social reform must be merely delusive.

To the capitalists we appeal to use their wealth, as many of their order already do, as a great national trust, and not for selfish purposes alone. We exhort them to aid in the completion of the work they have well begun, and, having admitted the workmen to political independence, not to shrink from accepting laws and carrying out plans of social reform directed to secure his material independence.

To the workman we appeal by the memory and traditions of his own sufferings and wrongs to be vigilant to avoid the great guilt of inflicting upon his fellow-citizens the injustice from which he has himself escaped. We call upon him to reform his own social and domestic life,—to put down drunkenness and brutal violence. Decent habitations and high wages are not ends to be sought for their own sake. High wages—now at least—are often a cause of crime. Material prosperity, without faith in God and love to our fellow-men, is as little use to man as earth to the plants without the sun.

I repeat, we demand increased material‘ welfare for those who labour with their hands, not that they may seize upon a few more coarse enjoyments, but that they may enter upon a purer and a higher life. We demand it also that the English workman may take his part worthily in the government of this country. We demand it in order that he may have the intelligence and the will to administer the great trust which fate has committed to his charge ; for it is not only his own home and his own country that he has to govern, but a vast empire—a duty unparalleled in the annals of democracy. We demand it, I say, in order that he, a citizen of this inclement island, washed by dark northern seas, may learn to rule righteously the dim multitudes of peasants who toil under the fierce light of tropical suns, in the distant continent of India. We demand that the material condition of those who labour shall be bettered, in order that, every source of weakness being removed at home, we, this English nation, may bring to the tasks which God has assigned us, the irresistible strength of a prosperous and united people.

THE EDUCATION OF CO-OPERATORS.[1]

ALL co-operators follow their great founder in denouncing individualism and the principle of competition; but I have recently observed among some social reformers a certain impatience and distrust of that opposite principle of association to which co-operators have so long looked for the ultimate regeneration of our social system. Though we may not attach much importance to this feeling, we cannot deny its existence. We recognise it in sarcastic descriptions of the motley throng of societies which jostle each other in modern civilisation, from societies for the salvation of souls and the spread of the gospel among the heathen, down to associations for the reform of bread, the promotion of early rising, and the burial of dead cats! It is hinted in these descriptions that most modern societies are trivial and ridiculous, or mere vexatious impediments to healthy individual action; and a comparison is sometimes instituted between them and the mediæval guilds, much to their disadvantage. The criticism is not entirely undeserved, nor the contrast entirely false. Putting aside great commercial companies, which are avowedly associations of capital trading for profit, we must, I think, admit that a large number of modern organisations are simply aggregates of money, with trivial or transient objects, instead of being, like the mediæval guilds, living groups of men animated by common principles of religious and industrial faith, and united for the satisfaction of the great permanent needs of human life.

I shall not here pause to consider the reason of this difference, but the comparison and the criticism will be of value if they lead us to ask what is the real function of the innumerable associations of the present age. A careful examination will prove that though not a few are useless and ridiculous, the majority of them are the legitimate products of the extraordinary variety of men's wants

[1] This paper was read before the Co-operative Congress held at Oxford in May 1882.

and aims, which, under the complex conditions of modern social life, it is beyond the power of the individual to satisfy or achieve. The Animals Necropolis Company, to which I have alluded, seems at first sight to be properly included under those societies which are foolish and useless, but it is in reality a fair if quaint illustration of the truth of the assertion I have just made. The tenderness for animals as companions, the crowding together of dwellings in great cities without a foot of vacant space, the strictness of modern sanitary regulations, are facts which explain and justify the existence of a society so apparently repugnant to common sense. I must resist the temptation which here presents itself to trace the genesis of other forms of existing associations, and content myself with drawing your attention to one singular fact, viz., that a considerable number of them are the direct creation of that State interference against which many co-operators entertain a generous prejudice. For this activity of modern legislation, which some co-operators censure, has strengthened, and not weakened the sense of moral responsibility and habits of voluntary co-operation. For example, the laws which punish the adulteration of food called into existence societies of master bakers, and of vendors of milk, to enforce the penalties against fraudulent tradesmen, and the laws which punish cruelty to animals gave birth to a society for the prosecution of offenders, thus rendering possible the effective expression of a moral sentiment which would otherwise have fretted in impotence.

If now we turn from modern associations in general to the consideration of workmen's societies, we shall find that though their aims cannot be described as transient or trivial, yet they too are in character usually aggregates of money limited to a single object, and making no attempt to embrace the whole of human life. Building societies facilitate the purchase of dwellings. Friendly societies make provision for sickness and death. Trades-Unions have rather a wider scope, and seem more nearly to resemble mediæval guilds in character and purpose. To the outward eye co-operative societies are smaller things than Trades-Unions and of slighter significance. Their aims—the promotion of thrift and the reduction of the cost of living—appear narrow and uninteresting; their energies seem entirely absorbed in the purchase of chests of tea and sacks of flour, and the ordinary coarse necessaries of daily life. Nor are their members (I think) in such close contact as those of a Union; the majority of them are often as unknown to each other as the shareholders in a great railway, and there are few opportunities of intercourse besides the quarterly meetings or the managing committee. A deeper scrutiny, however, shows that though not endowed with the fervent united life of the mediæval guilds, co-operative societies, by the possession of large ideals, approach nearer to them in reality than do Trades-Unions, which have a closer outward resemblance. I do not mean to disparage Trades-Unions, nor to assert that they have not moral aims because they have not large ideals; but I am inclined to think that the spirit which breathes in the fine inscription on the banner of the Glovers of Perth in the seventeenth century, "The perfect honour of a craft or beauty of a trade is not in wealthe but in moral worth, whereby virtue gains renowne," is more characteristic of co-operative societies than of any association formed in any particular modern trade. Trades-Unions which accept the facts of the present industrial system, and are engaged in a hand-to-hand fight with capitalists, have no time to indulge in dreams that are natural to bodies of men whose aim is the radical transformation of the entire conditions of industrial life.

For we know that, however seemingly immersed in the petty business of the shop co-operators may be, their real aim and their real determination is to put an end to competition and the division of men into capitalists and labourers—an aim and determination which again remind us of the mediæval guilds, where labour and capital were associated, and competition held in abhorrence. It is this large spirit, this resolute refusal to accept the present state of society as final, which marks off co-operation from all other movements, and gives to it an interest which is unique. I know it is said that "the one loud and universal shout of social regeneration," raised by Robert Owen, has, not only to the undiscerning ear but in reality, sunk into a mere debate about dividends; but this we will not allow to be true. The ideal of Robert Owen had to run the course of other ideals; it had to die that it might live. "That which thou sowest is not quickened except it die;" the co operative ideal had to be cast into the soil of material prosperity, in order that it might spring up into a new and more powerful life. The very fact that the subject I have to discuss to-day is the subject of education shows that the ideal is quickened, and is taking practical shape.

It may, however, be fairly asked why I have devoted so much time to the discussion of the general aim of co-operation, and the difference between mediæval and modern societies, instead of proceeding at once to consider the subject assigned to me? I reply that, as a matter of fact, directly I began to deal with that subject I found myself forced to determine what the exact work of co-operative societies is among the crowd of associations that catch our eye on every side; and my inquiry at least brought out one point very clearly, namely, that though they differ from other societies by the possession of an ideal aim, yet they do not attempt to cover the whole range of human life. Now if this be true, it is obvious that co-operation can only claim a part of education as its province, and that my business is to ascertain what that part should be.

The absence of any definite conception on this point will perhaps explain the hesitating and uncertain action of co-operators in regard to education and the small fraction of money they have hitherto devoted to it. Seeing that education is the function, not of one but of many associations, co-operators have had difficulties in deciding what their exact relation to it ought to be. Elementary education is provided by the State; intermediate education is met by the old foundations in their reformed character, and by the new high schools; what is called the higher education will be one of the principal functions of the university colleges which are springing up in the great towns. No one proposes that co-operators should venture to grapple with the seven times heated problem of religious education: that task must be abandoned to the Churches; but the fact that it is impossible for co-operators to adopt a distinct religious creed is again a point of difference between them and the mediæval guilds which is of deep significance. As regards technical education, it at first sight might seem admirably fitted for co-operators to undertake, but I believe it will be found that technical schools established by employers or by Government for each particular trade will do the work far better than could societies whose members are drawn from every trade.

What part of education then is left for co-operators to appro-

P

priate? The answer I would give is, the *education of the citizen*. By this I mean the education of each member of the community, as regards the relation in which he stands to other individual citizens, and to the community as a whole. But why should co-operators, more than any one else, take up this part of education? Because co-operators, if they would carry out their avowed aims, are more absolutely in need of such an education than any other persons, and because if we look at the origin of the co-operative movement we shall see that this is the work in education most thoroughly in harmony with its ideal purpose.

We all know what the circumstances were under which co-operation arose, and a hurried glance at the main features of the great industrial revolution of a hundred years ago will be sufficient to remind us of the nature of the problem with which Robert Owen had to grapple. The slowly dissolving framework of mediæval industrial life was suddenly broken in pieces by the mighty blows of the steam-engine and the power-loom. With it disappeared, like a dream, those ancient habits of social union and personal affection which had lingered on in the quiet homesteads where master and apprentice worked side by side at the loom and in the forge. Industry was dragged from cottages into factories and cities; the operative who laboured in the mill was parted from the capitalist who owned it; and the struggle for the wealth which machinery promised withered the old bonds of mutual trust, and made competition seem a new and terrible force. Of the innumerable evils which prevailed in this age of confusion, Owen fixed his eyes on two—isolation and competition: and to restore the ideas of brotherhood and citizenship, which had been trampled under foot, he proposed the formation of self-complete communities, with property in common, and based upon the principle of equal association and the pursuit of a moral life. The societies actually formed were not successful, but the aim of their founder is still the aim of the co-operative societies of the present day. Their task, however, is a more difficult one than Owen's, for whilst he bade men retire from the world and regain the idea of brotherhood in the life of small independent communities, co-operators are content that men should remain in the world, and seek to make them good citizens of the great community of the English people. Owen, in fact, would have replaced the isolation of individuals by the isolation of groups, which was to go back instead of to advance. The compact, close-knit life of the towns and guilds of the middle ages had to be broken up in order that the inhabitants of this island might become one nation. A great writer who brooded over the same problem that filled the mind of Robert Owen has cast a glance of regret upon the life of which the mediæval castle was the centre; but the isolation typified by the mediæval castle was infinitely greater than that suggested by the long rows of artisans' dwellings upon which its ruins look down, for it was the isolation of men united in close bonds by the spirit of aggression and the fear of violence; and it is the disappearance of the evils that produced union in the past which makes possible the seeming estrangement in which men now live. That estrangement is the price we have paid for national life and for individual independence; the problem for us is not to re-create union at the cost of national life, but to reconcile the union of individuals with national life; not to produce union at the cost of independence, but to reconcile union with independence.

Further, the workman is now not only independent, he shares likewise in the government of the State; yet at the very time that this responsibility is laid upon him he has entered upon conditions of industrial life which seem to exhaust his energies and dull his intelligence. A law of political development has slowly raised him from the position of a serf to that of a citizen; a law of industrial development has degraded him, by division of labour, from a man into a machine. These are the difficulties we have to face: the complicated character of modern citizenship and the deadening effect of minute subdivision of labour; and these it is which make the education of which I speak, the education of the citizen in his duties as a citizen, indispensable.

I shall draw, only in outline, a scheme for such citizen-education, it being my desire to prove to co-operators that they should undertake this work, rather than to discuss in detail what such education should be. The following is a sketch of the principal subjects which ought to be dealt with:—

I. *Political Education.*—1. A description of existing political institutions in England, local and central. 2. The history of these political institutions in England. 3. The history of political ideas, as found in the great writers, such as Burke or De Tocqueville.

4. The political relations of England to other countries and to her colonies.

II. *Industrial Education.*—1. A description of the present industrial system in England, and the main causes of the production and distribution of wealth.   2. A history of industrial institutions, *e.g.* the mediæval guilds, the Poor-Law, and Trades-Unions.   3. A history of the material condition of the working classes.   4. The history of social ideas, and of schemes of social reform.

III. *Sanitary Education.*—The duties of citizens in relation to the prevention of the spread of disease.

You will observe that the whole scheme is framed, not with reference to the education of the individual man, but of the *citizen*, with a view of showing what are his duties to his fellow-men, and in what way union with them is possible.   The mere vague impulse in a man to do his duty is barren without the knowledge which enables him to perceive what his duties are, and how to perform them ; and it seems to me that only through associations like yours can an efficient citizen-education be given to the great masses of the working people.   Men who still dream of the reconstruction of industrial life by the union of capital and labour will recognise at once that this education is the necessary preliminary to any such attempt.

Several objections to the proposal will, however, occur to every one.   Is there not a danger of political science being made a vehicle of partisan virulence ?   Is there not a danger that the attempt to deal with the perilous passing questions of the hour may sow division amongst co-operators?   I answer that it is no doubt difficult to handle the sensitive living interests of human beings in the same neutral and disinterested spirit in which it is so easy to approach the facts of physical science.   But just because the matter requires a larger spirit than that of men swayed by the ordinary petty considerations of a party or a class, is it one which co-operators, who seek to win such a spirit, should be eager to undertake.   It is for them, above all others, to prove that men's deepest interests are not the peculiar possession of factions and parties, but the rightful inheritance of every citizen.

But again, it may be objected, that even if co-operators were willing to adopt such subjects as part of their education, there are few teachers with the requisite impartiality of mind and width of knowledge. I do not think this objection a weighty one. In the ranks of co-operators themselves, and in the Universities, there are, I am convinced, persons who have studied political and social questions with all the keenness of partisans, but without their prejudice. The fact that these men will often, of course, have reached definite practical conclusions will not destroy their influence as scientific teachers. Another objection is that the expense of providing lecturers of this stamp would be greater than co-operators would be willing to incur. I do not deny that the cost might be considerable, but I think that if you adopt the suggestion thrown out by Professor Stuart, in his address at Gloucester (p. 23), that a Central Board should appoint lecturers to certain districts within which they should move from town to town, you would reduce the cost to a sum which co-operators ought not to grudge.

The greatest obstacle, in my opinion, to the success of the plan would not be the difficulty of finding competent teachers nor the greatness of the expense, but the apathy of co-operators themselves in the acquisition of knowledge. The difficulty of persuading workmen to listen to anything which does not concern pleasure or profit has long been acknowledged, and is, I think, even stronger than it used to be. Let me give you an example from the writings of one who was himself a workman, and spent the best years of his life in ardent and daring advocacy of the workman's cause. Speaking of the eager groups of artisans who could be seen discussing political questions forty years ago, Thomas Cooper remarks, with bitterness, in his autobiography : " *Now* you will see no such groups in Lancashire. But you will hear well-dressed working men talking, as they walk with their hands in their pockets, of 'co-ops.,' and their shares in them, or in building societies. And you will see others, like idiots, leading small greyhound dogs, covered with cloth, in a string ! They are about to race, and they are betting money as they go ! And yonder comes another clamorous dozen of men, cursing and swearing, and betting upon a few pigeons they are about to let fly ! As for their betting on horses—like their masters !—it is perfect madness. . . . Working men had ceased to think, and wanted to hear no thoughtful talk; at least, it was so with the greater number of them." We may, perhaps, allow something for the disposition of an old man to praise the generation to which he belonged, but I am sure that there are many workmen who could give similar evidence. Of course one explanation is, that workmen are less eager now about political and social questions, because they are more prosperous, and this is the danger co-operators have to meet —the danger that material comfort may diminish spiritual energy. We ought, moreover, in fairness, to recognise that it is not unnatural for men wearied by long hours of monotonous toil to indulge in sports and coarse amusements; that for them to devote their scanty leisure to intellectual exertion requires extraordinary efforts. But if political progress is not to end in political degradation, the efforts must be made. Languor can only be conquered by enthusiasm, and enthusiasm can only be kindled by two things: an ideal which takes the imagination by storm, and a definite intelligible plan for carrying out that ideal into practice. The plan I have ventured to hint at in this paper; the ideal is yours by inheritance—it is nothing less than that of brotherhood and a perfect citizenship. We have abandoned, and rightly abandoned, the attempt to realise citizenship by separating ourselves from society; we will never abandon the belief that it is yet to be won amid the press and confusion of the ordinary world in which we move. If, however, this great task is to be accomplished, if co-operators are to arrive at a correct solution of the social problems which are every day becoming more grave, if workmen are to rightly exercise the unparalleled political power of which they have become possessed, then they must receive a social and political education such as no other institutions have offered, and which I believe co-operative societies, by their origin and their aims, are bound to provide.

THE IDEAL RELATION OF CHURCH AND STATE.[1]

I.

The State and Freedom.—Plato's Republic is the ideal of a Greek state. In this ideal Plato does not introduce the distinction of Church and State; for to him Church and State are one. Let us try and see, in the modern world, what the State is, what the Church is, and what are their relations.

Man has two wants—freedom and religion. What is freedom? The power to do what I like. How do mankind obtain freedom? By the State, the organised power of the people. The visible embodiment of the State are judges, magistrates, courts of law, officers of justice, armed men. The primary function of the State is to secure freedom by compulsion.

If we think for a moment of a great nation we shall understand this. What is the picture which rises in the mind? A picture of myriads of separate living beings spread over the face of the land—thronging the streets of cities, tending sheep on lonely hills, going down to the sea in ships, hewing coal in mines, pondering in inner chambers, praying in churches—crossing each other's paths in ceaseless motion—a picture of millions of men, each doing what is right in his own eyes—thinking, preaching, sowing, reaping, weaving. What makes this possible? The State. To the eye of the senses these countless human beings move without restraint: to the eye of the mind they move within a network of compulsion. A web is cast around them within which they move, without which they could not move. Break that web and the picture vanishes; tumult unspeakable and bewilderment appear. The order of motion ceases, the plough is left untouched in the furrow, the sheep untended on the hills, the student closes his books, factories are ruined, arts and learning lost. That wonderful

---

[1] Notes of an Address delivered at a private meeting in Balliol College in the spring of 1879.

web of restraint is woven by the State; within its meshes man is safe, on breaking it he loses all. The primary function of the State now is to secure freedom by compulsion. To Plato the primary function of the State was to *put* every man into his place; to us it is freedom—to enable every man to *find* his place. There is no mention of freedom in Plato's ideal State; but the whole history of Western Europe is the history of the effort to obtain it. Freedom—the power to do what we like—a little thing it seems, but it has been bought with a great price. Only to-day has freedom ceased to be the gospel of English life; slowly has it been realised. For long the State, instead of the guardian, was the oppressor of freedom; only to-day do we see a just and transfigured State securing freedom for all.

II.

Religion.—But this moving life-pageant that we behold, what does it mean? What is the *end* of this freedom slowly won with tears? Religion alone gives the answer—religion the end and bond of life. Man loved freedom that he might love God; the right use of freedom is religion. But what, cries man, is religion? What *is* the right use of freedom? The ancient answer was—to love God. But to love God, I must have faith in God—how shall I have faith in God? The beginning of religion is the cry of man for a law of life to restrain his freedom. The consciousness of an ideal self which includes the good of all, the consciousness of this ideal enshrined within the temple of the mind gives the answer to that cry. When a man is aware of the presence of this ideal, the first stage of *faith* has come. The consciousness of an ideal is the first stage, the recognition of this ideal as the shadow of God, the beginning and end of all things, the eternal spirit of the universe, is the second stage. Faith is complete when a man beholds this ideal as the reflection of God within and without him, as God in the unexplored depths of his own soul, as God in the unrevealed secrets of the physical universe.

After faith comes *knowledge*—how shall we know God? How detain this ideal that hovers like winged light within the mind? To know God man must seek to become God—life is the ceaseless endeavour to become like God; to enact God in our own souls and in the world ; and though men must needs fail, failure here is the only success.

Thus by growth towards God within himself a man knows God; and he knows Him in yet a second way. He scans the human world, he learns how the civilisation he lives in was built up by the blind working of human instincts ascending out of the wild disorder of the primeval conflict; how institutions, laws, and knowledge, slowly formed in the lapse of ages, make possible his love of God. He wanders through the physical world, searches for the laws of wind and rain, and for the forces that move the heavens and make the corn to grow; and gathering up his knowledge, adapts to it his life, and learns how to transform the world. And though the procession of natural events treads man down, though he cannot transform the physical world as he transforms the human by faith and love and knowledge, yet both the physical world and the human are to him the awful veil of a personal God who inhabits eternity. God is a person—how else could man love and worship God ? What personality is we only faintly apprehend—who has withdrawn the impenetrable veil which hides our own personality from us ? God is a father—but who has explained a father's love ?

There is *limitation* to man's knowledge, and he is disposed to cry out, Why this impassable barrier ? He knows he is limited, why he is limited he knows not. Only by some image does he strive to approach the mystery. The sea, he may say, had no voice until it ceased to be supreme on the globe; there, where its dominion ended and its limits began, on the edge of the land, it broke silence. Man would have had no tongue had he been merely infinite; where he feels his limits, where the infinite spirit within him touches the shore of his finite life, there he too breaks silence.

After faith and knowledge come prayer and worship. The actual communion with the image of God within our own souls is prayer; worship is the adoration of God without us, thanksgiving for the human pity that seeks out suffering, for the labour of our fellow-men, for the ripened corn. Action is the realisation of our ideal, the love not of ourselves but of our fellow-men, the removal of sin and pain, the increase of knowledge and beauty, the binding together of the whole world in the bond of peace.

III.

The Church.—How does man maintain this religion which I have tried to define ? By the Church—the organised expression of the Spirit of God working through the whole people. As we call the people and the organised power of the people together the State, so we call the people and their religious organisation the Church. The visible embodiments of the Church are sacred buildings, sacred books, and ministers; the primary function of the Church is to secure the right use of freedom by persuasion. It is an organisation to keep alive in the hearts of men faith in God. Its ministers seek to cleanse the spiritual vision of men, to exalt men to the highest deeds they are capable of, by public worship, by public prayer, by exhortation. If we looked now once more at that picture of the human world, we should behold no longer myriads of isolated beings pursuing their own way, we should see the freedom which seems to sever men binding them together; we should see a vision of all men drawn together by the silken cords of persuasion, living no longer as divided beings but in the unity of the Spirit. Men separate in order to re-unite; sin is separation, faith is union.

Religion, the desire to do what is right! A great thing this! The whole of Plato's Republic is the attempt to draw men to do what is right. If it has taken man centuries to win liberty, how many more centuries must pass away before he learns the right use of liberty! Nay, what has not come down to us in the name of religion itself?—division, bigotry, persecution. If the State has oppressed and stamped out freedom, the Church has misguided men and stamped out religion. Picture the Founder of our religion sitting on that mountain on which the ancient prophet bowed his head in expectation of the rain-cloud, sitting with His face towards the western sea, what a world of spiritual ruin and calamity would He behold! If men were slow in building up a power to enable them to do what they like, how much slower in building up a power to enable them to do what is right! We are disposed to say the true Church is not yet come.

IV.

Relation of Church and State.—The State secures freedom by compulsion; the Church teaches the right use of freedom by persuasion. Our next question is, What is the relation between Church and State? We have seen that an ideal end is proposed for man's life, which we may shortly define as inward and outward purity, and religion organised in the Church seeks to attain it; but what has the State to do with this ideal end? Now religion organised in the Church has in times past pursued two lines of action—First, it has secluded itself from the world, gone out of the world, that is, of the State; and, secondly, it has striven to re-enter the world as a conqueror, to dominate the world, and thus to spiritualise the world through the organ of the world, the State. Framing a certain definite conception of the nature of man's destiny and of his relation to God, it has sought to impose this conception on the world through the State, to mould the whole world after its own ideal. The Church is an organisation which has sought to mould the world on an ideal, as Plato sought to mould it in the construction of his model State. In his State the whole power of the community is used to fashion life in the light of the conceptions discovered by philosophy. We need not pause over this attempt; but the history of the Christian Church is the history of an actual attempt to accomplish the same end that Plato only dreamed of. Here, then, we have the recognition of an ideal end and an organisation devoted to the accomplishment of this end; but we have by its side other organisations, and above all, the State. To find out what is the relation of the State to this ideal end, we must ask the question, What is the end of the State? And here two conceptions meet us which are fundamentally opposed. First, that the State is the organised power of the community to promote the *material* ends of life; as such it is subordinate to the Church, which seeks to promote the spiritual ends of life. Second, that the State has the *same* end as the Church, the promotion of the highest form of life In this case the Church is nothing more than the State in its spiritual aspect, instead of, say, its industrial or its intellectual aspect. According to this view, the State provides a spiritual organisation as it provides an industrial organisation for the people, and this spiritual organisation is the Church.

Here are two root ideas opposed to each other at every point. These two will struggle for mastery in the future. The conflict is between those who maintain the secular character of the State and those who maintain the spiritual character of the State. The first look on the Church as a light shining in darkness, as an institution separate from all other institutions in character and aim, an institution which, standing outside the world, seeks to re-enter it and spiritualise it. In this view, having been forced to abandon its claim to supremacy, the Church now seeks to establish its claim to independence. The attempt of the State to impose a creed or an organisation on it will be resisted to the death; a drunkard might as well administer the Sacraments. It is an institution not created by the world, but one which entered the world, and is at war with it to the end of time. The second conception, on the other hand, makes no sharp separation between the Church and the State; it asserts that the aims of both are the same, but it recognises that a special organisation is necessary to the right fulfilment of the spiritual objects of life. It points out that from the beginning of civilisation the two organisations have been bound up together. It admits that a war between light and darkness is going on in the world, but it declares that light is found in the world as well as in the Church. It asserts that the State is competent to impose certain restrictions on, and to exercise control over the Church, because their aims are the same. We must choose between the two conceptions, and we choose the second.

But the problem may be approached in another way. Which will provide the more efficient organisation for the spiritualisation of life: freedom, or the State? Should freedom not only clothe and feed men, but also teach them how to live? The passionate discussion of to-day is, whether freedom ought to satisfy the spiritual wants, as it satisfies the physical wants of the people? My answer is, Freedom should provide for the physical wants of men, because by freedom every man is clothed and fed in the best way with the least effort. Men's physical wants are satisfied in the best way by the outward pressure of competition; but men's spiritual wants are satisfied in the best way only by the inward pressure of the love of God. To satisfy men's physical wants you must be dependent, to satisfy men's spiritual wants you must be independent. The grower of corn and the weaver of wool satisfies men's wants as he finds them; the spiritual teacher does not seek to satisfy men's wants as he finds them, he seeks to give men higher wants. How can he whose mission it is to cleanse men's spiritual vision be supported by those who are convinced that their vision is perfect—how can he whose mission it is "to raise men to the highest deeds they are capable of" be maintained by those who are convinced that their morality is perfect? Where the want is greatest it is the least felt. To teach the people the ministers of religion must be independent of the people, to lead the people they must be in advance of the people. Individual interests are not always public interests. It is the public interest that a country should be taught a pure and spiritual religion, it is the interest of religious teachers to teach that which will be acceptable at the moment. It is for the public interest that religion should be universal, that it should be a bond of union, that it should be progressive. The State, and not the individual, is best calculated to provide such a religion. We saw before that freedom being obtained, it was religion that was to weld free but isolated beings into a loving interdependent whole. Which is the more likely to do this : a religion wise and rational, comprehensive and universal, recognising a progressive revelation of God, such as the State may provide, or a religion provided by individual interests which is liable to become what is popular at the moment, which accentuates and multiplies divisions, which perpetuates obsolete forms, and has no assurance of universality of teaching? It is scarcely too much to say that as an independent producer can only live by satisfying physical wants in the best way, the independent sect or independent minister can only live by satisfying spiritual wants in the worst way. If I thought that Disestablishment were best for the spiritual interests of the people I would advocate it, but only on such a principle can it be justified, and my argument is that spiritual evil, not good, would attend it.

What is really required is a body of independent ministers in contact at once with the continuous revelation of God in man and in nature, and with the religious life of the people. The State alone can establish such a Church organisation as shall insure the independence of the minister, by securing him his livelihood and protecting him from the spiritual despotism of the people. I believe the argument holds good for religion as for education, that it is of such importance to the State itself, to the whole com-

munity collectively, that it behoves the State not to leave it to
individual effort, which, as in the case of education, either does not
satisfy spiritual wants at all, or does not satisfy them in the best
way.   If I chose to particularise, I might here add that the connection of religion with the State is the most effective check to
sacerdotalism in all its different forms, and sacerdotalism is the
form of religion which can become fundamentally dangerous to the
State.   It injures the State spiritually by alienating the greatest
number and the most intellectual of the members of the State
from religion altogether, it injures the State temporally by creating
an antagonism between Church and State—a great national
calamity from which we are now entirely free.

But what religion is the State to accept?   It must accept the
historical religion of the people, and impose certain conditions such
as shall prevent a development inconsistent with its own existence,
which shall secure a religion universal, progressive with the
people's life and thought, and such as shall be a bond of union
thrown around them.   The ideal Church is the State.   As the
nation is a spiritual and secular community, so is the State a
spiritual and secular power.   In the pathetic words of Cardinal
Newman, Christianity is no longer the law of the land; but I
answer, True, yet by the very removal in such a church as I
contemplate of those restrictions, which seemed to create an artificial identity between the Church and the nation, you have
created a new and living unity through which the spirit of Christ
breathes as it never breathed before.   The outward and compulsory
bonds of the older union are fast disappearing in modern society;
they are to be replaced by better and stronger bonds, namely,
spiritual ones.   But as the State of old recognised and enforced
those past artificial and temporary bonds, so should it recognise
and identify itself with the new spiritual and eternal bond.
Christianity as a theological system may cease to be the law of
the land, but Christianity as a disposition of the mind lives in the
hearts of the people.   We recognise now that divine truth is not
the jealously guarded treasure of a sect, but the common heritage
of mankind, not a light held up by priests before a forsaken
multitude, but that inner light which illumines the face of the
whole people.   The State alone, we believe, can secure this purer
religion whose bond shall be, not rigid dogmas, but worship and

prayer, union in liturgy not in articles, whose sole object shall be the spiritualisation of life. To all free organisations of religion it will grant protection, while it seeks slowly to remove by persuasion what it will not sweep away by force.

For the spirit of God dwells not here and not there, not in this sect or that, but in the whole people. When we behold the desolation, the sin, the deformity of the world, how can we believe it? Nevertheless, God is there. An ancient Italian city is built upon a mountain torrent, and those who ascend the encircling hills hear the voice of the torrent above the hum and traffic of the streets. So it is with those who pause a moment to listen in the midst of the world—they hear, above the din and uproar of human life, the voice of the stream of God flowing from beneath the eternal throne.

Conclusion.—I have considered some ideal relations of the modern State as Plato considered the ideal relations of the ancient State. The actual relations of religion and the State, so difficult, so perplexed by a long history and by party politics, I have left untouched. But the ideal I have hinted at has a bearing on the solution of *the* problem of our time. The discussion of that problem awaits us in the immediate future. By the discussion of principles we get the most effective education for practice. I would further insist especially on the present importance of principles, because this is an age of transition. The constructive positive stage which is to follow it will lay tasks upon us splendid though difficult. While the struggle for a free State lies behind us in the past, the struggle for a pure Church lies before us in the future. A pure Church, so far from being won, dwells as yet only in the imaginations of men. Enough for us to-night to remember that the spring of all civilisation is the yearning for a deeper, wider personal life; that freedom and religion, both not one alone, are the conditions of that yearning. Before another generation is in the grave politics as a struggle for liberty will have faded away; but religion and a pure Church are not only not yet won for us, they are threatened as they never were before by intolerance and indifference. The struggle for religion will be a struggle beside which the struggle for freedom will seem a little thing, and upon us, who recognise every man as a priest of the Most High God, lies the burden of pressing forward to secure to the nation the religion by which it may live.

NOTES AND JOTTINGS.

NOTES AND JOTTINGS.

Religion.

THE basis of religion is independent of science. Theology, not religion, is the antithesis to science.

It is vain to chafe at mystery—it is as appropriate to consciousness as clearness to the intellect. We are very near the fount of all things when we feel that there *is* mystery. Often standing by the sea lulled by the monotonous roar of waves have we thrilled with the sudden sense of revelation in mystery; or moving swiftly through crowded streets, startled, awe-stricken, and henceforth lived for ever conscious of the mystery in human faces. So in the old days that were before us, ofttimes has the secret of things been unveiled to poets or prophets in a flash of consciousness that might not be translated into thoughts. But whence flashed the revelation? Immemorially has there been linked with the consciousness of the "not ourselves" the sense of right and wrong. If we abstract the two things and keep them apart, we ask in wonder what can be the connection between the sense of right and wrong, and the perception of wind and cloud, mountain, river, and sunshine? And yet in all ages they have been bound together in religion, whispering the spiritual communion of all things; a communion, says Bacon, that links the smile upon the human face with the rippling of waters; which we feel in outer things, in the sweet identifying of the wind-ranged clouds of heaven, and the wave-worn wrinkles on the sand, the moving of the breeze among the pines, and the falling of breakers upon the beach. Are there not moments when we stand before what lies without us, as on rising ground, the eye dilated, arm outstretched, our ears tingling with expectancy of coming sound, as of the heart of the wide world beating like our own? In those seconds we seem one with the "not ourselves;" we *live*, and it too lives within us; and only in hail-ing it as a being like ourselves can we chant our oneness with it. It is a form of speech, but it is the speech within us which has communion with the universe.

Many are the forms in which man has sought revelation of the great fact without him; for he could grasp it only as *expressed*, revealed. Under the dome of St. Paul's, we are awed by the feeling of vastness, of space—it is the infinite made finite; under the canopy of heaven the sense is lost in infinitude. And temporary, fading and passing as are the myriad expressions that have been, there is one form of immemorial age, the truest of all—the personal. For seeking sympathy of the universe face to face, has not man bitterly upbraided the changeless stars for shining coldly down upon his tragedies of passion? What language, in moments of unsearchable agony, can he grasp but the human, the personal? How can creation thrill him with sympathy and inspire him with strength, but as a man of sorrows and acquainted with grief? For most of us Christ is the expression of God, *i.e.* the eternal fact within and without us: In time of peril, of failing, and of falsehood the one power that enables us to transcend weakness is the feeling of the communion of the two eternal facts through Christ.[1]

Any attempt to preach a purer religion must go along with attempts at social reform.

It is a good thing that our religion is not bound up with all our creeds and institutions—progress would be impossible. But progress will never be organic until the religious spirit breathes through every act and institution.

Evidently the starting-point of religion and philosophy is the same. It is the faith that the end of life is righteousness, and that the world is so ordered that righteousness is possible through human will; that the end for which the universe came into existence is also its cause; that the idea of good is God, the Creator of the universe. Philosophy tries to show *how* this idea made the

---

[1] The above passages are from an essay on "The Objective Basis of Religion," dated February 5th, 1874; those which follow are from note-books, and of various dates.

world ; religion believes it simply, and asks no more. Philosophy is the proof of the end, religion is the assertion of the end.

Just as there was a stage in the history of thought, when abstract terms did not exist, when men spoke of natural events in terms of their own personality, so was there a time when men could conceive no other way of expressing the majesty of God except by miracles, by representing Him as moulding nature to His will. What they cared for was not the truth of *facts*, but the truth of *feeling* and *thought* : miracles and mythology in their beginnings were *language*.

The conception of a Fall is the conception of a possibility of good not realised—self-conscious man recognised an ideal which he had not reached, but which he felt he ought to reach, and had therefore fallen from.

The assertion, " I can alter my life and break the chain of habit," is an echo of the eternal act of creation.

The indestructible sense that somehow in realising our own idea of perfection, we are rescuing the sad world from a misery we cannot directly alleviate, is projected in the idea of the crucifixion of Christ for the whole human race.

It is not when we are resisting temptation that we feel at our best, but in some still moment of passionate vision or contemplation. Our idea of good has a full and positive meaning apart from the existence of evil either as a distinct force or negation.

Observe—man is placed at the centre of the religious and moral systems when he has ceased to be the centre of the physical universe.

Two mighty opposites have to be reconciled, the energy of spiritual affirmation that breathes in the Hebrew and Christian Scriptures, and the inquisitive search for truth of Greek philosophy. The two spirits cannot be better contrasted than by placing side by side two sentences, one from the Gospel of St. John, " I am the way, the truth, and the life ; " the other from the Republic of Plato : " Let us follow the argument whithersoever it leads us."

Had liberal theologians in England combined more often with their undoubted courage and warmth definite philosophic views, religious liberalism would not now be condemned as offering nothing more than a mere sentiment of vague benevolence. Earnest and thoughtful people are willing to encounter the difficulty of mastering some unfamiliar phrases of technical language when they find they are in possession of a sharply defined intellectual position upon which their religious faith may rest.

Note how English communistic ideas come from the New Testament; French from the Roman "law natural" extended to a "state of nature." Note also the enormous gulf between the abstract intellectual conceptions of the French, and their practical life before the Revolution—an intellectual idea thoroughly realised by all in abstract, continually denied and ignored in practice. Compare the intellectual acknowledgment of Christian morality elsewhere and its denial in practice.

Immortality and the End of Life.

A moral consciousness implies two things—God and immortality. I mean that God and immortality are the logical conditions of it. Tentatively one may say, (1.) All moral action implies *an ideal and actual order and end*=God. (2.) All moral action implies *permanence* of relations=Immortality.

We do believe it would be irrational to try to be good if the course of the world were not ordered for holiness and justice.

If an astronomer show that the earth within a limited time must be destroyed, and the race with it, where is our hope of the happiness and perfectibility of the race? We want an *eternal* end; and this cannot be found in the good of the human race.

The horror of thinking an impure thought is quite out of proportion to its possible effect upon the character, and therefore upon the race ; the horror at the wrong done in the face of a divine self transcending the limits of our personality, the feeling that it is wrong in the sight of a pure God, is to many the secret of God's existence, and the secret, that the end of life is to live to God.

Humanity is an abstraction manufactured by the intellect, and can never be the object of religion; for religion in every form demands something that lives and is not made. It is the vision of a living Being that makes the Psalmist cry, " As the hart panteth after the water brooks, so panteth my soul after thee, O God."

Is there a difference in seeking happiness for self and seeking it for the race ? Yes, undoubtedly. The latter involves the fundamental conception of living for an end other than self. The error consists in aiming at a lower good for the race than for the individual. What end, then, should the individual seek ? Should he seek the righteousness of the race ? Yes and no. Yes, for the end of life is righteousness ; yet not a righteousness dependent on the existence of the human race, but eternal. The human race may pass away as the individual passes away, but righteousness shall not cease. Action and life demand an eternal end to rest in ; happiness which each individual finds unreal, the human race, an aggregate of individuals, must find unreal ; it cannot be the eternal, unchangeable end either for the individual or the race. The race may, nay, will vanish ; what a pitiful end then must the happiness of it be—the unreal existence of a transient shadow ! And if righteousness were inseparably bound up with the existence of the race, it, too, would be but an unreal, unsubstantial end. But the righteousness which the individual seeks, and which results in the happiness of the race, as the condition of the search after righteousness in this world, is eternal and unchangeable ; the end and maker of all things, the rest the soul ever seeks, the divine peace.

There is, first, the selfishness of each man for himself; and, second, of all men for all men and each other. The true glory of life is the devotion of all men to an eternal principle.

What is immortality ? Is the self-conscious self immortal ?

Is the desire of immortality a mere shrinking from death? or a vain conceit of the dignity of human existence? What is the fundamental idea involved in the beliefs about immortality? This—that duty, passion, and pain have no meaning except in relation to an *eternal* something. All life is a search for the *real*: man seeks reality from the moment he feels and thinks upon his feelings; he rests not till he unveils the secret of existence.

The belief in immortality is the expression of the gradual consciousness of man of the order implicit in his history.

Most terrible is the effect of the Reign of Law on the belief in immortality. Fever and despair come upon action, and the assertion that this world is all in all, narrows and perverts the world of ethical science. And indeed it is very awful, that great contrast of the Divine Fate of the world pacing on resistless and merciless, and our passionate individuality with its hopes, and loves, and fears; that vision of our warm, throbbing personal life quenched for ever in the stern sweep of Time. But it is but a passing picture of the mind; soon the great thought dawns upon the soul: "It is I, this living, feeling man, that thinks of fate and oblivion; I cannot reach the stars with my hands, but I pierce beyond them with my thoughts, and if things go on in the illimitable depth of the skies which would shrivel up the imagination like a dead leaf, I am greater than they, for I ask 'why,' and look before and after, and draw all things into the tumult of my personal life—the stars in their courses, and the whole past and future of the universe, all things as they move in their eternal paths, even as the tiniest pool reflects the sun and the everlasting hills."

Like all great intellectual revolutions, the effect of the Reign of Law upon ethical temper has been harassing and disturbing; but as every great intellectual movement has in the end raised and ennobled the moral character of man through the purification of his beliefs, so will this great conception leave us the belief in God and the belief in immortality purified and elevated, strengthening through them the spirit of unselfishness which it is already beginning to intensify and which makes us turn our faces to the future with an ever-growing hope.

It is a little strange that the belief in universal order should have resulted in a conviction that there is no absolute end, that the fact of things must for ever remain unknown. The mood is due to the imagination rather than to the reason; for the conception of order without an end is contradictory; and if man is related to the world through his intellect, it is rational to suppose that he is related to it through the highest feelings of his nature. The men of science have forgotten the deep saying of him who first imagined modern science, that there are some things which can only be known rightly under conditions of emotion, and because they have reached all the results of their knowledge by a rigid elimination of emotion, they reject it as the interpreter of life and outer things, no longer daring to believe in that kinship of man and nature which makes the cry of a child, heard breaking the stillness of the open land, seem the voice of the whole world. Such emotions will some day find adequate expression in Reason; and man will learn that the mystery of life comes from his own infinity, and not because the truth of God can never be known.

Church and State.

The State divorced from religion becomes *Antichrist* in reality. All the most powerful emotions of society are enlisted against it.

It is said that the State ought to be secular, because history proves that the connection between Church and State has debased religion and injured the people. Answer: History proves that State interference with industry was bad; that is no reason for the State leaving industry alone altogether. So with religion—the most delicate and precious of all human interests. And a democratic State differs from a monarchical or aristocratic State. A State cannot found or initiate religion, but it can support and sustain religion.

Feudalism in the Church will be destroyed by the growth of democracy and the reformation of the land system. If we destroy feudalism, we must take care to substitute other *personal moral relations* between classes. Let us destroy feudalism, but let us institute a *divine* democracy.

Competition.

Competition, or the unimpeded pressure of individual on individual, has been from the beginning a great force in societies; but of old it was hindered and controlled by custom; in the future, like the other great physical forces of society, it will be controlled by morality.

———————

Competition has brought about two great opposing opinions; one that Government should do nothing, the other that it should do everything. The first arises from the contemplation of the immense wealth heaped up under a system of unimpeded individual action, and of the extraordinary folly and selfishness of the customs and legislation that controlled such action in the past. The second arises from the sufferings which unimpeded individualism has brought upon the working classes, who cry out that Government is bound to protect them from misery and starvation. Competition has been most successful in increasing the efficiency of production; distribution has lost perhaps more than it has gained by it. And the problem of distribution is the true problem of Political Economy at the present time.

———————

Cannot the principle of self destroy as well as found society? Yes; self-interest must be followed by self-sacrifice, or society will dissolve. Through the principle of self-interest society comes into being; through its annihilation will it endure.

———————

Individualism and Socialism.

There is an undoubted connection between the break-up of the old system of industry, the system of small manufacturers, and the growth of individualism,—a connection, that is, between the rise of factories and the development of individual liberty.

———————

The law of human movement in historical times is from *natural* groups to *individualism*, and from individualism to *moral* groups. The primitive blood associations re-appear after a stage of individualism in moral guilds. "Association is the watchword of the future." The problem of the genuine Socialist is to lay down the conditions of union and its purposes. In the past, all associations had their origin in unconscious physical motives; in the future, all associations will have their origin in conscious ethical motives. Here, as in many other things, the latest and most perfect development of society seems to be anticipated in its outward form by the most primitive; but the inner life of the form has changed.

———————

The differentiation of functions should promote the unity of spirit. Differentiation only takes place in order that a higher unity may be reached. Differentiation of functions and *not* differentiation of spirit is what we desire. The unity of spirit is the cause of the separation of functions; the separation of functions has for its end the unity of the spiritual universe.

The woman is only emancipated from the man that they may reunite in a higher communion of life and purpose. The workman is only emancipated from the employer that they may re-unite in a higher communion of life and purpose. The individual is only emancipated from the control of the community that he may consciously devote himself to more intimate union with the community.

The end and law of progress is the unity of the human spirit. This can only be attained through separation of functions. In the industrial world there is separation of functions—its ideal is unity of industrial purpose. This unity can only be attained through association; but association implies a higher unity than the industrial one. It implies a unity of the ethical spirit.

Differentiation is wrong where it produces division of spirit; it is right where it produces unity of spirit. Art, in order to progress, had to separate from religion; but the noblest works of art were created in the service of religion, the noblest buildings, the noblest statues; art, in order to be great once more, will be united, not to religion, but to the religious spirit breathing through the communities.

———————

Certain Fallacies.

If justice in its beginning was the compromise between the many weak against the few strong, it is inferred that this is the character of justice now. This is due to want of historic sense. The nature of a thing is always more than its origin tells of.

———————

Take note of two supreme fallacies: (1.) The confusion of definiteness with definition—because you can't define a thing, you haven't a definite idea of it—*e.g.* self, God, emotion. (2.) That to explain a thing is to explain it away—*e.g.* as if a man who was told that the seat of sensation is in the brain, not in the tip of the finger pricked, were to believe that he did not feel pain at the end of the finger.

Adam Smith generalised his laws of Political Economy from the assumption that all human beings were selfish; disregarding the fact of disinterestedness and the like, which make the science much more difficult, perhaps impossible. So scientific men have made their discoveries by looking upon nature as absolute and objective, by eliminating man and his interpretation of it in terms of his own experience. We are now in danger of forgetting the humanity of nature; we are all beginning to look upon nature as men of science look at it, to laugh to scorn the old ideas of man which found himself there.

It is in the Greek world that the action of the law of symbolism comes out most clearly. Under the impulse to interpret, man creates a symbolism, the reflex of himself, which in after generations, its original meaning forgotten, grows into a distinct world, veiling and transforming the real world, and seeking explanation for itself. From the ages when the Greek mythology rose like a bright exhalation in the morning out of the metaphors of the natural world to answer the first pulsations of man's spiritual life, to the later ages of modern history, the real world has remained almost unknown.

The Individual.

Philosophy can explain the world if it looks upon man as nothing more than a drop of acid or a bit of mineral; but the individual is the cross light which confuses the broad light of explanation.

The individual in physical science is nothing; in human science everything.

Expression.

How strange it is to put out one's most sacred and fullest feelings in carefully chosen words and set them before the world! How strange the contrast between the panic mood of utmost pain in which the feeling flashed upon one as a torment, and the quiet diligence with which one elaborates it in expression, thrusting it from one with cool deliberation, weighing word against word, and sucking in intensest pleasure out of the memory of deathly pain. Is it that our own feelings are not our own, our own agony not for ourselves, that God demands them for Himself, drawing from us what would madden if left within us? And yet, ah me! how cold and hard the soul seems when it dwells even on its own pain in the past, how the warm flush of feeling for the sufferer dies in the cunning working of the thing for God! Who shall bridge the chasm and be for ever impassioned and sincere?

Blank verse is upheld in tragedy as in fact more nearly approaching the language of men deeply and passionately stirred. Passion expresses itself in rhythmical language. This may be said of the language of all the great sailors of Elizabeth's time, indeed of all the prose writing of the time, more or less. Look at Gilbert, Raleigh, Spenser (on Ireland), Hooker, how the great passion thrilling the nation makes itself felt in their noble poetical language.

Sentiment.

The English Rebellion and the French Revolution have often been compared, but I do not know whether what seems their most marked and essential difference has ever been noted. The first was distinguished by an entire devotion to God and an absence of all sentiment; the second by an entire appeal to sentiment and indifference to God.

In no great religious movement has philanthropy been very strong, or rather sentiment or pity—the consciousness of *sin* has been too strong.

Some natures are intensely sensitive without being sympathetic. In these natures feeling is sentiment; for sympathy is feeling related to an object, whilst sentiment is the same feeling seeking itself alone.

Utilitarianism is a cause of sentiment in making the end of action the happiness or pleasure of human beings; sympathy with *pain alone* is sentiment.

Mere sensuous images cannot bring back love and sympathy in absence; the mighty conception of duty can.

Various Aphorisms.

The organisation of the world is not for happiness; from this fact are drawn the ordinary arguments against design; it is for something else.

Man first interpreted the outer world by himself—now himself by the outer world.

Man seeks pleasure and self—great unforeseen results follow: man seeks God and others—and there follows pleasure.

The secret of progress, the perpetual satisfying of wants followed by the springing up of new wants, is the secret of individual unrest and disappointment.

To the ancients the intellect was the most enduring part of man—to us the emotions.

Beauty and holiness are both indefinable; the belief in a perfect holiness is like Columbus's belief in a new world—some day we shall find it on the other side the ocean of existence. There are things in man which the eye of the mind can never see in life, as the eye of the body can never see the heart alive; life flies the surgeon's knife.

The sense of beauty is the greatest restraint upon fanaticism.

The soul demands not a refuge, but a resting-place.

Images.

A figure standing in relief against a cloudless sky-line is a solemn thing; it is man in the embrace of the infinite.

Some people's minds are like a place of public meeting—all kinds of opinions appear there in turn, and leave it just as they found it, empty and open to every comer.

We ascend the hill-tops of philosophy, not to gaze up at the ever-visible heavens, but to embrace in one grand view the human world beneath us.

It is upon the noblest natures that the greatest weight of sorrow falls; as the broad branches of the cedar are broken by the snow, which falls away from other trees.

A wonderful image of life—a fierce wind blowing at evening from a cloudless sky, rocking the great firs to and fro, and roaring amongst their branches, whilst upon their tall stems rests the quiet light of the declining sun.

After all, a learned man is often not much better off than a man who knows a great many commonplace people.

To make a politic speech is like being carried up a flight of steps by the pressure of a crowd.

It is well that the beaten ways of the world get trodden into mud: we are thus forced to seek new paths and pick out new lines of life.

A city lying in a wave of sunshine, with its spires and domes pale and unsubstantial as in a fairy's dream; the wave flows on and shadows follow, spires and domes are dark and clear, every detail is seen and marked—sorrow makes life and all things dark and real; spiritual joy makes the world a dreamland.

To sit in an old church, with the birds twittering in the eaves, looking through the open door at the far-off land and winding river, half curtained by the green glancing leafy boughs that overhang the porch—oh God! how sweet an image of those still moments of passion that steal like evening shadows over the fret and uproar of existence!

———————

Those laughing bells, those melancholy sobbing bells, how like our life—they fade and ebb, they swing in faintest waves of dying sound, and then the strained ear is left forlorn—but the unheard motion flows through the infinite for ever, and fills the heavens with joy.

———————

Our delicate, impalpable sorrows, our keen, aching, darling emotions, how strange, almost unreal they seem by the side of the gross mass of filthy misery that clogs the life of great cities!

What an odd thing this personality is with its strange vistas of complicated memory and association; how bleak and empty is the world outside it!

———————

Oh! Time, hast thou no memory? The bright pictures of glancing life, are they gone with those dead ones, who clasped hands and shouted? or not without a smile dost thou remember them, dreaming?

———————

Man is but a snowflake; he falls from the bosom of the clouds, a tiny separate thing blown and driven by bitter winds, and drops to earth at last, extinguished and trodden out by Fate or Time.

———————

Huddled together on our little earth we gaze with frightened eyes into the dark universe.

———————

Man lifts his head for one moment above the waves, gives one wild glance around, and perishes. But that glance, was it for nothing?